FAITHFUL PROMISES of God

guidance for today's living

FAE DUNN

FAITHFUL PROMISES of God

guidance for today's living

ELKHORN, NE

Faithful Promises of God
Copyright ©2019 Fae Dunn

All rights reserved. No part of this book may be reproduced, stored in a retrieval system, or transmitted in any other form or by any other means, without the prior written permission of the author.

Published by TeDaSe Publishing

ISBN: 978-0-9882407-3-5 Paperback

ISBN: 978-0-9882407-4-2 Kindle

ISBN: 978-0-9882407-5-9 EPub

Any similarity to real persons found in the text of this book is strictly coincidental and not intended by the author.

Scripture quotations are taken from the Holy Bible, New International Version, NIV, Copyright, 1973, 1978, 1984 International Bible Society. Used by permission of Zondervan Bible Publishers.

Scripture quotations marked NLT are taken from the Holy Bible, New Living Translation, copyright 1996, 2004, 2015 by Tyndale House Foundation. Used by permission of Tyndale House Publishers, Inc. Carol Stream, Illinois 60188. All rights reserved.

10 9 8 7 6 5 4 3 2

My Dear Reader,

I have been writing this book for the last three plus years, and during that time, I have also been praying for each of you. No, I do not know you by name, but God does and to that end, I prayed for God to touch your heart and mind as you read through the Bible using "Faithful Promises" as your encouragement.

I have chosen to capitalize the pronouns referring to God, Jesus or the Holy Spirit and referring to God precious Word. It has always been my practice to show respect and reverence to my Lord in this way. By the same token, I do not capitalize any reference to the evil one, satan or his demons.

I find it so encouraging that from the beginning when Adam sinned to this day, God awaits with open arms for our repentance and He will forgive us. He longs for us to walk daily with Him, to read His Word and to be mindful to obey that same Word.

"Jesus is the same yesterday and today and forever." Heb13:8. Thankfully, God never changes.

When I started this project, I was doing missionary work on the island of Tobago. No, it is not as romantic as it sounds and that might be a book somewhere down the road. But God used my time there, working with the children and then coming back to my humble apartment and writing. A quiet blessing that God called me to.

I am thankful to so many who cared for me during my time while serving on Tobago. My wonderful landlady, Claudia; the teachers and administration at Bon Accord Government School; the wonderful people at the Methodist church that were encouragers and my dear friends, Alvira, and Charmaine and her sweet daughter, Jireh-Elle, whom I have taken in as an adopted granddaughter. So many were caring for me when I was sick, and I appreciate the respect that I received from people of a different culture as I learned and asked many questions. I went down to minister to them, but they gave me so much more! Then I was extra blessed to make friends in Trinidad. I am ever grateful for friends who are like family, Damian and Allana.

Now to the many here in the States who helped make this project become reality. First and foremost, my encouraging friend, Deb, who encouraged me to write my first book, "Faithful Hope", and has continued to encourage me. Deb, I am so thankful to God that you are in my life!

To my dear friend, Ken, who for the last five years has encouraged me beyond the call of duty when I was so sick. He encouraged me to pull through and continue living when I just wanted to die because of the pain from the bite of a mosquito!

My children and their spouses, Dawn and Dave who rescued me by coming to Tobago when I could not fly alone, you went beyond the call of duty! Thank you and I am forever grateful for your love! To Sean and Sarah who took me in most every time I came back to the United States but especially when I came back very sick, they took me in for good. And to my grandchildren who are now giving me great-grands, I am praying that each of you will walk with Jesus!

For all of you who have prayed for me on my missionary journey, I am thankful for you! Most had no idea that a book was also part of this journey. I am thankful for those who came to Tobago to visit me. Kay came when I was sick, and Terry when I was healthy and could rent a car and take her around the island. What fun we had in both instances. God knew what we could handle and for that I am thankful!

Mostly, I am thankful to my Heavenly Father for allowing me to write another book guiding people to His Word. This book may seem to some to be repetitive, but the Bible can be seen that way too. I believe that I wrote what He was guiding me to write. You can start reading "Faithful Promises" at the beginning and straight through or just pick it up and read bits and pieces from time to time, let God be your guide, He wants you in His Word most of all.

This book is dedicated to you, the reader, as you mature in Christ.

Day 1

A NEW BEGINNING
Read: Genesis 1-5

If you have a hard time believing Genesis 1, it will be difficult to believe that anything in the Bible is true, or that it is written by our Lord God through some 40 different men. When you read through the Bible, from cover to cover you will be shocked at the continuity from the beginning to the very end. I contend that only God could do such a marvelous work.

So, let's get started. The creation of the earth and all the details of light and darkness, division of the waters, days, seasons, and years, the creation of life in the seas and on the land, and finally the forming of man and woman are almost too much for us to understand but it is our first step in believing it happened just as it is written. Faith that the entire Bible is true is our first challenge. Our faith is either strengthened by what we read, or we turn from the Bible and walk away. God has given us a choice from the beginning and we each continue to have that choice today.

The creation of woman from the rib of man shows how a husband and wife are to walk together as one. Furthermore, in Gen 2:24 (NLT), "This explains why a man leaves his father and mother and is joined to his wife, and the two are united into one." So often in modern society, this oneness does not take place and causes many problems in marriage, but we can see that God brought them together.

Prayer: Heavenly Father, open my eyes and my heart to Your Word. Help me daily to listen to the Holy Spirit and to learn what You are quickening my spirit to learn. Thank you, Lord, for the written Word and for giving me the capability to read it. Please walk with me on this journey I am about to take be with me each step of the way. In Jesus precious name, Amen.

Day 2

WICKEDNESS ON THE EARTH
Read: Genesis 6-10

I've often heard people say that we humans are basically good but according to Genesis 6, the people of the earth were so wicked that they were a disappointment to God. They had become totally evil! This behavior of the very people He had created broke God's heart. Do you suppose that He is disappointed with the behavior of man today?

Just as Noah was a righteous man and his family benefitted from his righteousness, Ham's wickedness and those consequences were passed down to the generations. This simple fact should make each one of us think about our actions, we need to flee from sinful behavior so evil does not pass down to our children, grandchildren, and great-grandchildren.

We have a choice: to walk in truth and integrity or to be rebellious which leads to behavior that is not pleasing to God. Not only must we keep a check on our behavior but watch what we say, for it will be repeated, and keep a check on our thought pattern as well.

Prayer: Father God, help me to keep a check on myself, to stay away from evil and to strive to do what is right. Help me, Lord, to seek Your will and to be obedient and do what You have called me to do. May the inclination of my heart be drawn moment by moment to You. May I always be thankful for what you have given me Lord and walk close to You. In Jesus name, Amen.

Day 3

COVENANT PROMISE
Read: Genesis 11-15

In today's reading we see Abram giving a tenth of all he recovered to Melchizedek, king of Salem. If each of us would discipline ourselves to give as Abram did, it would help us to always put God first. When we do this with a sincere heart, we are blessed beyond material means; we are blessed for being obedient.

As God makes a covenant with Abram, "Do not be afraid Abram. I am your shield, your very great reward." (Gen 15:1b NIV) Now, put your name in the place of Abram's and claim this promise. Abram was not afraid to tell God what he wanted most, a son, and we read, "Abram believed the Lord and the Lord counted him as righteous because of his faith." (Gen 15:6b NLT)

May we long for that sort of faith, to be so in tune with God that we believe without question. As we work our way through the Bible, let us work on our faith.

Prayer: Heavenly Father help my faith to grow, to believe like Abram. Help me to be generous of heart and give to Your work beyond the tenth that Abram gave. Help me to be obedient to Your Word. In Jesus name, Amen.

Day 4

ASSOCIATION COUNTS
Read: Genesis 16-20

No matter how spiritually strong we think we are, we and our family members will be influenced by those around us. In Lot's case, the men of Sodom were perverted and wanted to have sex with the two angels who came to town. Lot then offered his daughters to these men. Tell me, what father in his right mind would do that? Lot had been around this perversion so long that he saw nothing wrong with such an offer.

Then, as they were making their get-away to safety, Lot's wife did exactly what the angels had warned against, she turned around. This is totally speculation, but I think she looked back because she longed for her things that she had accumulated. I know it is hard to let go of what we value but when the Lord says it's time to let go, the consequences was being turned into a pillar of salt.

Next, we see Lot's daughters scheming in the most perverted way to become pregnant by their father. Even though Lot and Mrs. Lot may have protected their daughters while living in Sodom, the perversion of the town was still so obvious that these girls knew and chose to act on this incestuous corruption. And the children born were later to become enemies of the Israelites. It started way back then and continues today. Be careful who you hang with, who you count as a friend, for their thoughts and ideas will rub off.

Prayer: Lord, guide me to stay close to You, to be obedient to Your Word and to choose carefully those I befriend. Forgive the poor choices I have made and quicken my spirit to always keep my eyes on You. In Jesus name, Amen.

Day 5

GOD PROVIDES
Read: Genesis 21-25

Today's reading is full of God's provisions, from providing a sacrifice instead of Isaac to providing a burial spot for Sarah to providing a wife for Isaac, God was to be praised. True worship of God is shown when: 1) we completely obey God's Word, 2) we hold nothing back, surrendering our best for God and 3) we have the faith to wait for God to provide our needs. And provide, He will.

As a young man, Esau did not value his birthright and he seemed to be very self-centered as he proclaimed to his brother, Jacob, "Quick, let me have some of that red stew! I'm famished." (Gen 25:30 NIV) And further proclaiming, after Jacob asked him to sell his birthright to him, "What good is the birthright to me?" (Gen 25:32 NIV) Like so many today, he was only concerned with the here and now, he wanted food, and did not value what was important. May we be willing to sacrifice our wants and desires for the purpose of desiring God's will.

Prayer: Precious Heavenly Father, may my life be pleasing to You, not self-centered but help me to give up those things that seem important to me. Help me to let go of my self-indulgences and may my faith grow so that I trust You completely with my life. Thank You Jesus, Amen.

Day 6

DECEPTION GALORE
Read: Genesis 26-30

Just like his father, Abraham, Isaac shows up in Gerar, before the King. And just like his father, Isaac tells the men of Gerar that his wife, Rebekah, is his sister. Furthermore, he is caught in his lie and they send him on his way. Interestingly, Abimelech understood that if anyone had touched Rebekah, they would have been guilty of sin. Abimelech also saw that God was blessing Isaac with an increase in livestock, so they took an oath not to interfere with each other. They lived peacefully together.

As we move on, we see the deception of Jacob as his mother cooks a meal so that Jacob can receive Esau's blessing. And Jacob does just that, he dresses up like his brother in a hairy goat skin and comes off smelling like Esau and his father falls for it hook, line and goat hair. Isaac receives the kiss, he asked for it, from Jacob and smells Esau's cloths and blesses Jacob with Esau's blessing.

Esau is angry about Jacob receiving his blessing and vows to kill his brother. Once again, Rebekah gets involved and sends her favorite son to her brother's in the east. When he arrives, he meets Rachel and ends up at her father's house. His Uncle Laban deceives Jacob over and over for the next 20 years. But through all this deception, God is still in control. God uses all this for His good, just like He does today.

We can learn a valuable lesson as we read through the Bible, not necessarily to be deceptive but to know when people use us; God is there and will guide us. The most important part of His guiding us is for us to stay in the Word and to obey Him. Seeking Him daily is our best defense to responding to those who are cruel to us.

Prayer: Father God, help me to be honest and pleasing in Your sight. No matter how badly I am treated, may I always remember that You are there to teach me a valuable lesson. May I always be thankful for what You allow to come in my life. In Jesus name, Amen.

Day 7

GOD'S FORGIVENESS
Read: Genesis 31-35

Jacob's life took a turn for the good as he worked faithfully for his father-in-law. It seems that God used this time to teach Jacob. There are many today that God is doing the same thing with. These saints of God have not always walked the path that many think they should have. They have sinned but have repented and chosen to live the rest of their lives for the Lord. They have been humbled because of their actions of the past and want to live a life pleasing to the Lord. Yes, just like Jacob, God will use them.

So, God renamed Jacob Israel and then blessed him "You will become a great nation, even many nations. Kings will be among your descendants! ! And I will give you the land I once gave to Abraham and Isaac. Yes, I will give it to you and your descendants after you." (Gen 35:11b-12 NLT) Do you recognize this covenant blessing? Isn't it pretty much the same covenant blessing that God gave to Abraham? Jacob, now called Israel, is the seed that God is using to pass along this blessing. God chose a deceitful man, humbled him and then used him.

We must remember this as we look at people today who seem to have quite a past. Remember, God is in control and He will use whomever He pleases to bring more people into His Kingdom. He uses the broken, the rejected and the people that will humbly follow Him for His Kingdom purposes.

Prayer: Creator of the Universe, help me to learn these valuable lessons, as I read your Word. Thank you, Lord, for opening my eyes, to not be judgmental to those around me but to see the potential that You see in all mankind. Through the Blood of Jesus, Amen.

Day 8

GOD IS FAITHFUL
Read: Genesis 36-40

Just like in Joseph's dreams, God is telling each of us that He has a special plan for our lives. Even if you are in the midst of some very difficult times, He is there. This is your training time. This is the time to draw near to the One who loves you more than anyone. This is the time to learn those valuable lessons that are needed for the job He has for you.

In my own life, I prayed for 13 years to serve God and the children of Tobago. In those 13 years, God used every circumstance I went through to train me, teaching me compassion, reconciliation, resilience and so much more. During those times that I was broken with the situations of life, these are the exact times that God's glory can be seen. I had moved away from everyone, not even wanting to make friends. But God had other plans; He got me involved in a huge church. He allowed me to use my gift of exhortation in a ministry in the church coordinating the budgeting group. He put people in my life to encourage me to write and "Faithful Hope", my first book, was born. When I accepted that I would be alone and was content with it, He allowed me to come to Tobago and work with the children.

Is this the end of my journey in serving Him? I think not! In fact, I believe that He will care for me, continue to train me and bring other blessings into my life. Be encouraged, my friend. God has such a marvelous plan for your life, but He does require for us to live a life as Joseph did. Joseph remained faithful to God, knowing that God was guiding him, and did the right thing even when he was in prison. We encourage one another with our stories.

Prayer: Precious Lord, take my hand and guide me through the hard times as I become more like the Savior. Thank you, Lord, that You would value me and love me to care so deeply for me. In Jesus name, Amen.

Day 9

TESTING
Read: Genesis 41-45

In today's reading we see that the dreams that Joseph had as a young man are being fulfilled. We also see his brothers still covering up what they did to Joseph by using such words as "one is no more" (Gen 42:13 NIV) but also claiming to be "honest men" (Gen 42:11 NIV) to the exact man whom they wanted dead. Joseph needed to test their motives to see if they were the same or if they had truly changed.

True reconciliation does test the character of the person who wronged another to see if they have truly changed and are repentant of their sin. Covering the sin with words that do not make it sound as bad is still not a changed person. Joseph had to be firm with his brothers to witness if they had changed. We see that Judah backed his words with actions (see Gen 44:30-34) by putting himself as a slave in the place of Benjamin.

We learn a lot today about reconciliation. When we wrong another person, we first hurt God and then the person and then others around us. Our sin goes so much further than just hurting a person and covering that pain up with words that have no meaning behind them. If you are looking to reconcile with someone you have hurt, you need to be tested to check your true motive. Are you willing to name the sin and deal with the consequences? Are you only worried what will be said about you or are you truly concerned for the person you hurt?

Prayer: Heavenly Father, test my motives as to why I would want to go before the person I have caused so much pain. Test my heart that it is pure and that I am willing to do whatever is needed to bring healing to the one I hurt. Lord, I long for reconciliation that can only come through Christ, Amen.

Day 10

GOD INTENDED IT ALL FOR GOOD
Read: Genesis 46-50

Jacob calls all his sons together and speaks a word to each of them. By reminding them of their past short comings, perhaps those listening learned a lesson of what not to do. But once again we see that our actions do have consequences. As it was in the days of Jacob, it is still the very same way today. Once we've accepted Christ into our lives, we are forgiven of our sins, but we will still suffer the consequences for our past behavior.

With that said, don't we all wish we had a brother like Joseph, who could have been very cruel to his brothers for what they had done to him but instead, he pointed out, "Don't be afraid of me. Am I God, that I can punish you? You intended to harm me, but God intended it all for good. He brought me to this position so I could save the lives of many people." (Gen 50:19-20 NLT) Joseph looked at the overall picture of his life and realized if his brothers had not sold him, he wouldn't have been able to be in the position he was now.

Prayer: Father God, may we have forgiving hearts so as not to hold a grudge against another person. May we realize that what comes our way, You always have a purpose for it, using it to mature us in every way. Thank You Lord, Amen.

Day 11

GOD PROVIDES
Read: Exodus 1-3

Today we are reminded that our "fame" does not stay around very long after we die, for the Egyptian Pharaoh no longer remembered Joseph and what he had done in the land of Egypt, saving the people and making the government wealthy. So, Pharaoh did what many governments do when they want to destroy a people started killing the babies. In this case, he ordered that the boy babies be killed at birth.

At one point, a grown Moses tried to help his people, but they were not ready to accept him as their leader nor was he ready to lead these people. He was in need of some training that can only come from God. So, out to the dessert he goes, to work among sheep. Then one day, God comes to him speaking from a burning bush. God tells him that He's seen the abuse that the Egyptians have put upon His people. God is commissioning Moses to go back to Egypt this time ready to be the leader that the Israelites' need.

Many of us are called, maybe not from a burning bush, but all the same, we are called by God. Read the Word daily, pray, and be willing to go when He calls you.

> *Prayer: Father God, help me to be willing to listen to Your call on my life, help me to hear Your voice. I am ready to serve You and obey. In Jesus name, Amen.*

Day 12

PROTESTS AND PROMISES
Read: Exodus 4-6

Can you imagine telling God that you cannot do the job that God has called you to? But isn't that exactly what Moses did? This is a reminder that we are not much different than Moses when God calls us to an assignment. Remember that 1 Corinthians 1: 26-27 (NLT) reminds us that we are not considered useful according to the world's standards, but "instead, God chose things the world considers foolish in order to shame those who think they are wise. And He chose things that are powerless to shame those who are powerful."

As we read the Exodus passage, we see that God provided Aaron to be Moses' spokesman. And although it seemed that Pharaoh's stubbornness was hurting the Israelites, God was paving the way for a true miracle.

Once again, in Chapter 6, we see God reminding Moses of His promise to Abraham, Isaac and Jacob. He is reaffirming his covenant promise, that the land of Canaan is theirs. Many times God expects us to move, to go forward in action in order to bring His blessing to us. So, don't just sit back and say things like "I will just pray, and God will make it happen". Here is proof that God does expect us to do our part.

Prayer: Father in Heaven forgive me when I argue with You as you call me to a task. Help me to grasp what seems impossible to me and to believe that it will happen. Help me to step out in faith. In Jesus name, Amen.

Day 13

GOD'S PATIENCE, MAN'S STUBBORNNESS

Read: Exodus 7-10

The Lord pointed out, "But I have raised you up for this very purpose, that I might show you My power and that My name might be proclaimed in all the earth." (Ex 9:16 NIV) Pharaoh's heart was hardened for God's glory to be seen by all mankind. Not only for that time but it was the story of the Jewish nation and later a witness to Christians.

It is hard to understand how anyone could be so stubborn as to allow such horrible things to happen to a nation and not comply with what God is demanding. Sometimes I suspect that people see this as a fairytale story and do not comprehend that what happened to the Pharaoh of Egypt was directly from God's hand. Especially when it seemed that he was going to let the Israelites go, only to become even more hard-hearted as to stop them.

Today, we can see the world turning more and more evil and yet, many look to self, the government or other means for help rather than to the One who is capable of making it all better. But, do these people come to the Lord with repentant hearts? Or do they just want the bad to go away and have everything all better once again? Yes, even today we see many who harden their hearts just as Pharaoh did, unwilling to yield to God. We need to check our hearts, our motives and make sure we are not bent on evil, to soften our heart and fear God.

Prayer: Heavenly Father, I open my heart and mind to do your will. Help me to not harden my heart and to be willing to obey what You are calling me to do. In Jesus name, Amen.

Day 14

THE LORD'S DELIVERANCE
Read: Exodus 11-15

Once the Israelites are out in the desert and see Pharaoh's army coming after them, they whine, they complain, they think it would have been better if they would have stayed in their houses in Egypt. Still again, God shields them from the Egyptian army and paves their way of escape. They end up going through the Red Sea on dry land safe once again. But when the Egyptian army follows them, they are covered with water and drowned, later to wash up on shore.

Then they celebrate with a song of deliverance but within a short distance, there is no water for three days and the people turn against Moses, really, it is God leading them, they just don't trust what God is doing, once again. It is there that the Lord sets this boundary, "If you will listen carefully to the voice of the Lord your God and do what is right in His sight, obeying His commands and keeping all His decrees, then I will not make you suffer any of the diseases I sent on the Egyptians; for I am the Lord who heals you." (15:26 NLT)

It seems that we suffer the way we do because we are not following God's commands and decrees. There are times that we go through a sickness for the purpose of glorifying God but oftentimes we bring diseases upon ourselves because we are not following the one Book that God has given us, the Bible. Yes, it is for today!

Prayer: Heavenly Father, be with me and guide me in the ways I am to go. Give me an obedient heart as I walk this path with You. In Jesus name, Amen.

Day 15

DO NOT BE AFRAID
Read: Exodus 16-20

What jumped out at me today was "so that your fear of Him will keep you from sinning." (Ex 20: 20b NLT). Immediately I felt the Lord impressing upon my mind and heart that there are not many in the United States that fear God. Sadly, many have no understanding of God at all. Those who do just want to see God as a God of love and do not think He would ever judge their thoughts and behavior.

Now, let me remind you. The God of the Universe, Who created the heavens and the earth, does love us dearly. But when we love someone, we see the importance of correcting their wrong behavior. It is through that love for another person that we do not want to see them punished for wrong-doing. It is the same with God. He loves us enough to correct us to show us His justice. When we are not following His will and ways, He will show us the consequences of our behavior.

"Don't be afraid," Moses answered them, "for God has come in this way to test you, and so that your fear of Him will keep you from sinning." (Ex 20:20 NLT) Are you being tested today? Keep looking to the only answer there is, that is Jesus! Follow His Word daily to help you better understand what He expects out of you. Know that your wrong behavior will bring about judgment and you will feel the consequences of your behavior. But also know that He longs for you to stay close to Him, to walk in His ways, so that you might be kept from continuing in the same sin.

Prayer: Father in Heaven, thank You for loving me enough to test my motives and my inner thoughts. I am thankful for a healthy fear of You so that I will obey. In Jesus name, Amen.

Day 16

FURTHER LAWS AND REGULATIONS
Read: Exodus 21-23

These three chapters continue with laws that the Israelites were to keep. If you look closely, you will see that our forefathers fashioned the laws of our land directly from the Bible. Is it any wonder that today, when so much sin is taking place that people don't want to even acknowledge the Bible?

Once again, in Chapter 23, God reminds the people that He is to be their only God (see v 24) they are to worship only Him. With this, He promises to bless them with food and water and protect them from illnesses and to give them long lives (see verses 25-26).

In today's fallen world, please do not judge someone who is sick and try to tell them they have a hidden sin and why they are sick. Oh yes, some people arrogantly proclaim such foolishness! They proclaim that sin is there in someone else without looking at themselves. We need to be careful to always check ourselves daily on our behavior then we won't have time to be looking at those around us.

Prayer: Heavenly Father, I know that I am saved by the blood of Jesus but know these laws are for a purpose to guide me. Thank You for being so detailed. In Jesus name, Amen.

Day 17

EVERYTHING HAS ORDER
Read: Exodus 24-27

Although today's reading can seem a little boring, it can also be exciting. If our Heavenly Father took this much time and interest in building of the tabernacle and its contents how much more time does He take in us?

With these instructions that God gave Moses, we can say God set boundaries for the Israelites and many were quite strict. As we continue to read the Bible, we will see that He has set boundaries for each of us as well. A boundary for one person, may not be a boundary for the next person and it is important for us to respect that God knows what He is doing and respect our friends, for that is where God has put each of us.

Prayer: Heavenly Father, help me to comprehend the importance of this information about the tabernacle. Also, help me to learn where You want me and that I would be obedient. In Jesus name, Amen.

Day 18

A REFLECTION OF WHAT IS TO COME
Read: Exodus 28-30

Can you imagine each morning preparing to meet the Lord as Aaron and his sons had to do? Everything had to be perfect. They represented the people as well as themselves. Quite a responsibility! It was of the utmost importance that these men be pure before the Lord, so they could sacrifice for the people.

I am thankful that today Christ takes us just as we are (usually quite soiled) because He presented Himself as the perfect sacrifice in our place. Because of this, we can stand before God and He sees our Lord Jesus Christ has purified us.

Then we start on the most incredible journey of our lives, to live for Christ, we no longer desire to do the evil we once did, or this becomes quite a struggle in our lives. Our desire is to serve Him and to please Him in all that we do. That would be fantastic if it weren't for the evil one still trying to get us to fall. Oh, and then there is our flesh that pulls us to go back to our former way of life. Yes, we are in a battle, but we must remember to whom we belong, Christ Jesus. "I have been crucified with Christ and I no longer live, but Christ lives in me." (Gal 2:20 NIV)

Prayer: Thank you Lord Jesus for all Your preparation and showing us the importance of planning ahead, of thinking things through. Thank You for caring so deeply for me. In Jesus name, Amen.

Day 19

GOD'S GIFTS
Read: Exodus 31-34

May our prayer be, "If You are pleased with me, teach me Your ways so I may know You and continue to find favor with You." (Ex 33:13 NIV) Longing to be more pleasing to our Heavenly Father must be followed by our obedience. "I have filled him with the Spirit of God, with skill, ability and knowledge in all kinds of crafts" (Ex 31:3 NIV) Knowing that God has given us each a special talent leaves us to discover that special gift and use it for His glory.

Before we jump to feeling more superior than these people or anyone else, we must be reminded that we too, often take our eyes off the Lord. Our gods are not a golden calf but perhaps another car, another bigger TV, more electronics (the latest cellular phone or tablet), more clothes, shoes, purses, jewelry. Have I mentioned your god yet? And I know for many their god is their stomachs, for all we must do is look, there is an empty void within, that we try to fill but only Jesus can satisfy.

Prayer: Dear Lord, Help to remind me daily that You are patient with me, You are slow to anger, and You are faithful, forgiving my sin and rebellion. Draw me closer to You and help me to use the gifts You have given me. In Jesus name, Amen.

Day 20

A GIVING HEART
Read: Exodus 35-38

"Let those with generous hearts present the following gifts to the Lord." (Ex 35:5 NLT) May we, as Christ followers, be seen to have a generous heart, not withholding from the Lord, what already belongs to Him. The amazing part of this story is that the people gave and gave and finally Moses had to go to them and tell them that they could stop giving, there was enough.

As God guided His people, first out of Egypt and now in the wilderness, He provided. They were to keep their eyes on Him and listen to Him. Today He continues to provide our needs if we keep our eyes on Him and listen to Him. How? By reading the Bible daily and asking the Lord "what would You have me learn from Your Word today?" He will quicken your spirit so you can learn that valuable lesson He wants you to learn. Be sure to take time to listen during your prayer time, He can speak to your heart from His Word.

Prayer: Lord God, Thank You for caring so deeply for me. Thank You for being there to meet me not where I wish to be, but exactly where I am. Once I surrendered my life to You, You started me on a wonderful journey to become more like Your Son, Jesus. Let the journey begin daily! In Jesus name, Amen.

Day 21

GOD'S PRESENCE
Read: Exodus 39-40

All the work is completed for the tabernacle and Moses puts each item in its place. Then the glory of the Lord comes in the form of a cloud by day and fire by night to be with the people throughout their journey to the Promised Land.

Did you know that when you confess your sins and ask Jesus to come live in your heart, He is with you through thick and thin, day and night? He doesn't come and go according to your behavior, He is there to stay. If you read the Bible and your desire is to live for Him, He will guide you day by day, step by step through His Word.

Prayer: Heavenly Father, just as You had everything planned out for the Tabernacle, I know You have plans for me, that You long for the best for me so my life may bring glory to You. In Jesus name, Amen.

Day 22

AND HE CALLED
Read: Leviticus 1-3

God used the whole book of Leviticus to explain to the people how to live a holy life with a holy God. Although we no longer sacrifice an animal for our sins, there is plenty for us to learn from this book. When they saw the animal being killed for their sin, they had a better understanding of how their sin had consequences and how it affects others. The sinner's hand was on the head of the animal, so he was very close to the sacrifice. It was to teach full submission without selfish motives. The head represented the mind of the individual, the fat was abundance, the inner parts was the emotions and the legs were their outward walk and conduct. The pleasing aroma to the Lord represents our prayers.

The animal must be one without defect, just as Christ was without sin. These sacrificial animals were set apart from profane use or cultic pollution for service to God. This is symbolic and foundational for ethical holiness.

In today's world, we do not sacrifice but we are to set ourselves apart, away from evil, keeping our mind pure, our emotions in check and our outward walk and conduct pleasing to the Lord. What does that look like? As you read the Bible, God will show you the dos and don'ts for your life. Much is the same for all of us, as in the Ten Commandments, but there are other areas that are very individual to each of us and we will learn these areas as we draw closer to the Lord.

Prayer: Heavenly Father, thank you for today's reading and reminding me that my actions have consequences. Please Father God, guide me in the ways You desire that I live, and may I be obedient to Your calling. In Jesus name, Amen.

Day 23

UNINTENTIONAL SIN
Read: Leviticus 4-6

How many times have you heard or you have said "I didn't mean to hurt you."? Yes, it is an unintentional sin. Just because we didn't mean to does not make it any less of a sin. Here in Leviticus, we see that God made provisions for unintentional sins. If He found an unintentional sin important enough to offer sacrifices for, how much more should we pay special attention to people we hurt unintentionally?

In any close relationship, it is bound to happen, at some point unintentional sin or should we say, actions that we didn't realize would hurt the other person but does. Many will just say "I didn't mean to" and walk away, leaving the other person hurting even worse because they were open enough to tell you that your behavior hurt them but then you acted like it was nothing.

After reading the passage today, we should realize that unintentional sin is just as important as intentional sin. Today, we need to repent of that unintentional sin but also go to the person we have sinned against and ask their forgiveness. This process cannot be a flippant "I'm sorry" but a heartfelt apology to change our ways and not do the same hurtful action to them again. We must state a right behavior in place of the hurtful behavior. We must be intentional.

Prayer: Heavenly Father, quicken my heart to be aware of wrong behavior and help me to be humble enough to make things right with those I hurt. Forgive me Father and help me walk in Your ways. In Jesus name, Amen.

Day 24

OBEDIENCE
Read: Leviticus 7-10

Concerning the ordination of Aaron and his sons, God had Moses follow a certain procedure. To take some of the blood from the sacrifice and put it on the right ear, to make him aware enough to listen to God's voice; put some of the blood on the thumb of his right hand, to show him that it is a privilege to serve the Living God; and on the big toe of his right foot, to remind him that his walk should always be acceptable in God's eyes. This ordination took time and would have been a constant reminder to these men that being chosen by God for a purpose was truly a privilege.

In our lives today, do we recognize that God has also chosen us for a purpose? Do we listen to God's voice as we read the Word? Are we always looking for the message that God wants to give us each and every day? Do we recognize what a privilege it is to serve God in all that we do? Are we more interested in our own pleasure or what God wants us to be doing? And finally, do we make a conscience effort to be pleasing God in our daily walk? "May the words of my mouth and the meditation of my heart be pleasing in Your sight, O Lord, my Rock and my Redeemer." (Psalm 19:14 NIV)

Prayer: Father God, help me to be pleasing to you in all my ways. Help me to focus on what You want me to meditate on, what You want me to be doing, and to listen intently to You so I am pleasing to You. Thank you, Father, that You are drawing me ever closer to You each day. In Jesus name, Amen.

Day 25

BE HOLY
Read: Leviticus 11-13

In our modern world, these chapters seem a little foreign, but they are there for a purpose. From clean and unclean food to infectious skin diseases, we can see that all these regulations are important to God. And, if they are important to God, they should be important to us in the way we live our lives.

Are we eating foods that are making us sick because they go against God's purposes? We continue eating unhealthy food because it tastes good and we see sickness everywhere but never make the connection. We run to a conventional doctor, who most often does not know these regulations, so he treats you with another poison rather than getting down to the root of the problem. The root of the problem is that most of us are not living as God had intended for us to live. He gave us guidelines to live by, but we say that was for then, we are so much more advanced. But are we?

Prayer: Heavenly Father, help me to digest your Word and take to heart what You are showing me, to change my behavior. Help me to remember that You made each of us just as we are, and I am to focus on myself. I need to glorify You by knowing You and keeping my body pure for Your good work. In Jesus name, Amen.

Day 26

BE CLEAN
Read: Leviticus 14-15

God required that the Israelites not live like the people around them, "You must keep the Israelites separate from things that make them unclean, so they will not die in their uncleanness for defiling my dwelling place, which is among them." (Lev 15:31 NIV)

They were to be set apart just as Christians today should be set apart from the evil that is ever present in our world. Yes, it means we must make choices of spending time with people who do not acknowledge God or live for Him. We are to keep ourselves clean in all manner of behavior and go before God in repentance when we have been exposed to and given in to the infection of sinful behavior.

Prayer: Dear Lord, give me discernment to know right from wrong, especially when the activity seems to be so much fun. When I do make a wrong choice, may I be quick to come to You in repentance and determined to change my ways. In Jesus name, Amen.

Day 27

DENY YOURSELF
Read: Leviticus 16-18

"Keep My requirements and do not follow any of the detestable customs that are practiced before you came and do not defile yourselves with them. I am the Lord your God." (Lev 18:30 NIV) In chapter 18, we see a list of "do nots", which were all practiced by the nations around as the Israelites were settling in a new land. God gave them this list to shield them from the dangers of such practices and people.

The United States used to be a Godly nation that followed the instructions of the Bible but once the Bible was forsaken, people forgot those instructions. People started practicing evil pleasures, being lured further and further into such detestable practices, just as God warned against.

Yet, in chapter 16:29 and 31 (NIV), we read "you must deny yourselves". In denying oneself, we learn to control those desires, those actions that seem so pleasurable at the moment, but can have far reaching consequences. So, in denying ourselves, we are actually being protected as we seek God's perfect will for our lives. Sometimes we may not understand; but God does, and He knows what is best for us.

> *Prayer: Dear Heavenly Father, help me to live for You and follow Your regulations. May the Holy Spirit be so strong in my life that I listen to those warnings and turn away from my fleshly desires. And Father, when I fail, please quicken my spirit and keep me humble so that I may turn from my wickedness in confession to You. In Jesus name, Amen.*

Day 28

SET APART
Read: Leviticus 19-21

In the New Living Translation, the heading for Chapter 19 says, "Holiness in Personal Conduct". This chapter goes back through some of the Ten Commandments such as do not steal, but it also tells the people how to behave with others. Leviticus 19:19 (NLT) reminds us all to "obey all My decrees." And Leviticus 20:7-8 (NLT), God reminds us "So set yourselves apart to be holy, for I am the Lord your God. Keep all my decrees by putting them into practice, for I am the Lord who makes you holy."

If we, as Christ followers, would read Leviticus regularly, and take some of these decrees to heart, and work hard to follow them, putting them into practice, perhaps people would not look at Christians and say, "they do the same things we do, sometimes even worse". We are being watched by those around us; make sure our actions are not the reason someone says they do not want to be a Christian. May we get to a point in life that we desire to please God and follow His decrees.

Prayer: Lord God, help me to be set apart, different from those around me and pleasing to You. Thank You for Your Word so I have guidelines on what is pleasing to You. I love You Lord! In Jesus name, Amen.

Day 29

FOLLOWING HIM
Read: Leviticus 22-24

In today's reading, God gives the rules and regulations for the many festivals the people and priest must follow. My thought is that God gave these to the people because that way they would be thinking of Him constantly (or at least during the festivals). When we look back at what has happened so far, in our reading, to the chosen people, they forsook God quickly when Moses was on the mountain too long. They whined and cried for the food they had in Egypt until God took drastic measures and fed them.

God reminds them "You must faithfully keep all my commands by putting them into practice, for I am the Lord. Do not bring shame on My Holy Name, for I will display My Holiness among the people of Israel." (Lev 22:31-32a NLT) Not only the Israelites, but we today must be reminded to follow His ways according to Scripture, for when we claim to be a Christian but behave differently, we bring shame to His name. We don't often think of it in this way, but it is true.

Prayer: Lord, help me to stay in Your Word daily and to let the Holy Spirit lead me for I long to be pleasing to You in all my ways. Keep my mind fixed on You and may my desires always be true to Your Word and Your ways. In Jesus precious name, Amen.

Day 30

REDEMPTION
Read: Leviticus 25-27

As we finish the book of Leviticus today, we see that God elaborates on His instructions He gave to Moses on Mount Sinai. God further reminds the people "If you want to live securely in the land, follow my decrees and obey my regulations." (Lev 25:18 NLT) God expected the Israelites and He expects us to follow His instructions, His decrees and His regulations.

Many say the Bible is an ancient book and not for today. Those who say that have either never read the Bible or have no understanding of the Word and have chosen not to do what God has decreed. Here, as we read the first five books, we see definite decrees and regulations laid out before the people. Today, many say this is Old Testament teaching so we don't have to follow it. There are some decrees that don't apply to us today but there are others that we would benefit from following.

Prayer: Heavenly Father, I read today of boundaries You set for the Israelites. May I know Your boundaries that You have for my life and not want more than You want for me. Thank You Lord for caring so deeply and showing me exactly what You require. In Jesus name, Amen.

Day 31

COUNTING
Read: Numbers 1-3

There are some passages in the Bible that are hard to get through and that leave us wondering what the significance is. Today's reading would be such a passage. Counting. Can you imagine how long it took to count 603,550 (see Num 2:32) men? But if God had the Israelites do this, it must have been important, even if we do not get it.

What this highlights is the importance of how God values order. He wanted to number every man by name and then God saw it important enough so they all would camp around the Tent of Meetings. God had a purpose for each person and in all of these instructions, He expected them to obey and to live orderly lives within the camp. Even the Levites were expected to follow the order that God set up.

Is it any different today? God does expect His people to live orderly lives, following His commands. Commands on how to treat each other and how to care for what God has allowed us to have. We are not to live in confusion or following our own flesh. That never seems to work well. But God always allows us our free will, and sometimes we must go through a time of pain before we come back to Him in repentance.

Prayer: Father of Order and Justice, please help me to live according to Your Word. I may stumble but may I be quick to repent and live for You! In Jesus name, Amen.

Day 32

SERVING HIM
Read: Numbers 4-6

In this time period, people took vows before the Lord, in which they had to perform certain acts or completely separate themselves from other people. "When a man or woman wrongs another in any way and so is unfaithful to the Lord, that person is guilty and must confess the sin he has committed. He must make full restitution for his wrong, add one fifth to it and give it all to the person he has wronged." (Num 5:6-7 NIV) There can be no question on how this is carried out, the people who today call themselves Christian would make for a more peaceful world by doing this when they wrong another. It would also help them to check their behavior before doing wrong. Consequences do discourage bad behavior.

When we read about special vows, there is a list of dos and don'ts that many today would not understand but remember, God always has a reason for restrictions and it is always for our good. When we dedicate our life to Christ, we need to make choices to abstain from pleasures that interfere with serving Him and to avoid all manner of evil.

Prayer: Precious Lord, help me to always be mindful of my behavior and to make things right immediately so I am not offensive to the person I hurt. Thank you, Lord, that I have a desire to serve You and help me to walk in a manner that is glorifying You in all I do. In Jesus name, Amen.

Day 33

GIVING
Read: Numbers 7-10

In chapter 7, we see monotonous giving, each giving the same thing that are considered gifts for the Lord. When we give, we must realize that, even though the gift is going to a person, it is truly giving to the Lord. Our giving, just as in today's reading, ultimately benefits us. It opens our heart to the needs of others. It is done in obedience to the Lord. It is given out of need. God does great things for those willing to obey Him.

"Rise up, O Lord! May Your enemies be scattered; may your foes flee before you." (Num 10:35b NIV) God always goes before all of our situations, He knows what is best even when we think we know better. May we be trusting Him in all our life decisions and even when we do not understand, we must trust a little more. May our faith so shine as to bring glory to Him!

Prayer: Heavenly Father, I praise you for allowing me to have the resources to give to the needs of others. I thank you Lord that You do go before me and care for me. The enemy has no authority in my life and, Lord, help me to always trust You. In Jesus name, Amen.

Day 34

GLUTTONY
Read: Numbers 11-13

When the people started whining about all they were missing by not being back in Egypt, they went to Moses and demanded meat. God sent quail for them to eat but He also named the place Kibroth-hattaavah (see Num 11: 34 concerning meanings: "graves of craving" (NIV) or "graves of gluttony" (NLT).)

How often do we whine about wanting something, thinking that we actually need it? We may even pray about it, and then we get it. Then it turns out not to be what we expected. It does not satisfy that longing within us. It may even gratify for a while but all too soon, it is put aside, perhaps even tossed out.

Is the longing in our soul filled and totally content by Jesus or do we want something more? As we keep our eyes on Him, He satisfies that deepest longing. For some of us, it takes years to understand that Jesus is all we need. We can go to Him for the smallest of prayer request in our daily life and He is there. Nothing satisfies like Jesus. Do you know Him?

Prayer: Lord, may my faith grow ever stronger and may I always be humble before You and mankind. May I not crave what is not good for me and be satisfied with what You give. In Jesus name, Amen.

Day 35

SLOW TO ANGER
Read: Numbers 14-15

Once again, we see the Israelites rebelling, fearful of the people in the land that God has promised them. They disobeyed God and tested him over and over and certainly grumbled against God and the leaders He had chosen. But, there are consequences for such behavior, not only would all 20 years old and older die in the desert but "your children will be shepherds here for forty years, suffering for your unfaithfulness, until the last of your bodies lies in the desert." (Num 14:33 NIV) When they started seeing the consequences come to reality, then they cried out "we have sinned" (Num 14:40b NIV) but although admitting their wrongs, they did not truly repent, that is, turn away from their sin. They still were bent on doing things their own way.

Have things changed much since this historical event? Do people still grumble against God? Do people still want to do things their own way rather than how God is directing? Do people still confess their sins the moment they start to suffer but never truly turn away from their evil ways? If it did not work for the Israelites, it will not work for us either!

Prayer: Father God, may I have a heart to be obedient to Your Word and not follow the lusts of my own heart. May I be quick to repent of my sin and turn to obeying Your commands, for You have given us a better direction. Thank You Lord for being patient with me! In Jesus name, Amen.

Day 36

GRUMBLING
Read: Numbers 16-18

Here we find a group of men who rose up against Moses and Aaron. These two men were God's chosen, so this group really was rebelling against God. Their grumbling went on and on. Moses humbled himself before this group, then suggested that they come back the next morning, so they could go before the Lord. You would think that the consequences to the behavior of the leaders would have gotten the groups attention. As the earth swallowed these men and their whole household, which was a cleansing of evil, and then fire took the 250 men, one would have thought that the assembly would have known that Moses and Aaron were from God. No, not at all, they continued to grumble.

Are we not this same way at times? It seems we get on a grumbling kick and can't stop. Do we need to examine who we are grumbling against? Are we being rebellious against someone God has put before us as our leader? What lesson is God trying to teach us? We may not get a staff that has sprouted, budded, blossomed and produced almonds but we need to allow God to guide us through our leaders, unless they are going against God's Word. May we have the wisdom to learn from those around us, those God has put in our path, and grow in His grace and love.

Prayer: Dearest Lord, I am sorry for being rebellious at times and not listening to You through others, always confirmed through Your Word. Help me to grow to be a more pleasing person and willing to learn, especially from mistakes, and to bring glory to You. In Jesus name, Amen.

Day 37

COMPLAINING
Read: Numbers 19-21

It seems that the Israelites were complaining against Moses on a regular basis. Each time, God would meet their needs and yet, they would forget God's goodness and complain once again. Several times God had had enough and was ready to destroy them but Moses would petition God's mercy and God would let them live.

This time, Moses was told to speak to the rock and water would come out. Moses was angry at the people because of their rebellion and struck the rock instead. Unfortunately, for his disobedience, Moses would not go into the Promised Land. This is a great reminder that God does expect us to obey His Word. When we don't, we suffer consequences. It doesn't mean we can't repent and turn our lives around, but we will be reminded of our disobedience by that consequence. And many times, God will prove that He does work all things for our good. We don't always understand but He is all knowing and all powerful and will always do what is best for us.

Prayer: Father God, help me to remember that You want the best for me. Help me to be content where I am and not complain to all who will listen. Thank You Lord for Your mercy. In Jesus name, Amen.

Day 38

BLESSING OR CURSING
Read: Numbers 22-25

Balaam was supposed to curse the Israelites, but it seems the only thing he could do was bless them. Not once, not twice but three times he blesses them from afar. The Israelites had no clue what was happening.

But then we see in Chapter 25 that the Israelite men defiled themselves by having sexual relations with the Moabite women, who also lured them into sacrificing to their gods. One sin can easily lead us towards another. With our hearts already hardened because of the first sin, we often don't even feel the nudge to walk away from more sin. With our defenses already low, we walk into evil going ever so much deeper. Be careful oh, so very careful and always keep our eyes on Jesus, reading the Bible daily and looking to Him for all instructions. He cares for you but has given us free will to make choices of doing His will or going our own way. Our way is never better!

Prayer: Dear Heavenly Father, I long to be pleasing to You and yet I fall into sin just as easily as the Israelites. Help me Lord to keep my eyes on You and my heart away from self-pleasure. I long to please You! In Jesus name, Amen.

Day 39

PRAYER
Read: Numbers 26-29

God receives our prayers "as an aroma pleasing to the Lord" (Num 28:8 NIV). We also see this in Revelation 5:8 (NIV) "Each one had a harp and they were holding golden bowls full of incense, which are the prayers of the saints." This was especially a time for prayer as Moses is preparing his successor, Joshua, so the people are not "like sheep without a shepherd." (Num 27: 17b NIV)

Many today look to their pastor to guide them and care for them but we must know that any person can often fall short. No matter how close he walks with the Lord, he is not perfect. How often does a pastor lead a church and ends up sinning in some manner that causes many of the people to leave the church, often never going to another? May we "fix our eyes on Jesus, the author and perfecter of our faith" (Heb 12: 2a NIV), who is the only One who will not disappoint us. We must do our part, staying focused on what Jesus wants for our lives.

Prayer: Heavenly Father, help me to stay in Your Word and to be obedient to the instructions You have given. Every day may Your desire be my desire, and may I never look to a human being for my fulfillment, only to You! In Jesus name, Amen.

Day 40

FOLLOW GOD WHOLEHEARTEDLY
Read: Numbers 30-32

It seems that the Israelites wanted to go their own way over and over so when the tribes of Reuben and Gad went to Moses with the proposal to live on the east side of the Promised Land, Moses reminded them of the reason they wandered for forty years. Their forefathers were sinners, going against the Lord and now it appears that their sons are doing the same thing. But "the Gadites and Reubenites answered, "Your servants will do what the Lord has said." (Num 32:31 NIV) They would obey by going into the land the Lord was giving them and fight. Once the land was taken, they would go live to the East of the Promised Land.

Aren't we often the same way? We turn the Lord down and want to live our own life, partially obeying the Lord but living outside His promises? Does there seem to be more freedom over there? Do we not trust the Lord's promises? Do we really think we know better? "Trust in the Lord with all your heart and lean not on your own understanding; in all your ways acknowledge Him and He will direct your paths." (Pro 3:5-6 NIV) Next time you want to do something differently than what the Lord has directed, pray long and hard about your decision and then consider obeying God.

Prayer: Lord, Creator of the Universe, forgive me when I think I know more than you and want to do things my way. Quicken my spirit and heart to Your ways and help me to be content. In Jesus name, Amen.

Day 41

REVIEW
Read: Numbers 33-36

The Israelites receive final instructions and Moses reminded them of the history of how they got to where they were. This is a very good example of what should be done, even today, as we are a people who seem to forget how we got to where we are. Along with such privilege come rules of what to do and what not to do. Sadly, in today's world, we seem to have a bunch of privileged people who do not think they need to do anything in return. Many don't even have a desire to give back to society. Sadly, they are takers.

The answer lies in whom they have chosen to serve. Have they forsaken the One True God of the Universe? Even if some attend church, they have lost their heart's desire to serve Christ so all they do is for show, which puts the emphasis on themselves, not on Christ?

"For it is by grace you have been saved, through faith—and this is not from yourselves, it is the gift of God—not by works, so that no one can boast. For we are God's handiwork, created in Christ Jesus to do good works, which God prepared in advance for us to do." (Eph 8-10 NIV)

Prayer: Most Precious Father, thank You for Your love! Remind me often that I am nothing without You! Help me to always show gratitude to those around me and to never be a taker. In Jesus name, Amen.

Day 42

GO FORTH
Read: Deuteronomy 1-3

We, again, are reminded of God's loving guidance as the Israelites are wondering in the wilderness. But this 40-year journey was punishment because they had not trusted the Lord. God said He was giving them a land that was rich and beautiful. Yes, He expected them to do their part, that is, to go in and fight the inhabitants, to destroy the evil people of the land He was giving them.

Today, we often think it is coldhearted to destroy evil people. Have we forgotten what Paul warns us in 1 Cor 15:30-34?

"And why should we ourselves risk our lives hour by hour? For I swear, dear brothers and sisters, that I face death daily. This is as certain as my pride in what Christ Jesus our Lord has done in you. And what value was there in fighting wild beasts—those people of Ephesus—if there will be no resurrection from the dead? And if there is no resurrection, "Let's feast and drink, for tomorrow we die!" Don't be fooled by those who say such things, for "bad company corrupts good character." Think carefully about what is right, and stop sinning. For to your shame I say that some of you don't know God at all." (NLT)

Evil must be dealt with. We cannot sit around, praying and lifting holy hands, without going into the battle. God calls us to fight for rights of children and elderly and all in between. He expects us to take the necessary steps to win against evil.

Prayer: Heavenly Father, give me the strength for whatever battle is ahead. Thank You for preparing me. In Jesus name, Amen.

Day 43

BE CAREFUL
Read: Deuteronomy 4-6

Over and over in today's reading, we see Moses reminding the people to obey, watch out and be careful plus Moses told the people to listen carefully as he gave them the Ten Commandments once again. This was all in preparation for going into the Promised Land, the land flowing with milk and honey. Almost every time Moses gave a reminder of what God expected them to do, it was followed by a promised blessing, if they obeyed.

It is much the same way today. When God gives us a promise, it is followed by what we need to do. Today, many worship other gods because we are such a materialistic people. Be careful that you don't look down your nose at others or you look to what your neighbor has and desire it. God has given you just exactly what He wants you to have, but remember, you are expected to care for and appreciate what He has given you. Again, we see that we must do our part.

Prayer: Father God, help me and remind me daily to follow Your Word, that I will do what is right and good in the Lord's eyes. Thank You for Your Word! In Jesus name, Amen.

Day 44

CHOSEN
Read: Deuteronomy 7-10

As the Israelites are preparing to go into the Promised Land, God, through Moses, is giving them detailed instructions. As He tells them to burn the idols in the land, He reminds them "For you are a holy people, who belong to the Lord your God. Of all the people on earth, the Lord your God has chosen you to be His own special treasure." (Deut 7:6 NLT) Do you think these people really comprehended how awesome a statement that is?

Here is the Good News that Peter gave to us: "But you are not like that, for you are a chosen people. You are royal priests, a holy nation, God's very own possession. As a result, you can show others the goodness of God, for He called you out of the darkness into His wonderful light." (1 Pet 2:9 NLT) When we have made that all important decision to ask Jesus to come into our lives, when we have decided to change our ways and live for Him, when we look to Him and His Word for the answers in life, we too are chosen by God!

The Israelites were called to be obedient to God's commands, and then they would be blessed. As Christ followers today, we are called to that same obedience; to love those around us and to obey His Word. Get in the Word, read it daily and ask God to show you His direction for you this very day.

Prayer: Heavenly Father, help me daily to walk in Your ways, to love and serve You by loving and serving those around me. May I never take my eyes off of You! In Jesus name, Amen.

Day 45

CHOICES
Read: Deuteronomy 11-14

Although much of what we read today has been said before, our precious Lord continues to remind the Israelites to be obedient to His commands, decrees and regulations.

"I am giving you the choice between a blessing and a curse! You will be blessed if you obey the commands of the Lord your God that I am giving you today. But you will be cursed if you reject the command of the Lord your God and turn away from Him and worship gods you have not known before." (Deut 11:26-28 NLT)

When we have Jesus in our lives, walking along the right road can be trying. We can see evil at every turn, but James reminds us that we must "resist the devil, and he will flee from you" (James 4:7b NIV). Just as God tested the Israelites (see Deut 13:3b), He will bring testing into our life. This isn't punishment but instead He is checking to see if we have learned our lesson and can move on in serving Him. May we make the right choice and obey the Lord, giving Him the glory for all He has done.

Prayer: Holy Father, may I not yield to the temptations all around nor follow those who are bent on sin. May I worship only You and obey Your commands and decrees. In Jesus name, Amen.

Day 46

FOLLOW JUSTICE
Read: Deuteronomy 15-18

God continues to give the Israelites instructions on how to live. He knew the hearts of the people so well that He told them how to handle debt, He told them how to treat their servants (employees in today's world), He told them how to care for the widows and orphans, He told them the importance of worshiping properly and twice we read, "You must purge the evil from among you." (Deut 17:7b and 12b NIV) All these instructions are, once again, a reminder of what their forefathers had been given. Furthermore, God was blunt about the detestable practices of those they were to conquer. Such practices have become common place in our modern society. Although we think we do not sacrifice our children, we do, and we practice divination and sorcery, we engage in witchcraft and casting spells and we even consult the dead.

We continue to need the reminder of how to live a Godly life, including "do not pervert justice or show partiality. Do not accept a bribe, for a bribe blinds the eyes of the wise and twists the words of the righteous. Follow justice and justice alone, so that you may live and possess the land the Lord your God is giving you." (Deut 16:19-20 NIV) Wise words then and we would do well to follow them today. As we fall further away from the Lord, we see more injustices happening and people turning a blind eye. We see babies being killed, homosexuality being accepted, money being given in exchange for favors, the government providing for the needy where the people of God should be walking alongside these people, and we are accepting such sin. This should not be!

Prayer: Heavenly Father, give me a heart to follow Your Word, no matter how hard it feels, help me to persevere so that I may be pleasing to You. Help me to take a strong stand against evil and purge it from our land. In Jesus name, Amen.

Day 47

UNINTENTIONAL
Read: Deuteronomy 19-22

Have you ever tried to deal with children who have been arguing and one gets hurt? We usually hear the other one say, "I didn't mean to hurt him." In today's reading, we see that a city of refuge is setup for someone killing another unintentionally. We also read today what is to be done to those who sin.

This points out that even when something is done unintentionally, it still has consequences--the guilty person still must be punished. I have heard that when confronted with their behavior, an abusive man will say, "I didn't mean to. You took it wrong". Well, according to the Scripture reading today, a sin is a sin, whether you did it intentionally or unintentionally, it still happened, and you must still be punished, suffer the consequences, apologize and make things right.

In present day America, it seems that people think that they do not have to take responsibility for their behavior if they say, "I didn't mean to". What has taken a society to this depth of irresponsibility? Perhaps it is a lack of exposure to what is right, a lack of fearing God (and adults in their lives) and a lack of self-control.

Prayer: Father in Heaven, have mercy on me. Your Word tells me to purge the evil from my life and I ask that You start with me. Forgive my sins so that I may walk afresh with You all the days of my life. In Jesus name, Amen.

Day 48

RESPONSIBILITY
Read: Deuteronomy 23-26

In today's reading we see that God is interested in what some might call the small things in life as well as big decisions. In chapter 24, verse 5, God tells us that a man recently married "must be free to spend one year at home, bringing happiness to the wife he has married" (NLT). This shows the importance God places on marriage and the responsibility of the man to learn all about his wife and to make her happy.

I went to a wedding once and I truly thought the pastor gave such good advice during the ceremony as he said to the groom "for the rest of your days, you will be going to the University of this precious woman who is to become your wife today. It is your job to study her and to please her all the days of your life." Of course, the pastor also had wise words for the bride as well but if more men knew the importance that God places on the man to make his wife happy, they might take this responsibility a little more serious. As much as men would like to say, "yeah but she has responsibility too", it is still the man who was made first, he was to delight in his wife and please her. Moreover, God holds men as the spiritual head of the family and men must work to be a servant leader inside the bonds of marriage.

Prayer: Heavenly Father, may I be pleasing to You in how I treat others. Give me a willing heart to follow Your instructions. In Jesus name, Amen.

Day 49

CONSEQUENCES
Read: Deuteronomy 27-29

I'm sure, by now, you have noticed that God repeats Himself on certain topics. When something is repeated once, it means that God wants us to "get it" to grasp hold to what He is saying. But as we see 'obey these commands' over and over, we have to understand that God is trying to tell the people "what I am saying is of the utmost importance, pay attention!" God tells the people to obey and He tells them the blessings that will happen if they do obey but in today's reading, we also read the curses that will happen if they do not obey. He even went a little further in Deut 28:58a (NLT) and said, "if you refuse to obey". Just like the Israelites, we forget quickly what God expects from us.

Yes, even today we take that chance, not believing that God will really punish us, we disobey the Lord, and we refuse to follow the Word of the Lord. Can you imagine? The sad truth is: we all do it. And because many do not read the Bible or haven't in a long time, we walk, make decisions and go in our own direction with no thought of the Lord. Is this decision we've just made pleasing to the Lord? Perhaps we should pray and seek His face before plowing ahead in our own sinful way? Choices are always left to us, God wants us to follow Him, but He is not going to force us! Which do you choose? Obedience or disobedience? Life or death?

Prayer: Heavenly Father, help me not to turn aside from Your Word. Help me to fully obey You in all I do. In those times I sin, bring me to You in full repentance so my relationship with You is renewed. In Jesus name, Amen.

Day 50

ANOTHER GOOD-BYE
Read: Deuteronomy 30-34

Moses reminds the people of their responsibility, what God expects of them as they go into the Promised Land. Then he commissions Joshua, who will lead the people after Moses dies. The Lord reminds Joshua to "be strong and courageous" (Deut 31:6a NIV) as he leads the people.

In our own lives, once we have decided to live for Christ, to let Him guide us in all we do, we too must take courage in serving Him. Life is not always easy, but God will use everything we go through for our good and it will bring glory to Him.

As we close the book of Deuteronomy, we find Moses climbing up the mountain to look across into the Promised Land. I feel like Moses has become a good friend. He's made mistakes, but he has also cried out in repentance for his sins as well as for these people when God had had enough of their sinful ways. Even though God said Moses would not go into the Promised Land this side of heaven, we find in Matthew 17:4 that Moses and Elijah were with Jesus. What a precious Lord we serve, who blesses us even when we don't deserve it.

Prayer: Precious Lord, thank You for not leaving us high and dry but giving us instructions for life. May I always fall into Your everlasting arms and see You as my refuge and strength. In Jesus name, Amen.

Day 51

JOSHUA
Read: Joshua 1-3

"Be strong and courageous" (see Joshua 1:6; 1:7; 1:9; 1:18) are the words God says to Joshua several times as Joshua takes over the leadership of the Israelites. God instructs Joshua to be careful to follow all the instructions that Moses had given him and further, God says "not to deviate from them" (Joshua 1:7 NLT). God goes on to tell Joshua to "study this Book of Instruction continually" and finally to "meditate on it day and night" (Joshua 1:8 NLT). And God reminds Joshua of the promise connected with these instructions "only then will you prosper and succeed in all you do." (Joshua 1:8 NLT)

I'm sure you've heard before that God gives us free-will, we can make our own decisions. It has been that way since the beginning. Joshua could listen to the Lord's instructions or do what he wanted. When we have God speaking to us directly, like Moses and now Joshua, who would want to do any different? But, did you realize that the Word of God, the Bible, gives us instructions on how to live our lives? We must read it daily, meditate on it and finally make that decision to follow it or go our own way. Our choices are not always so wise, and we suffer the consequences, but God's way is the only way to be blessed and certainly for us to bring God the glory.

Prayer: Heavenly Father, I hold to Your promise that You will not leave me nor forsake me. Help me daily to obey You in all that I do. Give me strength for each new day, knowing my hope is in You. In Jesus name, Amen.

Day 52

SIN FOUND OUT
Read: Joshua 4-7

As the Israelites cross the Jordan and take Jericho, they are witness to God's sustaining power and care for them. We see that God also gives instructions on how Jericho will be defeated and what must be destroyed and what must be consecrated to the Lord very clear and precise instructions. Achan chose not to obey and stole what was set apart for destruction; he saw a beautiful robe and some coins along with a gold bar and decided that he would go against the Lord's instructions. As a result, his whole family was stoned, and their bodies were burned.

I do not think people understand the importance of being honest and living a life of integrity and the destruction that can happen to our whole family if we go against the teachings of the Lord. Achan was an example to the whole community to obey the Lord's instructions but further, he is an example for us today. As we live our lives, each person has a responsibility to be in the Word of God and to obey what God is telling you. Walking with the Lord, walking with the intention of serving Him and doing what He expects will not only guard you but your family from certain destruction.

Prayer: Dear Heavenly Father, I confess to You that I have been disobedient to You and Your Word. Father forgive me for my rebellion and help me to walk before You in honesty and integrity of heart and mind. In Jesus name, Amen.

Day 53

DESTROY EVIL
Read: Joshua 8-10

Some may see today's Scriptural reading as war and killing and say how horrible it was for the Israelites to kill everyone. But, remember, God had instructed Joshua that they were to destroy everyone when they crossed the Jordan to take the land. Why? Because what these people did was evil. They worshipped other gods, they sacrificed their children, and they were a very immoral people.

This is a good lesson for us today because nothing has changed. Paul said in 1 Corinthians 15:33, "Do not be misled, bad company corrupts good character" (NIV). In today's society, we cannot go around killing those evil people, the best that we can do is to totally stay away from such people and pray for them.

We must protect ourselves from immoral, evil people by shutting them out of our lives. Yes, I've heard the arguments that perhaps we can love them to Christ and goodness. But I will present to you an abusive person who belittles you, who eggs you on to a point that you strike back. So, in a way, you become like them. The best thing to do is to close them out of our life, not having contact with evil. You can continue to pray for such a person but don't subject yourself to evil. Proverbs 22: 24-25 confirms this, "Do not make friends with a hot-tempered man, do not associate with one easily angered, or you may learn his ways and get yourself ensnared." (NIV)

Prayer: Heavenly Father, please help me to stay away from evil and to be pleasing to you by doing good. Help me to listen to You and to obey. In Jesus name, Amen.

Day 54

CALEB COLLECTS
Read: Joshua 11-14

    Caleb had been faithful when he went with the men to explore the land some 45 years before. He had seen that it truly was a land flowing with milk and honey, but ten other spies discouraged the people concerning going in and thus began their 40 years of wondering in the desert. Caleb wholeheartedly followed the Lord and now, at 85 years old, he was given the land promised to him.

    This is such a great reminder that sometimes we must wait many years before our prayers are answered. Never give up and certainly keep on fighting for the Lord as He strengthens and matures us to be able to handle the precious gift He is giving us.

Prayer: Dear Lord, help me to be like Caleb, to stand with You and not the crowd and to follow You wholeheartedly. In Jesus name, Amen.

Day 55

TAKE POSSESSION
Read: Joshua 15-18

We can see that God likes order as He sets boundaries for each tribe, and more importantly, God expected them to take possession of what He was giving them.

Just as Joshua had to tell the descendants of Joseph when they came to him and said they didn't have enough land for all their people, to clear out the hill country, God expects us to go in and clear out what He has given us. To maintain what He has given us. To take care of what He has given us. There are times that He expects us to fight for what He wants us to have and once we have it, we are to clear that forest and take possession.

God had allowed me to serve Him on the island of Tobago, I had to prepare for this journey by selling my house, selling and giving away almost everything I owned, preparing for a move to a foreign land. Each day while there, I prayed for God's protection for the work being done. I had taken that step of faith and went forward, despite the obstacles that the evil one tried to put in my way. I also knew when it was time to come back home. What do you need to prepare for, to step out in faith with the strength that can only come from Him?

Prayer: Precious Lord, sometimes I am weak or afraid, help me to step out in faith to take possession for that which You want me to have. When I am weak, may Your strength keep me going. In Jesus name, Amen.

Day 56

A WITNESS
Read: Joshua 19-22

As the Reubenites, the Gadites and the half-tribe of Manasseh returned to the land on the east side of Jordan, Joshua reminded them, "be very careful to keep the commandment and the law that Moses the servant of the Lord gave you: to love the Lord your God, to walk in all His ways, to obey His commands, to hold fast to Him and to serve Him with all your heart and all your soul." (Joshua 22:5 NIV) The Lord had handed their enemies to them! "Not one of all the Lord's good promises to the house of Israel failed; every one was fulfilled." (Joshua 21:45 NIV)

May we learn a lesson or two from today's reading. Even if our intentions are good and honorable, we need to communicate to those around us what we are doing. First, it is an accountability factor and secondly, then no one has to guess what we are doing for we are forthright and open.

Prayer: Lord Jesus, help me to always be open in my actions and willing to sit and talk to those around me as to why I am doing things the way I am. Also, Lord, help me to not rebel against You and that I would worship you from my heart. In Jesus name, Amen.

Day 57

FAREWELL
Read: Joshua 23-24

In our reading today, we find the well-known phrase that we see on plaques as we enter a home, "choose for yourselves this day whom you will serve but as for me and my household, we will serve the Lord." (Joshua 24:15 NIV)

When we make a choice to serve the Lord, it is more than with mouth service. He expects us to serve Him with our whole heart. Remember that God is a jealous God and has given us instructions as to how we serve him. In Joshua 23: 6-8, He tells us "so be very careful to follow everything Moses wrote in the Book of Instruction. Do not deviate from it, turning either to the right or to the left. Make sure you do not associate with the other people still remaining in the land. Do not even mention the names of their gods, much less swear by them or serve them or worship them. Rather, cling tightly to the Lord your God as you have done until now." (NLT)

Those instructions are as much for today as they were when Joshua was giving them. Truly, they are not meant to make life less fun for us. No indeed, God gave these instructions so our lives will be more full. We will know true contentment if we chose to serve God only, to worship Him daily, to seek His face in all our decisions. I don't know about you, but I have strayed from the Lord from time to time, seeking my own pleasure but it has always come back to bite me. Who do you choose to serve?

Prayer: Dear God, may I yield my heart to You and obey. May my heart be bent on loving God only and be reminded of His faithfulness. Thank You Lord for always bringing me back to You. In Jesus name, Amen.

Day 58

FAILURE
Read: Judges 1-3

God had given the Israelite instructions to take the land; that is to destroy all the inhabitants. The reason they were to destroy everyone is because the people were evil, they worshiped false gods, they presented human sacrifices, and they chose to serve themselves. By not obeying God's directions, it was just a matter of time before the Israelites would be following after the people of the land.

Even today, we must be careful who we keep company with. It may not be acceptable to kill those evil around us, but we can stay away from them. Have you ever noticed how easily we are drawn towards evil? First of all, evil oftentimes seems fun. If we are not careful, we can be drawn to evil like a magnet. And once we are in its clutches, it seems that we have to experience more and more evil before we wake up and repent. But, just as Jesus told the woman caught in adultery, He also expects us today to, "go now and leave your life of sin." (John 8:11 NIV)

Prayer: Holy Spirit, fall fresh on me. May I never forget the regulations God has put before me and may I obey His Word. In Jesus name, Amen.

Day 59

GOD USES DEBORAH
Read: Judges 4-5

Deborah was a prophet and was also judging the Israelites. I think this very important for we can see in Acts 10:34 when Peter says, "I now realize how true it is that God does not show favoritism." (NIV) So, we can better understand that God can just as easily use a woman to fulfill His plan as a man. What Peter also realized is that God can use a gentile as easily as a Jew. So, Deborah called Barak to go fight against Sisera, but Barak did not want to go without Deborah. She agrees but tells him that victory will be given to a woman, instead of him.

This reading is very important for each of us who does not have the right concept of how important we are to God. Truly, He does not show favoritism. Years ago, I had a pastor tell me that he thought that if the men (of the church) did not take on their leadership roles, God would use the women, not only as leaders but also to teach the younger generation of men leadership so they could fulfill what God has called men to do.

Prayer: Dear Lord, may my heart always be willing to obey Your calling. Give me the strength to daily obey You. In Jesus name, Amen.

Day 60

TESTING
Read: Judges 6-8

Over and over we have read how the Lord used different leaders to remind the Israelites of the law and regulations they were to observe. Unfortunately, they, like us, seem to want to take a different road. How many times do we read that they did evil? Or that they did what was right in their own eyes? Worshipping other Gods. Wanting what others have. Not listening to those who are trying to tell them to turn from our wicked ways. Failing to show kindness.

God had used Gideon to bring the people back to Himself but as soon as he died, they "again prostituted themselves to the Baals." (Judges 8:33 NIV) We, in today's modern world, are not any different. We are pulled away from serving and following the Lord by entertainment, playing or watching sports. We are pulled away from the Lord because we have to work to make more money to buy things that we do not need. We are pulled away because we are trying to impress someone who could care less about what we do or what we have.

Today's reading should be an encouragement to us as we face battles in our own lives. But know, if He is calling you, it is OK to test Him to make sure He is the one doing the calling. When you get the confirmation, get busy and do exactly what He has called you to do. He will bring about the victory!

Prayer: Father God, help me to listen to You and then act upon what you have told me. I am so thankful that You would see me worthy of serving, help me to walk forward in faith. In Jesus name, Amen.

Day 61

REPENTANCE AGAIN
Read: Judges 9-12

Once again, the Israelites went their own way, choosing to not please the Lord with their behavior. And again, they suffered the consequences of such behavior. When things got bad enough, they did cry out to God, "We have sinned against You, forsaking our God and serving the Baals." (Judges 10:10 NIV) But God answered, "you have forsaken Me and served other gods, so I will no longer save you. Go and cry out to the gods you have chosen. Let them save you when you are in trouble!" (Judges 10:13-14 NIV) Again, we see the Israelites confessing their sin, and "got rid of their foreign gods among them and served the Lord" (Judges 10:16 NIV) and God accepted them back, once again.

This is a good lesson for us to remember. Whether it is God's forgiveness we are seeking or that of another person, we may need to go ask forgiveness and repent of our behavior more than once. We may need to change our ways to show that we are a changed person. But, if you are sincere about wanting them back in your life, you will do whatever it takes to show them you are sorry and have changed.

Prayer: Heavenly Father, forgive me of my wrong behavior and help me to be successful in You. Help me to stay on the straight and narrow path in doing what is right in what you have told me to do. In Jesus name, Amen.

Day 62

SAMPSON
Read: Judges 13-16

As children, many of us heard the story of Sampson and his great strength. What we often failed to grasp is that Sampson was a womanizer and quite disobedient, but God never gave up on him.

During her pregnancy, Sampson's mother never drank fermented drink or ate any unclean food, for her son was set apart to God for the purpose of delivering Israel out of the hands of the Philistines. He seemed to be somewhat of a wild, undisciplined young man as he insisted (to his parents) that he wanted a Philistine wife. When his marriage to her did not work out, he moved on in his anger. In his final choice of women, she too was not faithful to him but was more interested in getting some cash from her fellow countrymen.

Sad to say that many of us today have also made bad choices and focused on a person rather than God. But as we see in today's reading, God can use our mistakes and bring us back under His wing. God longs for us to recognize that He is all we need, and He will use us and care for us just as we need. Do not let those around you who think they are better than you, tell you that God can no longer use you. For when we are at the end of ourselves, we can grab hold of His hand and gain new strength from Him.

Prayer: Father in Heaven, I have sinned more times than I can remember, forgive me. Help me to walk with You all the days of my life and when I stumble, get back up and start on the path to serving You. Thank You for Your love! In Jesus name, Amen.

Day 63

EVERYONE DID AS HE SAW FIT
Read: Judges 17-19

I find it quite interesting how the Israelites were given instructions on how to behave, what to do and what not to do it couldn't be any clearer. Yet, in today's reading we find a man from Ephraim who confessed to his mother that he'd stolen her silver. When she got the money back, she took some of it and had an image and an idol made and placed these in Micah's house. Sometime later a young Levite is invited to stay at Micah's house and be his personal priest. This priest lives in a house with idols and as long as he is getting his 10 pieces of silver a year and a change of clothes and food to eat, that's all he cares about.

The sad part is, it is not much different today. We have people who will sell their soul for a position at their job or choose to overlook evil, dishonesty and immorality because, they insist that it is a different world today and it is accepted. Are we going to serve God, bring glory to Him in all our behaviors or overlook evil and follow that path?

Prayer: Heavenly Father, give me strength to stand against evil and to live my life so I am pleasing to You. In Jesus name, Amen.

Day 64

PURGE EVIL
Read: Judges 20-21

The Israelites wanted to do what was right. They went before the Lord for answers. They were to purge evil from the land. The Benjamites had "committed this lewd and disgraceful act". (Judges 20:6b NIV) At first they asked that the wicked men of Gibeah be turned over to them so that they could be put to death, in fact purging the evil from the land. It was not that easy, they ended up in battle where both sides lost a great number of men. Because of Benjamin's great loss, the Israelites had to figure out how to provide wives for the men who were left. With this problem solved, they continued to do what was right in their own eyes.

And so, we see that nothing is new today, we sin, we try to make things right and then we have to decide how to settle the matter. We may even look to the Lord for short periods of time, but we think we know better, we have a better plan than following the Lord's direction. Aren't we a strange people? To have the Lord of the Universe to care for us and have His Word to guide but we want to do things our own way?

Prayer: Dear Heavenly Father, walk along side of me and give me a willing heart to serve You, to listen to You and obey You so that my days here on earth may be pleasing to You. In Jesus name, Amen.

Day 65

A REDEEMER
Read: Ruth 1-4

The relationship between Naomi and Ruth was quite unique. Even though Naomi encouraged her daughters-in-law to return to their families, Ruth wanted to stay with Naomi. "But Ruth replied, "Don't urge me to leave you or to turn back from you. Where you go I will go, and where you stay I will stay. Your people will be my people and your God my God. Where you die I will die, and there I will be buried. May the Lord deal with me, be it ever so severely, if anything but death separates you and me." (Ruth 1:16-17 NIV) Indeed, Ruth was faithful and Naomi very blessed.

Today, we don't gather grain, nor do we hope for a family redeemer, but we will do well to seek God in all that we do. For God has called some to be single and God has called others to marry. In either case, we should set the Lord always before us.

Prayer: Lord, may I always be faithful to those near and dear to me and most of all, may I be faithful to You. May You be the One I seek to redeem me, and may I always be reminded that you care so deeply for me. In Jesus name, Amen.

Day 66

GIVING TO GOD
Read: 1 Samuel 1-3

In Genesis, we saw that God asked Abraham to sacrifice Isaac to test his faith. In today's reading, we find Hannah childless and very discouraged. She goes before the Lord, "pouring out my soul" (1 Sam 1:15b NIV). She wants a son so badly that she makes a vow to give this boy child back to the Lord so he can serve the Lord his entire life. And God grants her request.

May we be like Hannah and "sing" a prayer of praise to the Lord as He molds our precious loved ones into the image of His Son, Jesus. May we keep our loved ones in our prayers and see that they will grow "in favor with the Lord and with people". (1 Sam 2:26b NLT) May we give to God all who are of great importance to us and cover them in prayer.

Prayer: Heavenly Father, You lift up the needy, You humble and You exalt and You look at my actions and weigh them. May I possess the humility of Hannah and let go of whom You have given me and allow You to direct their ways. Thank you for my children! In Jesus name, Amen.

Day 67

REPENT AND SERVE THE LORD ONLY
Read: 1 Samuel 4-7

We see in today's reading that Eli's two sons were killed in battle and the Ark of God was captured by the Philistines. When Eli was told of this news, being old and fat, he fell over backwards and broke his neck. Why would the Bible tell us that he was overweight? For one thing, it showed he was self-indulging. When we are self-indulging, we usually are putting our own self-interest before those of the Lord. Oftentimes the Lord asks us to give up something that is of great importance to us. It might be food, it might be certain reading material or a TV program, it might be certain people, but God makes it very clear that He doesn't want it in our life.

God shows us and gives us choices. He never forces His will on us. Because of our great love for Him, we should want to do what He's asking us. Wouldn't it be wonderful if it were that simple: He shows me, and I do it? That's not often the case, sometimes we have to be shown a couple of times before we get the hint. But it is important to remember that He guides us to make our life more pleasing to Himself. Our obedience does not get us a higher place in heaven no, only the blood of Jesus and our accepting Him as our Lord and Savior will get us to heaven. But when we love someone, we want to please Him. The choice is ours.

Prayer: Lord, help me to be willing to confess and turn away from my sin, to help me release those things that are pulling me away from You. Do whatever is necessary to keep me close to You. In Jesus name, Amen.

Day 68

THE SPIRIT OF THE LORD
Read: 1 Samuel 8-11

Saul was God's chosen, the King that Israel had longed for. The Lord gave him a new heart and the Spirit of the Lord came upon him and he prophesied. (see 1 Sam 10:10) We read several times in today's reading how the Spirit of the Lord came upon Saul and he did what the Lord was calling him to do for he was "changed into a different person" (1 Sam 10:6b NIV).

Today, the Spirit of the Lord doesn't come and go. Once we've accepted Jesus into our lives, in repentance, we humbly ask the Lord Jesus to come dwell in our lives and our hearts desire changes. We want to live for Jesus, no longer wanting to please only ourselves. The Holy Spirit comes in to dwell in our lives, not to leave but to help us live a life pleasing to our Father. As we daily read the Word, He daily speaks to our heart to guide us in the little things as well as the bigger things through His Word.

As we press on towards the goal of such a high calling as to serve the Risen King, our Lord and Savior, we may stumble from time to time. The important thing is for us to humble ourselves to Jesus and ask Him to forgive our sin that we may be able to move forward in serving Him. He loves us so much and His desire is to draw us ever closer to Him, to guide us and take us by the hand. His great love is unfailing!

Prayer: Heavenly Father, thank You for Your great love. We see it in our daily reading and we need it every day of our lives. Help me to stay close to You. In Jesus name, Amen.

Day 69

FOOLISHNESS
Read: 1 Samuel 12-14

Saul found out pretty early in his reign that he was not pleasing to God and the Lord was seeking a man after His own heart to take Saul's place as king. Saul and his men were waiting for Samuel to offer a burnt offering and a peace offering, Saul became impatient and made the offering himself and when Samuel arrived, Saul gave him a lame excuse for his behavior. But Samuel told Saul right then that he had done a foolish thing by not keeping the command of the Lord. Furthermore, Samuel told Saul, "now your kingdom must end, for the Lord has sought out a man after His own heart." (1 Sam 13:14a NLT)

Each and every day we find in our daily reading how important it is to God for us to follow His instructions (the laws and commands that God directs us with). Are we any different than Saul much of the time? Even when we know what we should do, we still tend to do it our own way. When we fail, have fallen on our face, we will then (sometimes) consider the way of the Lord. His ways are higher than our ways, we don't necessarily understand how they can work but when we follow His direction, things turn out. This can be a hard lesson to learn but it is a good lesson to learn.

Prayer: Lord, help me to learn the lessons You are teaching me and to not be stubborn. Help me to grasp those lessons You have for me. In Jesus name, Amen.

Day 70

OBEDIENCE IS BETTER THAN SACRIFICE
Read: 1 Samuel 15-17

Although we have the well-known story of David killing Goliath in today's reading, I want to concentrate on Saul's rebellion. As we read 1 Sam 15:22-23(NLT), "But Samuel replied, What is more pleasing to the Lord: your burnt offerings and sacrifices or your obedience to His voice? Listen! Obedience is better than sacrifice, and submission is better than offering the fat of rams. Rebellion is as sinful as witchcraft, and stubbornness as bad as worshiping idols." This is straight forward. It is plain. God wants obedience.

Saul tried to look spiritual by saying he had been disobedient, so he could offer the animals as sacrifices, even though God had given explicit instructions to kill everything. And this exact same thing is going on today. You have preachers telling the congregation to give, give, give with the promise that they will receive tenfold the blessings, this for their own benefit. We find so many who let everyone know what good deeds they are doing for Christ, but their heart is far from what God has called them to do. Obedience to His Word is better than sacrifice. So walk along humbly and walk in obedience to the Word of God.

Prayer: Lord, the battle is truly Yours. Help me to read Your Word and obey so You can fight my battles and let victory reign. In Jesus name, Amen.

Day 71

TRUE FRIENDSHIP
Read: 1 Samuel 18-21

True friendship is a rare finding. We see this type of friendship between Jonathan and David. They were there for each other but not necessarily inseparable. For many today, this is hard to understand. We don't have to be together in body, but we are together in spirit, praying for one another and always helping the other to draw nearer to the Lord.

Jonathan asked David to "treat me with faithful love of the Lord as long as I live. But if I die, treat my family with this faithful love " (1 Sam 20:14-15 NLT) In our fast-paced world, full of many who control their friends (or at least try), we seldom find friendships that are deep yet give each other the freedom to serve the Lord. If you have a true friendship, hold on tightly yet allowing the Lord to use each of you where He will.

Prayer: Father God, thank You for giving me loving and supportive people in my life to encourage me when I am down and to love me through it all. May I always be faithful and kind to the friends You have given me. In Jesus name, Amen.

Day 72

FAITHFUL
Read: 1 Samuel 22-24

Much of today's reading concerns Saul chasing David from one place to another, accusing him of trying to kill him. But when David had a chance to take Saul's life, he could not do it. In the midst of Saul's craziness, his son, "Jonathan went to find David and encourage him to stay strong in his faith in God" (1 Sam 23:16 NLT). Jonathan comforts David by these words, "Don't be afraid" (1 Sam 23:17a NLT).

It is truly a special friend that is an encourager. It is the person who we want to share the day with. The person who listens to us when we are hurting. The person who is there through the hard times as well as the good times. Always be thankful for special friends but for those of us who have accepted Jesus in our hearts, we also have Him as that special friend who is there for us.

Prayer: Precious Lord, thank You for loving me and always being there for me. Help me to be an encouraging friend and to always point the hurting to You. In Jesus name, Amen.

Day 73

WICKEDNESS
Read: 1 Samuel 25-27

Nabel was crude and mean in all his dealings and furthermore he was wicked and ill-tempered. His wife was sensible and beautiful. Have you ever noticed in life that it seems that opposites seem to marry? In this case, it certainly seems to be true. When we see the arrogance of Nabel when David's men came and asked for provisions, especially when David's men protected Nabel's shepherds and his flocks, was beyond understanding and certainly common sense.

If Nabel was wicked, ill-tempered and mean in all his dealings, he most likely treated Abigail, his wife, the very same way, yet she went to David to ask his forgiveness of Nabel wicked behavior. David recognized her wisdom in doing this and blessed her as she kept David from killing Nabel and his men.

There are many men today that are arrogant, mean, wicked and certainly ill-tempered. Today we call it abuse but remember, it is sin to treat anyone like that. Even when a man is shown his evil in the way he treats his wife and others, he often ignores this insight. God brings our behavior before us for the purpose of repentance and change. It is our choice. But do remember, if we choose not to repent and change, we may not die immediately like Nabel did, but we will certainly die spiritually even if we pretend to be Godly.

Prayer: Heavenly Father, may You give me wisdom like Abigail with good judgment and reward these efforts. May this draw those around me to a relationship with You. In Jesus name, Amen.

Day 74

STRENGTH IN THE LORD
Read: 1 Samuel 28-31

In today's reading, we see that Samuel has died as well as Saul and his sons. When David and his men were gone from Ziklag, the Amalekites destroyed it and took the women and children. David's men were angry and talked about stoning him, but David sought the Lord. The Lord assured David that they would recover all that had been taken. David found strength in God!

No matter what we are facing, whether large or small, may we gain our strength, our guidance, our hope in the Lord our God. May we never be selfish in what the Lord has given us, and may we always be willing to share the hope that comes from Jesus. Not only will He strengthen us, but He will also comfort us, care for us, protect us and also allow us to grow in character. Of utmost importance, we must always look to Him and His Word to learn how to mature and be pleasing to Him in all we do.

Prayer: Heavenly Father, may it always be said that I found my strength in You. When I am weak, discouraged or saddened, may I look to You. In Jesus name, Amen.

Day 75

MOURNED, WEPT AND FASTED
Read: 2 Samuel 1-4

Can you imagine the sorrow David felt when he found out his dear friend Jonathan had died? But David was an honorable man and also lamented for Saul as well. There was a lot of years that they had known one another, and David had such deep feelings for both Saul and Jonathan.

There are people who are a part of our lives but yet, the other person does not seem to care much about us. That does not stop our feelings, but we must respect their wishes. We may not have contact with them or be able to talk to them, but we can talk to the Lord about that person. Sometimes we lament over a lost friendship, sometimes we lament over the loss of a dear friend. A loss is a loss! We feel that pain. We may not understand but God does. God has His reasons for taking a person out of our lives. God knows best.

Prayer: Father God, thank You for loving me and watching over me even in choosing my friends and those near to me. Help me to accept and move on when you take someone out of my life. In Jesus name, Amen.

Day 76

ETERNAL BLESSINGS
Read: 2 Samuel 5-8

May we all have David's heart, "And now, O Lord God, I am Your servant; do as You have promised concerning me and my family. Confirm it as a promise that will last forever." And further on, "For You have spoken, and when you grant a blessing to Your servant, O Sovereign Lord, it is an eternal blessing!" (2 Sam 7: 25 and 29b NLT)

May we look to the Lord, seeking His will for our lives with humility of heart. May we give up "self" and be willing to do His will moment by moment. This can only happen as we read the Bible to see what God expects from us. This is not a quick fix in life but a process. As we read His Word and internalize it, our behavior starts to change. Our attitude also takes on new character and the longer we look to God for the answers to our everyday living, the more we develop the character of Christ.

Prayer: Heavenly Father, may I see joy in the gifts you bring to me from family and friends to precious pets. May I be willing at all time to do what is right and just. In Jesus name, Amen.

Day 77

DOING HIS WILL
Read: 2 Samuel 9-11

In Chapter 11, we read that David chose not to go out to war, as kings were accustomed to doing. He took a break from what was expected of him. Not being able to sleep, he wandered around on the roof and observed a woman bathing. "But each one is tempted when, by his own evil desire, is dragged away and enticed. Then after desire has conceived, it gives birth to sin; and sin, when it is full-grown, gives birth to death." (James I: 14-15 NIV) Seeing Bathsheba bathing, in the middle of the night, caused David to have desire for another man's wife, but he did not control his evil desire, instead, he fed that desire and it gave birth to sin.

Although we may not end up murdering someone, when we take our eyes off Jesus and start sinning instead of staying close to the will of God, we can find ourselves in the midst of big problems as well. The very moment we realize we are on a downward spiral, we need to go to the Lord and repent of our sin. Repentance means to turn away from the sin and walk with Jesus.

Prayer: Dear Lord, thank you for allowing me to read about David's sin and reminding me how vulnerable I am. It may not be the same sin, but I have areas where I am weak. Keep me close to You and obedient to Your Word. In Jesus name, Amen.

Day 78

CONSEQUENCES
Read: 2 Samuel 12-14

It is apparent that, although David was a man after God's own heart, he did not teach his children the laws and regulations of God. Amnon lusting after his sister, then devising a way to rape her and then hating her should have resulted in great punishment by his father but David did nothing. Absalom does kill his brother for what he did to their sister and again David does nothing. In fact, when Absalom does finally come home, King David kissed him.

Are we quick to bring the consequences of sin to our children so that they learn a lesson? Punishment is not bad, although it should be feared, because with punishment should come repentance for such behavior. But without immediate consequences for sinful behavior, we can think such behavior is acceptable and we will continue with sinful actions. Proverbs 5:23 reminds us "He will die for lack of discipline, led astray by his own great folly." (NIV)

Prayer: Heavenly Father, remind me often to speak Your truth to those you bring in my path but especially my children. May I be strong in Your Word and always wanting to bring life to those whom I love and those you bring into my life. Give me strength for this task. In Jesus name, Amen.

Day 79

RUNNING
Read: 2 Samuel 15-17

Absalom has now devised a plan to take over the kingdom and become king in place of his father. How very sad that David, a man of God, who fought and won many battles is running from his own son, like a scared animal.

This should be a lesson to men on how to father. Never overlook a sin your children commit! Children, no matter what age they are, need guidance and discipline, otherwise we will see them in trouble with the law or worse, they will die. Like many today, Absalom was arrogant. He thought he could do anything he wanted and get away with it. He looked for one thing after another to offend not only his father but the people of the kingdom. And, like many today, he justified himself.

Prayer: Father in Heaven, always keep me humble and willing to do Your will. Allow me to be a strong parent, looking to You for my guidance. In Jesus name, Amen.

Day 80

MOURNING
Read: 2 Samuel 18-21

Whether right or wrong, Absalom is killed and this news is taken to King David. Rather than being thankful for his men protecting him from Absalom, he is shaken and goes into great mourning for his son. Joab was right in confronting the king, "Today you have humiliated all your men, who have just saved your life and the lives of your sons and daughters and the lives of your wives and concubines. You love those who hate you and hate those who love you. You have made it clear today that the commanders and their men mean nothing to you. I see that you would be pleased if Absalom were alive today and all of us were dead." (19: 5-6 NIV)

We often see this sort of behavior today as well. People who are cared for in their final years by a dear child, who does so unselfishly, is not even thanked and certainly not left anything upon the parent's passing. The wisdom in a fellow friend or close family member to step forth and speak truth is of utmost importance. Let us make sure that we are not behaving like David did. Let us draw close to God and seek Him.

Prayer: Heavenly Father, may I always be grateful for those around me and show appreciation at all times. Teach me to be a blessing to others as well. In Jesus name, Amen.

Day 81

MY ROCK
Read: 2 Samuel 22-24

"The Lord is my Rock, my Fortress, and my Savior;
My God is my Rock, in whom I find protection. (2 Sam 22: 2-3a NLT)

How comforting is that? We continue to find comfort in verses 18 and 19, where it assures us that "He rescued me from my powerful enemies from those who hated me and were too strong for me. They attacked me at a moment when I was in distress, but the Lord supported me." (Chapter 22, NLT)

Isn't that the way the enemy does? When we are down, when we are in pain physically or mentally, he uses certain people, even those who call themselves Christian, to attack us further. Why would you want to work for evil? Why would you continually want to hurt another person? We can only conclude it is the evil in your heart, especially when you hide behind the Lord's name. Your behavior is far from the protection of Christ. You only think of yourself, not what you are doing to another human being. You prey on us when we are weak, but my Jesus is stronger than all the evil you can present.

Prayer: Lord, thank You for your protection and Your Word for guidance. Thank You for Your shield of victory. In Jesus name, Amen.

Day 82

FAITHFULNESS
Read: 1 Kings 1-2

As we start 1 Kings, we see that David is about to die. But more importantly, we learn that the character of a man is much more important than what he has accomplished when in a leadership position. This is true throughout time. We can see this in the leaders of nations as well as the leaders of families. When we are considering a leader, we need to look at the character of that person. How many years have I heard that what happens in the candidate's personal life should not be considered when making a choice for public office? So, these people are saying the exact opposite as what the Bible says. What God considers!

The family leader, the husband, should understand how important his role as husband and father is and in how closely he follows God's Word. He also needs to understand the effect of his behavior will have on his family. Raising children with a stress on the importance of good character might be a start in our modern society where we've fallen so short on character qualities. Add this to teaching children that their behavior has consequences and following through as the parent with such consequences will help build that character.

Prayer: Heavenly Father, thank You for the leadership You have put over me. Guide me towards obedience with those You have chosen. In Jesus name, Amen.

Day 83

OBEDIENCE
Read: 1 Kings 3-6

When Solomon is given a choice from the Lord to ask for anything he wanted, God is very pleased in what he asks for wisdom. "Give me an understanding heart so that I can govern Your people well and know the difference between right and wrong." (1 Kings 3:9a NLT) God replied in verses 11-14, "Because you have asked for wisdom in governing my people with justice and have not asked for a long life or wealth or the death of your enemies—I will give you what you asked for! I will give you a wise and understanding heart such as no one else has had or ever will have! And I will also give you what you did not ask for—riches and fame! And if you follow me and obey my decrees and my commands as your father, David, did, I will give you a long life."

This is not only a good lesson in obedience, knowing that we must do our part in order to receive God's blessings, but we must never be self-centered in our prayers. Our attitude and focus must be on serving others at all times.

Prayer: Precious Lord, may I serve the people You have put in my path with a discerning heart and may I walk in Your ways all the days of my life. In Jesus name, Amen.

Day 84

REPENTANCE
Read: 1 Kings 7-9

Solomon had good intentions and worked hard at pleasing the Lord, but he also married ungodly women and they were an influence on his life and decisions. He built a temple where the Ark of the Covenant would dwell, and the dedication prayer was sincere. "O Lord, God of Israel, there is no God like You in heaven above or on earth below—You who keep Your covenant of love with Your servants who continue wholeheartedly in Your way." (I Kings 8:23 NIV) The people were also hearing this prayer, so this leader brought the heart of the Lord to his people. Solomon reminds each of us, through his prayer of dedication to God that we must do our part and walk with God and when we sin, we must recognize that sin and repent and turn back to Him. May we turn our hearts to Him and keep His commands.

Often times we look at a man's (or woman's) accomplishments when judging them. Whether considering them for president or as a mate (and everything in between), we frequently forget that the character of a person is of utmost importance. Character is what a person is or does when no one is looking. Are they considerate of their family members? Do they show kindness to the down and out person on the street? Would they commit adultery even if no one would ever find out? Do they listen to people around them, and do they surround themselves with Godly people?

Prayer: Heavenly Father, I am thankful that You care so deeply for your creation, for each of us. Lord, help me to recognize and admit my sin daily so that I may walk closer to You each day. In Jesus name, Amen.

Day 85

IDOLS
Read: 1 Kings 10-12

Solomon, who started out with a heart that wanted to please God, was pulled away from God by his wives. He ended up wanting to please them more than God. When his son, Rehoboam, took the throne, he suffered the consequences of his father's unfaithfulness to the Lord. He followed the advice of the young men rather than the older men. He was harsh to the people and many turned away from him and his rule.

We must realize that our actions are an influence on our children and others around us. Also, our behavior has consequences and those consequences can be passed on to our children and grandchildren. We must also be careful to stay close to God for we can fall into sin easily, and if we do not think this is true, we are more vulnerable than we know. Always be ready to confess our sin and always be willing to teach those around us to do the same. Follow only the Lord God and no other person.

Prayer: Father God, help me each and every day to draw closer to You and when I sin, that I will confess that sin and turn back to You. Guide me each step. In Jesus name, Amen.

Day 86

CHOICES
Read: 1 Kings 13-15

As we start seeing the choices of each of the kings of the northern and southern kingdoms, we also see the consequences. Each one either made the choice to obey or disobey the commands of God. As we read, "the people of Judah did what was evil in the eyes of the Lord, provoking His anger with their sin" (1 Kings 14:22 NLT), it is sad that these people would treat the Lord this way.

In our society today, do we think about what we are going to do and how the Lord will feel or respond. May we make a conscience effort to do that what pleases the Lord. Many of us live a pretty good life, and we think we are good people. It is not until we start reading the Bible daily, reading through the Bible each year, that we are made aware, through the Holy Spirit, what God expects. Truly, He is faithful in teaching us His ways and His grace covers us as we repent of our sin. He knows our heart and He is there to walk with us as we learn His ways. Are you ready to take His hand today?

Prayer: Dear Heavenly Father, help me to be pleasing to You in all of my ways...Help me gain wisdom as I read Your Word daily. In Jesus name, Amen.

Day 87

BE CAREFUL WHAT YOU WORSHIP
Read: 1 Kings 16-18

In Chapter 16, two verses stick out 13b (NIV) "so that they provoked the Lord, The God of Israel, to anger by their worthless idols." and 26b (NIV) "so that they provoked the Lord, the God of Israel, to anger by their worthless idols." The people angered God by worshipping worthless idols. When God repeats Himself twice in such a short reading, He is trying to get a message across to the reader. Are we listening?

The sad part about living in the United States is that we have so much that we often forget Who gave us what we have. We often forget to thank Him for such provisions. And we often do not seem to appreciate His generosity towards us. We act like we deserve it rather than it being a gift. It is the same attitude that we afford to Jesus He gave His life for our sins. Yet we show no acknowledgment of this great gift for without it, we would not be reconciled with the Father. Let's take a look at the great love the Father has shown to us and be grateful.

Prayer: Lord God, please help me to check my behavior and attitude, including my motives, to be assured that I am not looking to other gods. May my guidance be from the Lord only. In Jesus name, Amen.

Day 88

GENTLE WHISPER
Read: 1 Kings 19-21

Our quiet time with the Lord each day is of great importance. Here we see the Lord took Elijah out on the mountain, alone and came to him in a gentle whisper. God was not in the windstorm nor in the earthquake nor in the fire, no, the Lord came to Elijah in the quiet, gentle whisper. And as we are spending time in God's Word, may we be alert to what He is speaking to us about in the quietness of the day.

Have you ever been in a church where, it seems, each person tries to out-sing the next, and seemingly trying to convince those around them how spiritual they are? Some raise hands, or dance, or shout to show those around them how holy they are. But truly remember, that is not necessarily what God is using to speak to us. He doesn't need the showy evangelist who prances and dances around, shouting a message supposedly from God. What God wants for us is when our hearts are drawn to Him, and in the quietness, He can talk to us and guide us. Are we listening?

Prayer: Father God, may I be ever alert to Your gentle whisper and ready to obey. May my heart be turned to You each and every day. In Jesus name, Amen.

Day 89

THE LORD'S DOOM
Read: 1 King 22

In this final chapter in 1 Kings, we see King Ahab thinking he can bypass the judgment of God by not wearing his royal robes into battle. In fact, the wickedness of Ahab becomes apparent as he directed King Jehoshaphat to wear his kingly robes. This diversion only lasted a short while because even the enemy figured out that Jehoshaphat was not the king they wanted dead. God predicted that Ahab would die in battle and no matter how much deceitfulness Ahab put forth, it happened he was shot by a "random" arrow and bled to death.

As we seek God's will for our lives, may we always remember to be honest and to follow the Lord. May it be said of us, after we are gone, that he did what was right in the eyes of the Lord and was pleasing in His heart.

Prayer: Heavenly Father, may my will follow You in all I do and say. May I willingly read Your Word and learn from it daily. In Jesus name, Amen.

Day 90

HOLY SPIRIT
Read: 2 Kings 1-3

Elisha had become Elijah's companion. Elisha was a prophet in the making as he was learning how to be a Godly man from Elijah. Elisha was close enough to the Lord that he had some idea that his mentor was about to be taken away (to heaven) and wanted to stay with Elijah. He even asked Elijah for a double share of his spirit. Elijah said that was totally up to the Lord but did tell Elisha if he saw Elijah taken, he would get his request.

In today's society, we are blessed to have the Holy Spirit with us at all times (if we have invited Jesus into our lives). But I do not think most of us really seek a greater indwelling of the Holy Spirit on a regular basis nor do we see the need for it. When times get hard, and they certainly will, some will have regret that they did not seek out the Lord much sooner. Others will wish they had read the Bible and may have some idea what it says but in that future day it will be taken away. So, while you have time, seek the Lord with your whole heart and be prepared for ministering to those around you.

Prayer: Heavenly Father, help me to keep my focus on You. May I have a longing to grow ever closer to You through what I read, the movies and other media I watch and the people I associate with. In Jesus name, Amen.

Day 91

CHARIOTS OF FIRE
Read: 2 Kings 4-6

In today's reading, we see miracles one after another, from oil flowing so the widow can pay her debtors to a young boy being brought back to life and onward we see Naaman being healed of leprosy to the floating ax head. But, may I suggest the biggest miracle of all is the Lord's protection "he saw that the hillside around Elisha was filled with horses and chariots of fire." (2 Kings 6:17b NLT)

Reading this helps us to be reminded of His great protection over us. And even though we may not have seen any chariots of fire protecting us, let us imagine them all around us in time of danger. This may seem foolish to some but to others it is great hope! Hope to set out on a journey that most would not take whether a short trip across town for that person who is afraid to leave the house or for that missionary, all alone, setting out for a strange land. We need this hope that only the Lord can offer each and every day. Remember, He loves you and has set chariots of fire round about you. Go forth!

Prayer: Lord God, thank You for Your protection and love. May I always know the hope that You give. In Jesus name, Amen.

Day 92

PROMISES
Read: 2 Kings 7-9

In today's reading we see lots of bloodshed. We also read how many of the kings did evil in the Lord's eyes. They received warnings and yet, continued to go their own direction. Doing what they felt was right not paying any attention to what the Lord had cautioned them on.

We have the Bible, we can read it every day or let it sit on a shelf getting dusty. We truly have no excuse as to not knowing what the Lord expects out of us because if we read the Word daily, He speaks to us. If we read and still do not understand, then get a different version of the Bible, one that is written in your heart language so you can comprehend. Having a Bible that is not written in your heart language is like living with someone who speaks a foreign language. Get in the Word and seek God's promises, His instructions and learn to grow in His love. Be open to the Holy Spirit's guiding.

Prayer: Father God, may I grow and learn as I read the Bible daily. Although my thoughts and ways are not Your thoughts and ways, may I soak a bit of You into my heart and mind, so I may walk in Your ways. In Jesus name, Amen.

Day 93

DESTROY EVIL
Read: 2 Kings 10-12

Today we see how Jehu destroyed all Baal worship, from the priest to the objects of worship. And yet, with Jehu following the Lord's instructions in destroying Ahab's family and this evil form of worship, he did not follow the Law of the Lord with all his heart.

That can be hard to understand because Jehu was diligent in carrying out what the Lord had commanded but yet, kept a certain part of himself back. If we are honest with ourselves, we know that we too, can be following the Lord but not with our whole heart. We seem to think that we need to hold on to a part of something that is better than what the Lord has for us. We can even justify it to ourselves and others. Our God is not forceful, He waits for us to be willing to give all we have to Him. He is the one person we do not have to guard our heart against. He only wants what is best for us.

Prayer: Heavenly Father, even though I understand You look out for me, I still struggle when I realized that there is yet another area in which I have held back but need to turn over to You. May I always be willing to give You my whole heart! In Jesus name, Amen.

Day 94

PARTIAL OBEDIENCE
Read: 2 Kings 13-15

We find in today's reading that Amaziah, Azariah, Jotham were kings who followed the Lord and were pleasing to Him. (see 2 Kings 14:3a; 15:3a; 15:34a) but the problem was they still left "the high places, however were not removed; the people continued to offer sacrifices and burn incense there" (see 2 Kings 14:4; 15:4; 15:35a).

Isn't that like us today, we do some of what the Lord is calling us to do but when it becomes too difficult, we do what we want or what we see as good in our own eyes? Partial obedience is still disobedience. When we do this, we are not pleasing to the Lord. It is especially difficult when we have loved ones who we need to take to the Word of God and yet, we do not do it. We are frightened that they will reject what we say to them, or maybe we just do not know the words to say. This is difficult but pray and take courage and the Lord will lead you.

Prayer: Holy Father, keep me close to You so that I may be pleasing to You in all that I do and say. May I care more for those around me than myself and be willing to step out in faith for You. In Jesus name, Amen.

Day 95

WORSHIP WORTHLESS IDOLS EQUALS FEELING WORTHLESS
Read: 2 Kings 16-17

I do not think I can say this enough or express to those around me this important principle. When we look to people to fulfill that void in our lives or to material possessions to give us our happiness, we will always be disappointed. Our total fulfillment is in Christ and Christ alone.

"They followed worthless idols and themselves became worthless." (2 Kings 17: 15b NIV) The verses before this one says that the people had become so hard headed and would not listen and rejected the Lord's wisdom. They seemed to think that those around them knew more than God's instructions and followed after them.

Oh how my heart hurts for so many today have followed in this example. Whether we look to food, shopping sprees, fast cars, big houses or name brand fashions, the counselor or the professor (this list could go on and on), we are never satisfied with any of this for very long. Our spirits long for God! That is where true fulfillment is found! The best purchase you can make is buying a Bible that you can understand, start reading it to find out that God loves you dearly and what He expects from you. Then surrender to Him. This truth set me free and I long to give that gift to you.

Prayer: Father God, I do not want to be stubborn and not listen! I want to daily turn from my wicked ways and follow after You. Help me to keep my eyes on You and not long for the "stuff" around me. In Jesus name, Amen.

Day 96

HEZEKIAH
Read: 2 Kings 18-20

We read about so many of the kings who did what was evil, that it is refreshing and a blessing to see that Hezekiah sought to please the Lord. It takes a great leader to go against the majority of the people and remove the pagan shrines and the idols. Remember, God did not want these people associating with the heathen nations and yet within time, they not only associated with them, but they grabbed hold of evil practices, embraced them and took them into the Temple of the Lord.

May we be strong in our walk to turn away from the evil practices of our day, of those around us who say there is nothing wrong with what is being done and to walk with the Lord in the truth of His Word. May we keep humble in our actions and loving all people, quick to apologize and make things right with those we have wronged. May we care deeply for those around us and lead them towards light and truth and life.

Prayer: Lord God, deliver me from the evil of this world and help me to walk closely to You. May You hear my cries for mercy and save me from evil. In Jesus name, Amen.

Day 97

IF ONLY
Read: 2 Kings 21-23

We see in today's reading how important it is to have a Godly leader, for people are like sheep and follow along doing what the leader does. God had said He would watch over the people if only they would follow His whole Law but since the leader did evil in the eyes of the Lord, so did the people, they followed him in doing evil. Josiah, on the other hand, pleased God. He was reading the Book of the Law and immediately repented and in turn, the people repented and humbled themselves. The evil articles that Manasseh had put up were now destroyed and burned. Josiah had a heart to please the Lord and do what the Word of God said.

As we are in the Word, with a desire to follow its instructions, may we recognize our sin and come to Him on bended knee in humble repentance. This is not a one-time occasion, but once we invite Jesus into our lives, we will daily recognize that we fall short and need His forgiveness. No sin is too small to come before the Lord and confess. No sin is too large to come to the Lord in repentance.

Prayer: Dear Heavenly Father, I come before you and ask that you forgive me for the words that I said that were not kind, and the thoughts that passed through my mind, perhaps lingering a bit too long. And Lord, please forgive me for my behavior is not always pleasing to You. I thank You for loving me so much. In Jesus name, Amen.

Day 98

SIN TAKES THEM DOWN
Read: 2 Kings 24-25

The sadness of today's reading is closely related to what is happening in the United States at this time. Many Christians have seen it coming for years and have tried to sound the alarm, but it has fallen on deaf ears. A country, a people, even one person who goes against the Lord, His commands, decrees and laws cannot stand. It may seem that things are going well for such people, but He is paying attention and, just as He gave the Israelites time to turn around, he is giving us a chance to repent.

He also does not force Himself on any of us. We have a choice to accept Him or reject Him. He did not force Himself on the Israelites and over and over they would go their own way. They did what felt good instead of pleasing God. And the result was that they went into captivity, experiencing a much worse life than if they had stayed close to the Lord all this time. So often, we will go astray, doing our own thing, enjoying our newfound freedom but at some point, our own way starts to hurt. We find our freedom wasn't free. Often times we must experience quite a bit of pain before we will turn from our evil ways and repent, looking to God for what is best for us.

Prayer: Dear Lord, help me to always be obedient to Your Word. I praise You for Your patience in not wanting anyone to perish but that they would turn to You. In Jesus name, Amen.

Day 99

ANCESTORS
Read: 1 Chronicles: 1-3

These days there seems to be a lot of emphasis on family history, more people want to know where they came from because it helps with our identity. As we read these first three chapters, we read many, many names that don't necessarily mean a lot to us, especially if you are reading this for the first time. But, let me assure you, if your name were in this long list, or one of your ancestors, it would take on meaning.

My encouragement to you is to read the whole Bible enough times, that you recognize some of the names in this long list. I like to underline the ones that I remember who they are or at least remember a bit about them. This helps me to become a little more familiar with God's Word and the people who God chose. Some did not make good choices and others followed God completely. We make choices, some not so good, others are made with more wisdom. The Word of God will help us make choices that are pleasing not only to Him but to you and those around you. It's taken me a long time to learn this valuable lesson, I pray that you will learn it more quickly and grasp onto the Lord and His wisdom.

Prayer: Father God, through all these names, may I gain wisdom in knowing that my actions not only affect me but generations to come. May I humbly repent when I have sinned. In Jesus name, Amen.

Day 100

HIS PURPOSE
Read: 1 Chronicles 4-6

In chapter 4: 9-10, we read about Jabez, being more honorable than his brothers. His mother experienced pain when he was born so it stands to reason that his name sounds like the Hebrew for pain. "Jabez cried out to the God of Israel, "Oh that You would bless me and enlarge my territory! Let your hand be with me and keep me from harm so that I will be free from pain." (NIV) Interesting that pain is part of his name and that he would ask God to keep him from pain. But most focus on the first part of his prayer, "Oh that You would bless me and enlarge my territory!" (1 Chron 4: 10 NIV) We really do not know any more about Jabez, whether he experienced pain or was blessed, but it is a nice prayer.

When we see someone suffering, do not automatically think they are not close to God or that they have sin in their lives. That seems to be the teaching of some pastors. Often God uses the pain a fellow Christian goes through to minister to those around them. God always has a purpose for allowing us to go through hard times and suffering, may we keep our eyes on Him and know that He possesses all wisdom and knows what is best for us.

Prayer: Heavenly Father, You care deeply for me and allow me to go through the pains of life to help me mature in Christ. Help me to learn my lessons quickly so I am pleasing to You. In Jesus name, Amen.

Day 101

DESCENDANT AFTER DESCENDANT
Read: 1 Chronicles 7-10

In today's reading, we finish up on all the descendants listed. In Chapter 10 King Saul and his sons are discussed. The saddest thing is these words, "So Saul died because he was unfaithful to the Lord. He failed to obey the Lord's commands, and he even consulted a medium instead of asking the Lord for guidance." (1 Chron 10:13-14a NLT) This is so sad. He was chosen by the Lord and he even experienced the Spirit but decided to go his own way.

May we understand the importance of looking to the Lord for our answers to life's problems and may we never look to the dark side for answers. Mediums, card readers, spiritualists, sorcery and divination, to name a few of the evils that can pull you into the wrong realm and down the path of destruction. May we not follow the path that Saul took when he could not get answers as quickly as he wanted. The Lord has the answers to living a life pleasing to Him and they are found in the Bible. Take time to read it daily.

Prayer: Lord, I have failed and fallen short so often but am thankful for your grace. You love me when I cannot even love myself and You are there to pick me up and start me on the right path once again. I am grateful Lord. In Jesus name, Amen.

Day 102

SEEK GOD
Read: 1 Chronicles 11-14

David's desire was to bring the Ark of God to the City of David but as we read of his excitement, we also see tragedy with the death of Uzzah because in this process, they did not follow the directions the Lord had given. This put the fear of the Lord back in David and he sought the Lord.

May we find through the years, that the times that we seek the Lord before we act, are the times that the best choices are made. May we not act hastily on our own thought or intuition, may we wait for clear guidance from the Lord. This can look different in each circumstance, but it usually means getting in the Word of God and reading. The answer can also come through prayer or another person's wise words. Whatever the case may be, waiting is an important factor.

When we get the answer, be prepared for some people around you to ridicule you, to discourage you, to even turn their backs on you. But when you know God has given you an answer, be prepared to act. To move forward in the battle against evil. And pray for those who demean you.

Prayer: Heavenly Father, give me the wisdom and strength to seek Your face as I serve You each and every day. Help me to remember that my service may not look like the next person's service, that You called me and will be there for me. In Jesus name, Amen.

Day 103

PRAISING GOD
Read: 1 Chronicles 15-17

Today we are given an excellent example of David's praising the Lord. From chapter 16:8-36, we are uplifted and taught how to praise God. Let us all give it a try and see what happens… "give thanks to the Lord and proclaim His greatness". (1 Chron 16:8a NLT) "Tell everyone about His wonderful deeds."(1 Chron 16:9b NLT) If we "continually seek Him". (1 Chron 16:11b NLT) As we repeat David's words, do you feel the joy springing up in our heart? "For great is the Lord and most worthy of praise; He is to be feared above all gods." (1 Chron 16:25 NIV)

Would the world be a different place if we took these words to heart and proclaimed them to everyone we meet? If we gave the Lord the glory He deserved, this world would be a better place because people would want the Lord in their lives! We would long for the Lord's salvation and would give Him thanks and rejoice and praise Him.

> *Prayer: Heavenly Father, I can change my behavior, my thoughts, my speech to reflect Your glory. Remind me by what I read, what I put before my eyes and listen to that You are my all in all. In Jesus name, Amen.*

Day 104

...WHAT IS THE COST?
Read: 1 Chronicles 18-22

At one of those moments in David's life in which he did not seek the Lord (and we all have such moments), he ordered a census of the people. This action was displeasing to the Lord and the Lord allowed David to choose his punishment. David decided it was better to "fall into the hands of the Lord" (1 Chron 21:13a NIV) than that of man.

As David saw the angle of death standing to destroy Jerusalem, he approached Araunah to buy the threshing floor. Instead, this generous man offered to give David the oxen and the wood for such an offering to the Lord. But David responded with "No, I insist on buying it for the full price. I will not take what is yours and give it to the Lord. I will not present burnt offerings that have cost me nothing!" (1 Chron 21:24 NLT)

In our lives, how often do we make that choice to offer something to the Lord that truly cost us nothing? May we check our hearts and be honest with ourselves to be assured that what we give to the Lord cost us. This does not have to be financial but often it is. It could be our very lives, to give of ourselves to the Lord so totally that we no longer insist on our own way. What are you presenting to the Lord?

Prayer: Heavenly Father, I come before You with a willing heart to serve You in whatever way You need. Help me to develop my gifts so I may serve you completely. In Jesus name, Amen.

Day 105

OFFICIALS
Read: 1 Chronicles 23-27

In today's reading, we read of the duties of different people who served in David's government. David valued the priests, the musicians, the gatekeepers, the treasurers and other officials along with the military commanders.

Let us focus on the priests and musicians for a brief moment. If it was so important to have such officials serving the government in David's day, why don't we see the value in governments around the world today? To seek the Lord in making all decisions is also important in our personal lives as well. Just because our government has forsaken the Lord God of the Universe, does not mean that we should. So, go before the Lord daily and humble yourself. Read the Bible daily. Pray daily. Turn your life over to Him and He will guide you. If our leadership does not give us a good example on how we should live, we do not have to go their way. Step out and reach out for Him.

Prayer: Lord, there is no other one like You, creator of life itself and all the universe. Help me to stay close to You and to walk in Your ways. In Jesus name, Amen.

Day 106

FURTHER INSTRUCTIONS
Read: 1 Chronicles 28-29

Today is a powerful reading! I cannot write anything more powerful than what has already been said: "Be careful to obey all the commands of the Lord your God, so that you may continue to possess this good land and leave it to your children as a permanent inheritance. And Solomon (put your name in here), my son, learn to know the God of your ancestors intimately. Worship and serve Him with your whole heart and a willing mind. For the Lord sees every heart and knows every plan and thought. If you seek Him, you will find Him. But if you forsake Him, He will reject you forever. So take this seriously Be strong and do the work." (1Chron 28:8b-10 NLT)

"Be strong and courageous, and do the work. Don't be afraid or discouraged, for the Lord God, my God, is with you. He will not fail you or forsake you." (1 Chron 28:20 NLT)

May we always be seeking the Lord's will for our lives. May we understand that following Him is our strength and wisdom for each new day!

Prayer: Father in heaven, I know that you test my heart. May my desire always be loyal to You, may I freely serve You and help me to not be discouraged or afraid, for I know You are with me. In Jesus name, Amen.

Day 107

WISDOM
Read: 2 Chronicles 1-3

As we start to read 2 Chronicles, we are reminded of what is important. God asked Solomon what he wanted, and Solomon answered that he wanted wisdom and knowledge so as to lead God's people. God granted this to Solomon, plus God gave him wealth, riches and fame.

Today, we must check ourselves often to be sure we are staying focused on what God wants for our lives. It is easy to get involved in self-fulfilling endeavors to the point that we forget about the Lord. If we start using phrases such as self-worth, self-confidence or anything dealing with self in it, be careful! When we look to "self", we are not looking to God to help us in our everyday life, let alone seeking His wisdom in our decisions. True wisdom is knowing that we cannot look to ourselves for all of life's decisions. We are first to pray to see what God would give us, and then we are to seek council from others with wisdom on the subject and their advice will be confirmation as to what God has already shown us. In this way, we can make a wise decision that will be pleasing to God, which in turn brings joy to our heart.

Prayer: Heavenly Father, may I always seek You and listen to Your guidance and obey each step of the way. In Jesus name, Amen.

Day 108

PRAYER
Read: 2 Chronicles 4-6

Solomon's prayer in chapter 6 starts out with "O Lord, God of Israel, there is no God like You in all of heaven and earth." (2 Chron 6:14 NLT) He reminds God of His promises to his father, David and perhaps it also was a reminder to himself for God said, "If your descendants guard their behavior and faithfully follow My Laws " (2 Chron 6:16b NLT).

Once again, we are reminded that our behavior does make a difference as to God keeping His promises. We need to follow Him, read His word daily and keep our focus on Him. When our heart is right, then we have such a deep desire to do His will, but when our heart is into pleasing self, we look more to people and not to God's will for our life. "When they turn back and confessed Your name praying and making supplication before You then hear from heaven and forgive the sin of Your people...(2 Chron 6:24b-25a NIV) "Forgive, and deal with each man according to all he does, since You know his heart (for You alone know the hearts of men), so that they will fear You and walk in Your ways all the time " (2 Chron 6:30-31a NIV)

Prayer: Father God, truly there is no one like You. May I be ever willing to confess my sins and turn back to You. You alone know my heart; may I walk in Your ways. In Jesus name, Amen.

Day 109

GOD RESPONDS
Read: 2 Chronicles 7-9

In God's response to Solomon's prayer, which we read yesterday in chapter 6, we read the often stated "prayer" of many "Then if my people who are called by My name will humble themselves and pray and seek My face and turn from their wicked ways, I will hear from heaven and will forgive their sins and restore their land." (2 Chron 7:14 NLT) But many have failed to understand why God said this. In the verses before this, God says that there might be times that He causes rainfall to cease or grasshoppers to destroy the crops or send a plague, and then we read verse 14.

Further on Solomon is reminded that the people must serve God faithfully, "obeying all my commands, decrees and regulations" (2 Chron 17b NLT) and also reminds Solomon "if you or your descendants abandon me and disobey the decrees and commands I have given you, and if you serve and worship other gods, then I will uproot the people from this land that I have given them." (2 Chron 19-20a NLT) This ought to be a great reminder of what God not only expected from the descendants of David but what He expects from all who call themselves Christ followers.

May we, who are Christians daily seek God on every decision we make. May we humble ourselves before Him and repent of our sins, whether in thought or deed. May we teach our children to honor our Lord and to serve Him all the days of their lives.

Prayer: Dear Lord, thank You for reminding me daily that I must obey You in order to receive Your blessings. May I faithfully follow You. In Jesus name, Amen.

Day 110

REJECTING WISDOM
Read: 2 Chronicles 10-13

Both David and Solomon have died. As much wisdom and leadership as they had, it was not taught or grasped by Solomon's son, Rehoboam, who is now king. The people come to him asking to be relieved of some of the taxes that his father had imposed. Rehoboam goes to the older counselors first for advice. They tell him to give them a favorable answer to keep them as loyal subjects. Rehoboam rejects their advice and goes to the young men. They advise him to tell the people if they thought his father was hard on them, just wait, he will be even harder. There was little wisdom in Rehoboam's decision to listen to the young men.

Now, this little story can be a valuable lesson to us today. From being a parent and raising our children to the head of a company to the leader of a nation, seeking the Lord's will would mean reading the Bible, praying and listening to God's answer. But most importantly, it would mean being obedient to what God is telling you to do. And yes, it is always wise to seek counselors who are also into the Word of God and seek Him daily. Most importantly, we need to cry out to God daily with a humble heart.

Prayer: Heavenly Father, help me to remain close to You, to have wise people around me and to keep my ears open to Your truth and obey. Keep my mind clear and attended to Your Word. In Jesus name, Amen.

Day 111

PLEASING GOD
Read: 2 Chronicles 14-17

The excitement of reading that Asa (and Jehoshaphat) were pleasing to God brings joy to my heart and puts a longing within me to also be pleasing to the Lord in all that I do. Furthermore, realizing that we must do our part in pleasing the Lord, when our heart is turned to the Lord with a longing to seek His will for our lives and then to obey His law and commands, we find a peace that passes all understanding. (see Phil 4:7) Isn't that what most of us long for?

As Azariah spoke to Asa, giving further instruction from the Lord, we must be reminded that we, too, must do our part, "The Lord will stay with you as long as you stay with Him! Whenever you seek Him, you will find Him. But if you abandon Him, He will abandon you." (2 Chron 15:2b NLT) I do not think such instruction could be any clearer than these words. We must remember that God also tests us so there are times in which we may suffer, or hardships come our way. In 1 Peter 2:21, we are reminded "For God called you to do good, even if it means suffering, just as Christ suffered for you." (NLT)

> *Prayer: O Lord, may I never grow tired of pleasing You and always stay on guard to not fall away from the One True God of the Universe! In Jesus name, Amen.*

Day 112

SHEEP WITHOUT A SHEPHERD
Read: 2 Chronicles 18-21

Interestingly, this phrase "like sheep without a shepherd" is not only found here in chapter 18, verse 16 but we also find it in Numbers 27:17 and Matt 9:36. Since the Bible was written on scrolls and not put together as a book for years and years after it was written, one man could not know what another wrote. To me, this is evidence of God being the author of the whole Bible because it is consistent in its writings. That is exciting news, to see confirmation that the One True God penned the Words we read today known as the Bible.

The passage we read today has lessons to be learned but the main lesson is that no matter how close we are to the Lord on any given day, the evil one can get us when we take our focus off of the Lord and he will use us for his purpose. We must have friends and family nearby to remind us often of God's great love and guidance for our life. We will never "arrive" at being so holy or spiritual here on this earth that we should ever put our guard down. We need to constantly pray and seek God's face for our daily living. We need to be in the Word of God to know what He expects out of us and then live that life as closely as we can in pleasing Him.

Prayer: Living as a Christ follower is work, it does not just happen! I must study to be approved by God (see 2 Tim 2:15). May my outward conduct be consistent with my profession of faith. In Jesus name, Amen.

Day 113

INFLUENCED
Read: 2 Chronicles 22-24

When Joash became king, he was greatly influenced by Jehoiada the priest. Up until Jehoiada's death, Joash pleased the Lord by restoring the Temple of the Lord and following Jehoiada's directions. Once Jehoiada died, King Joash was persuaded by the leaders of Judah to abandon the Lord and His Temple and worship Asherah poles and other idols. What a sad commentary that is!

This is a great example that we cannot hang around or become friends with those who are not Christ followers and if we do, we must be very cautious. No matter how strong we think we are, we can be pulled into following evil ways before we know it. It is also a great example of how easily it is to start worshiping idols today, many worship idols without even realizing it. Our position in life can be an idol, what we own can be an idol, our children/grandchildren can be an idol and so much more that we often do not even think about as being idols. Search your heart daily to be sure that you are seeking God and God alone.

Prayer: Dear Lord, may I check my heart and motives daily so as to be ever before You in all my ways. Thank You Lord, for Your Word that guides me and for people You put in my life to keep me on a straight path. In Jesus name, Amen.

Day 114

PRIDEFUL DOWNFALL
Read: 2 Chronicles 25-28

Once again, we are reminded of how important it is to keep our eyes on the Lord and to follow Him all the days of our life. We see that King Uzziah was 16 years old when he became king and he reigned 52 years. He was pleasing to the Lord as he sought God through Zechariah. When he feared the Lord and sought His guidance, God gave him success. Then we read, "But when he had become powerful, he also became proud, which led to his downfall. He sinned against the Lord his God" (2 Chron 26: 16a NLT)

This is a great reminder that we must always be on our guard because the evil one wants to destroy us and pull us away from our Precious Lord! We must be totally aware of how vulnerable we are and never get prideful. If you have already fallen, repent at once and turn your life around. If you have never known the Lord, now is the perfect time to acknowledge your sins, ask His forgiveness for your sins, deciding to turn from your sins, and to invite Jesus into your heart. Make a choice to live for Christ and to reject the evil that will take you down that road to hell.

Prayer: Heavenly Father, without You I am weak but when I am weak and grab Your hand, I have strength to fight the enemy. Remind me often to keep my pride in check and may I always be faithful to You. In Jesus name, Amen.

Day 115

TURNING TO THE LORD
Read: 2 Chronicles 29-32

Throughout these four chapters, we see how Hezekiah directed the priest, the Levites and the people to worship the Lord and to serve Him. Hezekiah reminded the people to "return to the Lord" (2 Chron 30:6a NIV), not like their relatives before them who abandoned the Lord and became contemptible people. Instead, Hezekiah encouraged the people in verse 8, same chapter, "Do not be stubborn, as they were, but submit yourselves to the Lord." (NLT) Not only did the people worship the Lord but they brought their tithes to the Lord and purified themselves.

In today's society, some do come before the Lord in repentance. Few know that repentance means a turning around of your sinful ways. Our behavior, the evil within us, needs to change and sometimes that can take many years! In the new life, we must not only ask the Lord's forgiveness when a sin is brought to mind, but we are to go to those we have used and hurt and sincerely ask their forgiveness. We can learn about that sincerity as we read the Bible, for there are many examples of Godly men and women who show us how to ask another's forgiveness. We should work the rest of our lives in pleasing God, not ourselves, with joy in our heart.

Prayer: Dear God, I long to be a pleasing person in Your sight. Help me with each new day, to turn from the evil I once knew and to do Your will. Help me to go to those I have hurt and with a sincere heart ask their forgiveness. In Jesus name, Amen.

Day 116

THE LORD ALONE IS GOD
Read: 2 Chronicles 33-35

In today's reading, we see that Manasseh started out his reign as an evil leader. He led the people towards sorcery, fortune telling and witchcraft as well as consulting mediums and psychics (see 2 Chron 33:6b). As the principle states, as goes the leader so go the people, and the reading today says that Manasseh led the people to do more evil than the pagan nations (see 2 Chron 33:9). King Manasseh had to go through tough times when the Assyrian army bound him and put a ring through his nose and led him away to Babylon. It was only then that Manasseh sought the Lord and humbled himself. The Lord heard his simple prayers and brought Manasseh back to his kingdom. Finally, at this point, the king recognized with his heart and mind "that the Lord alone is God". (2 Chron 33:13b NLT)

Manasseh's life is like many of us, we go our own way and choose to sin until something happens in our lives, usually something that causes pain, and wakes us up to the fact that we need more than ourselves. We need a Savior, Christ the Lord. The Lord guides us today with the written Word, the Bible. We need to read it daily and systematically read through the Bible to learn the ways God expects us to go and how to behave and be pleasing to Him. We can learn so much about life, how we should treat others, what God expects from us, by daily Bible reading. May we always have a heart that seeks truth and wisdom.

Prayer: Lord of the Universe, You alone are all knowing. You long for each of us to open our lives to You. Lord, I long for You, to love as You love, to be kind and to make a difference in this world. In Jesus name, Amen.

Day 117

HOPE EVEN IN DESTRUCTION
Read: 2 Chronicles 36-Ezra 3

What sadness we see for a nation! As Judah fell further and further into idolatry and rejecting the Lord. They even rejected the message from Jeremiah concerning what God would allow to happen if they did not turn, in repentance, back to Him. As 2 Chronicles closes, we see the fall of Jerusalem, the burning of the Temple of God and palaces but then Jeremiah had a message of hope a future king would set the exiles free to rebuild the Temple. Not only did Jeremiah prophecy this but he named that future king: Cyrus.

With great joy after being in exile for 70 years, a new king named Cyrus (only God could have given Jeremiah that insight), comes to reign. God stirred his heart to let the exiles return to Jerusalem to rebuild the Temple. Not only that but their neighbors were to give them gifts for the journey gifts of silver and gold, livestock and other valuable gifts for the journey.

This should be a reminder for each of us. When God closes one chapter of our lives, He has plans for us for the next. Hopefully we can grow and mature and it will not take 70 years to serve Him willingly where He calls us. The best way to mature in Him is to read the Bible daily and listen to His voice with your whole-heart and be willing to obey Him. There is hope in Christ even when it is dark all around us.

Prayer: Dear Lord, may my heart be moved in humble repentance to do Your will. May I shout in praise all the great works You have done. May my children, grandchildren and every generation to come bow before the Living God in humble adoration. In Jesus name, Amen.

Day 118

GOD'S PROTECTION
Read: Ezra 4-6

Have you ever noticed that often when God calls you to serve, satan will bring people in our life who oppose this work? We see this in today's reading. First these deceitful people wanted to come alongside the builders of the Temple. They even said that they worshiped and sacrificed to the Lord. But God gave wisdom to the leaders and they politely said, "no thank you". Next the enemies tried to discourage and frighten the people of Judah and finally they bribed some to work against the work that King Cyrus had sent them to do bringing frustration to their plans. When none of these evil deeds worked, they send a letter of accusation to King Artaxerxes, who ordered the work to be stopped. Sometime later the Israelites started building on the Temple once again with encouragement from the prophets Haggai and Zachariah. Another letter was sent, this time to King Darius and, because of a search of the records, he issued a letter affirming that King Cyrus had indeed sent the Israelites back to Jerusalem to rebuild the Temple. Darius even said that anyone who violated the decree would be punished.

When we are being opposed, we must stand strong in serving the Lord. The more we are opposed, the more we should understand our work for Him is needed. The opposition will strengthen us for the task that He has called us to. He loves you, dear friend, and is with those who have invited Jesus to live in their lives through repentance.

Prayer: Heavenly Father, thank You for the task You have set before me. Give me strength and wisdom to fulfill this great mission. And when I lose heart, put encouraging people in my path. In Jesus name, Amen.

Day 119

PURIFYING THE SIN
Read: Ezra 7-10

God's protective hand was on Ezra and the people who made their way from Babylon back to Jerusalem. But in preparation for their travels, they fasted and humbled themselves before God. We also see when Ezra reaches Jerusalem, he found out that some had married pagan women and even had children by them. Again, he went before the Lord and fasted and sought His face. He did not make any decisions without first wholeheartedly seeking the Lord.

Some say they only seek the Lord about big decisions in their lives but as Ezra is our example, let us seek Him for all matters in our life. Whether big or small, we can make wrong decisions that lead to sin or are sinful. We can be persuaded by our own sinful nature. Many of us can be talked into sinning by a friend or loved one. With this insight, can we not see that we need to seek God in all we do? Let us, like Ezra, fall on our face and lift our hands to the Lord as we seek guidance for our lives.

Prayer: Dear Lord, I come before You ashamed and disgraced because my sin is higher than my head and my guilt has reached heaven. I have been unfaithful with one detestable practice after another. Forgive me O Lord, for You are righteous. May my desire be always to please. Forgive me O Lord, for You are righteous. May my desire be always to please You. In Jesus name, Amen.

Day 120

NEHEMIAH IS CALLED
Read: Nehemiah 1-3

Nehemiah talked to some men who had come from Jerusalem and found out that the walls and gates, which protected the city, had not been rebuilt. This caused Nehemiah great distress, so much so that he cried, which brought him before the Lord in mourning, fasting and prayer. This also brought about confession as Nehemiah prayed to "the great and awesome God who keeps His covenant of unfailing love to those who love Him and obey His commands". (Neh 1:5 NLT) Finally Nehemiah asked God to give him success as he went to the king.

Even as Nehemiah stood before the king, answering his questions, he shot a prayer to God and answered the king. After the king said Nehemiah could go to Jerusalem, Nehemiah was ever so bold to ask the king for letters for safe travel through the territories west of the Euphrates River. Not only did the king grant this part of the request but he also sent Army officers and charioteers as protection for Nehemiah.

In our lives, whether faced with a big or small project, do we seek God's direction and permission? If we are reading the Word of God daily, we should not be asking for things beyond what He is calling us to do. We will have a better understanding as to the direction He wants us to go and to know to pray and seek His direction. Let us not forget to confess our sin, to repent and go before our Lord with humility.

Prayer: O Lord, God of heaven, Your unfailing love to those who obey You is beyond my understanding. I confess that I have sinned by not following Your Word. May I be ever before You in obedience and I ask You to grant me success in doing Your will. In Jesus name, Amen.

Day 121

INTIMIDATION
Read: Nehemiah 4-6

In today's reading, we see the enemies of Israel mocking the Jews, urging them to stop the work before them. In Nehemiah 6:15 (NLT) we read " the wall was finished—just 52 days after we had begun." This could only have been done with the Lord's help.

So, we see such encouragement in today's reading because it helps us to look back on our lives, as we have stepped out to serve the Lord, realizing those attacks from supposed friends was the work of the evil one. What is the one thing satan draws on when God calls us? He will remind us of our past, of our mistakes and sin that makes us unfit to serve. Then he will remind us that we are not educated enough or do not have the experience to serve the Lord. These tactics are not any different than what Nehemiah experienced.

Remember that Nehemiah, the servant leader, who not only directed the people in rebuilding the wall and the gates around Jerusalem, he himself also was right there working hard. He did not take money from the people in taxes but set an example for all generations to see what a true servant of the Lord does.

Prayer: O Lord God, hear my prayer. When people come along to discourage me, turn their insults back on their own heads. Lord, You are great and beyond my understanding, and You fight for those who have a heart to serve You. Remember me, God, with favor. In Jesus name, Amen.

Day 122

GOD'S JOY
Read: Nehemiah 7-9

Through our readings so far, we have seen God's blessings when the people obeyed the commands, regulations, and instructions of the Lord. Quite the opposite happened when they turned away from the Lord and His Word. They become self-absorbed people, looking to meet their own pleasures only, they become stubborn and very proud. "But You are a God of forgiveness, gracious and merciful, slow to become angry, and rich in unfailing love. You did not abandon them." (Ne 9:17b NLT)

When we turn from our sinful ways in repentance and determine to live our lives in obedience to God's Word, we find joy. "Do not grieve, for the joy of the Lord is your strength." (Ne 8:10b NIV) We have choices, who do you want to serve?

Prayer: O Lord God, when I go my own way, when I am more interested in serving myself than You, open my heart to repentance to seek Your forgiveness and to turn my life and my ways back to You. In Jesus name, Amen.

Day 123

FOLLOW GOD'S WORD
Read: Nehemiah 10-13

At the end of chapter 9, the people had made a binding agreement, in writing and sealed it. A short time later, Nehemiah went back to Babylon and the people seemed to forget this agreement. The priest provided a room for Tobiah, truly an enemy who was deceiving to make them believe he was there to help them. God had specifically told them to not allow these evil people to live around them. They were reminded that Solomon was a Godly man until he married women who worshiped other gods. The wives pulled Solomon away from God, "even he was led into sin by foreign women. Must we hear now that you too are doing all this terrible wickedness and are being unfaithful to our God by marrying foreign women?" (Ne 26b–27 NIV)

Even today, we must realize and be reminded often that when we stray away from God's Word or we start bringing ungodly people into our lives, we will fall away from the Lord and His Word. When we allow people to live in our country whose only purpose is to destroy us, we are not being kind to them and certainly are not protecting our children and wives and the widows. We are allowing evil to reign in our once Godly nation. A nation that was founded for freedom of religion and set up on Godly principles has become wicked and detestable in God's sight. We need to repent and turn back to the Word of God.

Prayer: Father in Heaven, remember me in Your great mercy and according to Your unlimited love. Give me strength to speak your Word, even when it is not popular to say. I am thankful to be Your servant, remember me with favor, O precious Lord. In Jesus name, Amen.

Day 124

HADASSAH
Read: Esther 1-5

This is quite a story of how Vashti was banished from the presence of the king because she refused to parade herself in front of a group of drunken men. Some commentaries have suggested that King Xerxes expected her to come before these men with just her royal crown on her head. In this case, she was not being a disobedient wife, as some say. She was actually a modest woman who was humble and could not do such a thing. God used this act to usher in a new queen. Although many women around the kingdom were oiled and prepared to go before the king, we are given extensive information about Hadassah, also called Esther.

God used Ester's position to influence the king to stop the planned killing of the Jewish people, which Haman had declared because of his hate for one man. As Esther's cousin, Mordecai, told her of what was going to happening, he pointed out that perhaps she was made queen by God for this very situation.

This story in history shows us how important it is for us to pray and seek God's face before we set out to do His work. No matter what the size of the task, He has called you to fast and pray. Ask others to join you in preparing for the battle that is about to take place.

Prayer: Heavenly Father, I do not understand Your ways, but I know that I need to seek Your will in all that I do and all that happens in my life. May I grow ever deeper in obedience of Your Word and love for Your people. In Jesus name, Amen.

Day 125

JUSTICE
Read: Esther 6-10

In a nutshell, we see that Haman plotted the killing of Jews and Esther exposed his plot to the king. Haman and his sons were hung on the very gallows he had intended for Mordecai. Esther and Mordecai were able to issue a decree, so the Jews could defend themselves, which resulted in the death of many who hated the Jews.

This is a great reminder of how God watches over His own and will bring justice to those who do not treat His chosen with love and fairness. It is also a reminder for each of us to treat others in a manner that is glorifying to God. God gives the sinner time to repent, to turn from their evil ways and then it is over for them. He will turn away from them. Too many people think they can push God and continue to do evil but read Romans 1 and see that there comes a time when God lets them go. Are we making the right choices in life, to be fully committed to God and have a heart to please Him?

Prayer: Holy Father, You alone are worthy of praise and honor. Help me to love Your Word, reading it daily and to obey. For my words are nothing if my behavior is not pleasing to You. In Jesus name, Amen.

Day 126

TESTINGS
Read: Job 1-3

If you are like me, there are times when you have gone through a painful situation, whether health, finances or other personal hardships, and you have wondered why God is allowing it. All we have to do is read chapter 1 of Job and we will have a better understanding as to why we go through such horrendous situations. So it is, when satan goes before God, please notice it is God who points out Job to the evil one. God even brags that Job is a blameless man, with integrity who fears God and stays away from evil. Always full of what he sees as an excuse, satan tells God that the only reason Job has such integrity is because God has protected him and given him so much. Indeed, God had put a hedge of protection around Job, but God knew Job well enough to allow him to be tested, knowing that Job would remain faithful.

Let the testing begin! Reading Job each year helps us to remember that when we go through difficult times, God has allowed it and knows that we will not fall away. God trusts us enough to allow these hard times and loves us even more to give us strength to withstand.

God gives us the Book of Job to learn. To be chosen by God for such a testing as this, and so many more through the years, is a privilege. It does not seem to get easier but knowing that we will go through the Refiners fire for the purpose of glorifying God as we draw ever closer to Him, is a comfort.

Prayer: Heavenly Father, may I look at times of suffering as a gift to seek you to a new depth. May I grasp the realization that You count me strong enough to go through such trials. May Your name be praised. In Jesus name, Amen.

Day 127

LIFE IS A STRUGGLE
Read: Job 4-7

Eliphaz thought he was giving Job words of wisdom as he accused Job of not being close to or pleasing to God. It seemed that his thought was if you are close to God, doing His will, you will be kept safe. All we must do is read all the Bible to see that many Godly men and women suffered in this life on earth.

Job's response is such good advice for each of us, "One should be kind to a fainting friend" (Job 6:14a NLT). Yes, be kind. It never seems to amaze me how cruel people can be. Yes, those close friends of ours can be terribly cruel when we are going through a difficult situation. It seems that when it is a physical problem, people are even more ready to point a finger at the wrongs in our life to justify why we are suffering. It does seem like Job can teach us a lesson or two as we watch him suffer.

Prayer: May I be willing to be taught during my painful times. May I be willing to listen to words of truth and be willing to change my lifestyle or attitude to be more pleasing to You. May I look at where I am and be thankful that You love me so very much. In Jesus name, Amen.

Day 128

QUESTIONS
Read: Job 8-10

Bildad seemed to have some false ideas about how God works. He said, "But if you pray to God and seek the favor of the Almighty, and if you are pure and live with integrity, He will surely rise up and restore your happy home." (Job 8: 5-6 NLT) He had the same thoughts as so many today have, that is if you are good then God blesses you. But we have already seen in Job 1 that is not true. God saw that Job was a righteous man and yet tested him.

Be careful to not be a Bildad in someone's life! Work hard on having compassion for those who are hurting. Give the same mercy that God has given you, love people where they are. Do not judge someone going through a difficult time, walk alongside them, supporting them. No matter how old we get, it seems that we can always continue learning to be kind to those around us. God's love is deeper than surface and let us work on sharing this same kind of love.

Prayer: Father, You formed me in my mother's womb, nothing happens in my life without Your approval. Through it all, help me to become stronger in Your ways. In Jesus name, Amen.

Day 129

ATTENTION TO DETAIL
Read: Job 11-14

Here we have another one of Job's friends accusing him of being such a great sinner. Apparently, these men do not really know Job but go by what they think to be true. "May the words of my mouth and the meditation of my heart be pleasing in Your sight, O Lord, my Rock and my Redeemer." Psalm 19:14 NIV)

What comes to mind during this reading is the importance of parenting with grace and kindness but also with allowing our children to go through hard times when they are growing up so as to build Godly character in them. Job 12:13 (NLT) says, " But true wisdom and power are found in God; counsel and understanding are His." We may not understand why we are going through such hard times but stand assured that God is allowing it for our good to grow and mature into one of His perfect children. And remember, our family and friends need love and acceptance and encouragement, not condemnation.

Prayer: O Lord, I have failed so often, forgive me for not being more encouraging to those in my life. Help me to walk in truth and newness of life to love those around me and draw them closer to You. In Jesus name, Amen.

Day 130

DISCOURAGEMENT
Read: Job 15-17

Oh the discouragement Job is feeling! Eliphaz spoke again but he just seems to pound on Job as being such a sinful, wicked man. And Job nails it when he responds, "What miserable comforters you are!" (Job 16: 2b NLT) He goes on in Job16:20–21 (NLT), "My friends scorn me, but I pour out my tears to God. I need someone to mediate between God and me, as a person mediates between friends."

I am so thankful for Jesus, the Mediator that Job saw was needed. Jesus offered himself as the Lamb of God who takes away the sins of the world, the sacrificial lamb. Unless we understand the filthiness of our sins, we cannot comprehend the depth of what Jesus did for us. We must realize that we are not "good" people, we are born in sin and have a sinful heart. Only when we are covered by the blood of Jesus are we washed as white as snow. Praise God for His great mercy on us.

Prayer: Heavenly Father, help me to never forget that I need a compassionate heart that can only come from Jesus, our Mediator and our Savior. Help me to grasp my own worth that You see in me and to be pleasing to You. In Jesus name, Amen.

Day 131

BLAME AND INSULTS
Read: Job 18-21

We continue to experience the blame and insults handed to Job from his so-called friends. They seem to have a great need to blame Job for his pain and heartache. Isn't that so like mankind throughout the history of the world? We justify a reason why we or someone else is going through the pain of life and we readily blame the person. The Book of Job should teach us that our justification thinking is not always right. We are fortunate to see the communication between God and satan, so this can give us a better understanding when those around us are suffering. We strive to have more compassion because we are given so much more and yet, we are just as ready to insult and blame as Job's friends were.

In Job 21:34a, Job asks, "how can you console me with your nonsense?" (NIV) May we check our spirit and thoughts and not try to console those who are hurting with nonsense. May we understand that God has a purpose when allowing us to go through the pains of life, so much deeper than our microscopic understanding. May we walk alongside those who are hurting in silence and in depth of heart to show our love and concern without being condemning. May we always remember that we do not have the mind of God and only He knows why He allows us to go through what we do.

> *Prayer: Dear Lord, help me to be careful with my words and have compassion on the hurting. May I proclaim, in the midst of my pain, that I know God lives and He has a purpose for my suffering, but, none the less, I will one day see my Savior face to face. In Jesus name, Amen.*

Day 132

NO HOPE
Read: Job 22-24

Eliphaz seems to have all the answers as to why Job is suffering. He says one suffers because we are wicked and full of sin. He also contends that if you submit to God, you will have peace in your life. Wouldn't it be wonderful if it were that simple? How wrong Eliphaz was! And how wrong we can be when we make judgments about why people are going through a tough situation. We need to be so very careful! Isn't it hard enough just checking ourselves to make sure we are walking the path that God has called us to, let alone judging others?

Job has many questions but also has to defend himself as he responds to his friend. Would it not be frustrating to know you have done the right things and yet, now are suffering? I wish I could be so confident to know that when He tests me, I would come out as pure gold. This path we walk when we come to Jesus is full of stumbles and even falling down. Having to let go of our old nature and learning the direction that God wants us to go is a daily struggle and full of learning experiences. The important thing is we DO have a Mediator now, Jesus. When we sin, we need to sincerely go to Him and repent, asking God for forgiveness. "He is faithful and just and will forgive us our sins and purify us from all unrighteousness." (1 John 1:9b NIV)

Prayer: Father God, You test me and care for me. Your goal for me is to teach me integrity of heart, that one day I will stand before You and You will be pleased with me. I long to be pleasing to You, dear Lord. In Jesus name, Amen.

Day 133

THOUGHTS
Read: Job 25-28

How much can one defend himself? It seems that Job is told by Bildad once again how God is powerful, and man is nothing. In Job's response, Job seems to talk and talk, words that do not always make sense in light of his suffering and being accused of being such a bad person by his comforters. It would be nice if wicked, evil people suffered the consequences of their behavior and that Godly people were rewarded for their goodness. But Job's final words in chapter 28, verse 28 pretty much says it all, "the fear of the Lord—that is wisdom, to shun evil is understanding." (NIV)

To be sure that we understand that fearing the Lord is also respect for His Word and our working to obey that Word as we read it daily. That is one of the ways to gain wisdom!

Prayer: Lord, I long daily to have that sort of wisdom and to stay away from evil. I long for Godly wisdom and understanding and know that it can only come from You. I am thankful for Your Word! In Jesus name, Amen.

Day 134

JOB SEARCHES HIS HEART
Read: Job 29-31

In today's passage, Job looks at his former blessings and does not understand what he has done so wrong as to now be in such anguish. He does realize that God has humbled him, but he cannot understand the depth of his suffering, for now even Job believes if you do good acts, you will not suffer. Such a confusing concept! But satan is the author of confusion and wishes that in each of our lives.

Job even goes back over his actions and thoughts "I made a covenant with my eyes not to look lustfully at a girl." (Job 31:1 NIV) Through all this questioning, we can see that Job is truly a man of integrity and God's testing of him only brings him to a more right relationship with God.

Prayer: Father God, through the hard times, may I examine myself to make sure I am drawing ever closer to You. May I know Your intimate friendship as You watch over me each step of the way. May I not walk in falsehood nor any sort of deceit and may my heart grow ever closer to You. In Jesus name, Amen.

Day 135

SPEAKING WHILE ANGRY
Read: Job 32-37

Elihu has waited to speak because he was younger. At least he did show respect to those around him by letting them speak first. But in his respectful waiting, he has become more and more angry. He was angry at Job for not admitting his sin. He was angry at Job's three friends. It even appears that he is angry with God. Perhaps the lesson here is to keep your mouth shut when you are angry.

Elihu admits that he is young, and wisdom comes with age, but he still tells his friends to listen to him as he expresses his thoughts. And his thoughts are extensive! It seems that he even tells God what He is thinking and why He has done this to Job. Certainly, with youth can come stupidity and this reminds us that we should speak less and listen more.

Prayer: Gracious Father, help me to listen to You. To speak only Your words and to hold my tongue more than I do. Teach me Your ways so that I have true understanding. In Jesus name, Amen.

Day 136

JOB'S BLESSINGS
Read: Job 38-42

We finally hear what God has to say after all that has been said by Job as well as his friends. God does not answer their questions but asks them question after question as he tells Job to be a man (see Job 38:3 & 40: 7). Job then confesses in 40:3-5 (NLT), "Then Job replied to the Lord, "I am nothing—how could I ever find the answers? I will cover my mouth with my hand. I have said too much already. I have nothing more to say." And in 42:6 (NLT), Job responds with "I take back everything I said, and I sit in dust and ashes to show my repentance."

How very important to show humility when we are wrong! Not only did God accept his repentant attitude but he told Job's friends that Job would pray for them and Job did. What a blessing when God restores Job's material losses. He is given twice as much as what was taken away plus more children. He lived long enough to see four generations and died after a full life.

What can we learn from Job's life? For some, it is to realize that even through the pain of health problems, financial woes, personal situations and so much more, God is with us. He has allowed the pain for a purpose, a purpose that we may not understand but it is for our good. To mold us to be more Christ-like, humble, patient and loving. That is our blessing, not material gain but a change of character.

Prayer: I pray that my children and grandchildren and every generation till the coming back of Christ can endure God's tests and will praise God in all they do! May I be the example that glorifies You. In Jesus name, Amen.

Day 137

PROTECTION
Read: Psalm 1-6

When you do not know what to say to God, when the words will not come to you during your prayer time, go to the Psalms and read them out loud. There is instruction on how to live our lives as in Psalm 1: We should stay away from sinners, do not even sit with the wicked, and certainly do not keep company with those who intend to hurt others. It further tells us to delight in the Word of the Lord! In Psalm 3:3 (NLT) we read, "But You, O Lord, are a shield around me; you are my glory, the one who holds my head high."

No matter what we are going through, God is there for us and we must call out to Him and obey His Word; but most importantly, we must open our lives up to Him, invite Him in and determine to live a changed life for Him. We cannot do it on our own, we need to be reading His Word daily because the life instructions are there; we must desire to be obedient and follow His Word.

Prayer: Because You, O Lord, care for me, guide me daily to stay on the right path, and to run into Your arms. I take refuge in You when people use me, when their cruel words sink into my heart and almost crush me. Thank You for Your mercy, love and protection. In Jesus name, Amen.

Day 138

SINCERE HEART
Read: Psalm 7-15

The Psalms are a comfort to those who are hurting "I come to You for protection, O Lord my God." (Psa 7:1a NLT) He is our protection in times of trouble. He does not abandon those who continually seek His face. In good times and in time of trouble, the Lord is with us. We must have a sincere heart that seeks Him. Our greatest desire must be to serve Him in all we do and to glorify His name.

Prayer: When I am afflicted, O Lord, I run to You for You hear my cry and comfort me. You will never reject me, but long for me to draw ever closer to You. You protect my mind and my heart from evil men. I find joy and peace in You. In Jesus name, Amen.

Day 139

PLEASING GOD
Read: Psalm 16-20

There is such great encouragement in today's reading. In these words, we are reminded that He is always with us (see Psa 16:8), He is our protection (see Psa 17:8-9), that He rescues us from our enemies (see Psa 18:17) and He gives us strength to stand firm against the enemy (see Psa 18:39). I especially like:

"To the faithful You show yourself faithful; to those with integrity you show integrity. To the pure You show Yourself pure, but to the wicked You show Yourself shrewd. You rescue the humble, but you humiliate the proud." (Psa 18:25-27 NLT)

Not only are we to see how He cares for us but in Psalm 19:13-14 (NIV), we are reminded, "Keep your servant also from willful sins; may they not rule over me. Then will I be blameless, innocent of great transgression. May the words of my mouth and the meditation of my heart be pleasing in your sight, O Lord, my Rock and my Redeemer."

Prayer: You, O Lord, are my strength and my protection, in You alone I take refuge. When I am sad, You are there. You give me joy beyond my circumstances. May my desires always be Your desires. In Jesus name, Amen.

Day 140

FEAR HIM
Read: Psalm 21-26

"O Lord, do not stay far away! You are my strength; come quickly to my aid!" (Psa 22:19 NLT) May we look to the Lord for our help and hope. The Psalms help remind us of His great love for us and also His mercy. He is forgiving but we must fear the Lord and strive to walk a life of humble integrity.

We cannot earn our salvation. That was done on the cross, through the blood of Jesus. To know that if we are not walking in His Word, obeying His laws, we cannot expect His protection and care for us. We have a responsibility in our walk with the Lord, just as we have responsibilities in all walks of life but walking the straight road with Jesus is the most important!

Prayer: Father God, may my hands be clean and my heart pure, may I not look to idols for comfort nor tell lies for my cause. May I have a healthy fear of You for I love to draw ever closer to You. In Jesus name, Amen.

Day 141

HE IS MY REFUGE
Read: Psalm 27-32

Psalm 27: 1 (NLT), "The Lord is my light and my salvation—so why should I be afraid? The Lord is my fortress, protecting me from danger, so why should I tremble?" As a new Christian I clung to that verse and still find comfort in it today. Even when I am being threatened, I must remind myself of this Psalm and know that He is there for me. He will take care of the evil one who uses people and discourages.

May the Lord always remind us of His great love for us and that in the worse of circumstances, He protects us. At times, He allows us to go through some pain or threat to make us stronger for He knows what is best for us! May we see His great love and protection and know that His unfailing love is with us at all times.

Prayer: Lord, teach me Your ways, keep me safe as Your mercy is revealed to me each day. Listen Lord when I cry to You for help, when I feel so alone, may You remind me of Your closeness. Give me joy in the morning as we step out together in the dance of life. In Jesus name, Amen.

Day 142

FEAR THE LORD
Read: Psalm 33-39

As we read today's encouragement, we are reminded over and over that we are to "Fear the Lord, you His Godly people, for those who fear Him will have all they need." (Psa 34:9 NLT) And further on, we are reminded, "Then keep your tongue from speaking evil and your lips from telling lies! Turn away from evil and do good. Search for peace, and work to maintain it." (Psa 34:13-14 NLT) God is a God of justice and although we may not always understand what goes on around us, what does not seem right in our eyes, is exactly what God knows is needed. Sometimes it is not for us to understand why something is happening a certain way, we just have to trust that God knows exactly what He is doing. That, my friend, is simple faith. Faith that He is in control and knows what is best for our lives.

I think there comes a time in our Christian walk when we really do let God have full control of our lives. For me, this has been a long, hard journey! I have felt that I have been a burden on my friends and especially my family. I have not understood true, unconditional love from anyone. I have felt that I had to preform by giving of myself, my possessions or they would not love me. No indeed, when I did give, they would reject me or act like they wanted or expected more from me. So, the time is coming when I will be weak and not be able to give. I will not have any means to give, it will be gone. Will those who care about us, who are there for us, be the ones we least expect? They will be our joy at the end of life.

Prayer: My heart rejoices in You, dear Lord, and I put my hope in You. You Lord, promise to be close to the broken-hearted and I long for You when my spirit is low. You protect me and deliver me from my enemy as I take shelter in You. In Jesus name, Amen.

Day 143

UNFAILING LOVE
Read: Psalm 40-47

"God is our refuge and strength, always ready to help in times of trouble." (Psa 46:1 NLT) Even when we are going through difficult times, when it seems that no one is there, God is not only here to help us through those rough times, but He is allowing it all to happen. It is truly not for us to understand! In our minds, we think if God is there to care for us, He will not let anyone touch us. He will not let anything bad happen to us. But if that were the case, we would become soft marshmallows, depending on Him and not gaining strength ourselves. He loves us beyond measure, more than anyone else but He also knows exactly what we need to gain a stronger character, to become more like Christ.

Each and every day, we need God in our lives. We need to read His Word and soak it in. We need to determine in our hearts to live daily for Him. And to grasp His great love for us. He is our all in all, who will take care of us even when the world around us looks like it is falling apart. He cares for each of us!

Prayer: You, O Lord, work wonders far too amazing for me to understand. Your love and truth always protect me. May Your law dwell within my heart and may my heart desire to please only You. In Jesus name, Amen.

Day 144

GOD'S MERCY
Read: Psalm 48-54

May we always go to Psalm 51 when we have sinned may we humbly go before God and confess our sin and ask that He restore our joy and that we will strive to obey Him. It is so important to remember that He does not want us to make a big production, so we can pridefully tell others about our great acts and why God forgave us. No, He longs for us to have a broken spirit and a repentant heart. That attitude is between you and the Lord, and, at some point, a humble heart will go to the hurt and offended and make restitution.

When we recognize our sin, the damage it has done to others and the pain to God, our Father, we can go before God in great humility. When we recognize that what we have done is so destructive to those around us and that we need God to help us turn away from our sinful ways, then we are ready to make changes in our life. When we are ready to make restitution with those we have sinned against, we are becoming a new creation. Are you ready to give up the old self and present yourself to God with a repentant heart? Only then can you know the joy that comes with salvation because you are letting go of your sinful nature.

Prayer: May my eyes always be on Him. May I long, at all times, to be pleasing to Him. May I be pleasing in His sight. May my attitude always be humble. In Jesus name, Amen.

Day 145

GOD'S JUSTICE
Read: Psalm 55-62

Make no mistake, God watches us and expects us to follow His Word. In Psalm 59:7a (NLT), He says, "Listen to the filth that comes from their mouths; their words cut like swords." It seems that in today's society, filth comes out of so many mouths and people use the excuse "it is only words". But in this way of thinking, they give no consideration to the people listening and whether they would be offended by the words that are coming out of their mouths. Many have no respect at all for another person.

God is a God of justice and when He considers what comes out of your mouth, are you going to be ashamed? First, repent and ask God to forgive you for your sin, the many obscenities that come out of your mouth. Then ask Him to show you other areas where you need to change. You have a choice His justice will either be punishment for your unrepentant heart or rewards for wanting to be a better person, not only pleasing to those around you but also pleasing to God. It is important to be pleasing to God in our behavior, but He looks at the heart that has accepted Jesus and now lives to please Him.

> *Prayer: Lord, You are my Rock, I find my peace in You only. No matter what happens around me, may I keep my focus on You and not be shaken by such evil. May Your protection be upon me. In Jesus name, Amen.*

Day 146

HIS UNFAILING LOVE
Read: Psalm 63-69

The last verse in chapter 69 tells us that even our descendants will be blessed, and safety is given to those who love Him. Often times we do not realize that our actions will have results on our children. Not in just the way we act, but even our attitudes are important to keep in check. So, when we are obeying God and doing what is right, that will also reflect on our children, grandchildren and future generations. We must remember that our responsibility goes beyond ourselves.

We are also reminded in this section of reading that He will protect us from evil and our enemies will end in defeat. It is ever important to keep our eyes on Him and set our mind to doing His will. But there are times when He allows us to go through trials, to refine us to produce pure gold and silver. (see Psa 66:10)

Prayer: Dear Lord, May I see Your greater goal as I go through suffering and the pains of this life. From unfaithful friends to the sufferings of growing old, may Your hand be on me and guide me. I long to hear You welcome me into the Kingdom. In Jesus name, Amen.

Day 147

THE GOODNESS OF GOD
Read: Psalm 70-76

What joy I feel when reading today's selection! We are assured of His caring for us and protecting us and He will judge the evil ones and they will be brought to destruction. When people say, 'God is Love', they do not want to face the truth that God is also a God of Justice. He is good! If we only see Him as Love, then we will think that we can do anything, and He will just love us. But when we see the truth that He will judge us, then we will put our thoughts and actions in check. This is a form of fearing the Lord. We all must have boundaries in order to be better people. Have you allowed the Word of God to help set your boundaries?

As the world is getting crazier and certainly more evil, I sometimes wonder if I will be cared for. With not having a husband, I feel so alone at times. But then, I read, "Now that I am old and gray, do not abandon me, O God." (Psa 71:18a NLT) And yes, that is exactly how I feel. David, as great as he was, felt so alone at times just like me. God had David write those words so it would one day encourage me (and so many others, like you). And we are reminded that He is right by our side, holding our hand and caring for us. I am so eternally thankful for Him!

Prayer: Thank You Lord for Your love and defending me from my enemies. You test my faithfulness but also give me strength to get through the test. May I draw ever closer to You. In Jesus name, Amen.

Day 148

REBELLION BRINGS PAIN
Read: Psalm 77-80

In today's reading, we are reminded that past generations have rebelled against the Lord but also that we sometimes follow in their footsteps. Why don't we learn from their mistakes? Why are we such a stubborn people? When we are young we think we are different and that this generation is the enlightened one who will change the world. If we have changed anything, it is for the worse. The Bible needs to be taught to the young. It tells us that there is nothing new under the sun. It tells us to love one another. It is the only way that the world can become a better place. We must read and do what the Bible says.

Such simple instructions but we continue to go our own way again and again. When the United States was founded, we started out right, the Bible was our forefathers guide. Sadly, each generation since then thinks they know better, that things are different, and we must modernize. What are we getting as a result? People only worried about themselves. More selfishness, more hatred, more prejudice, more and more evil! Is it too late to turn back to God, to obey His Word?

Prayer: O Lord, if only I would follow You rather than my fathers. May my heart be cleansed to the purity and integrity that only You offer. I long to be loyal to You, keep me away from my own selfishness and rebellion. In Jesus name, Amen.

Day 149

GOD'S BLESSINGS
Read: Psalm 81-86

Much of the Psalms are wonderful prayers! Psalm 86: 11-13 (NIV):

"Teach me Your way, O Lord, and I will walk in Your truth; give me an undivided heart, that I may fear Your name. I will praise You, O Lord my God, with all my heart; I will glorify Your name forever. For great is Your love toward me; You have delivered me from the depths of the grave."

May we learn to see the Psalms as guidelines to seeking God's face and pray the very words that the Psalmists were given. May we long for a pure heart and a truthful mind that we find such comfort as we are reminded that He not only cares daily for us but that He has rescued us from the depths of hell.

Prayer: You, O Lord, are my comfort and help. You are there to protect me from the enemy, who seeks to destroy me. I accept the goodness You have for me, I accept Your grace as I keep on Your path. All glory to You! In Jesus name, Amen.

Day 150

GOD, MY REFUGE
Read: Psalm 87-91

It is good to remember what the Lord has done but sometimes He has to get our attention and we go through a time of hurting other times He is there protecting us, covering us with His great love and we hardly seem to notice. "Because he loves me," says the Lord, "I will rescue him; I will protect him, for he acknowledges my name. He will call upon me, and I will answer him; I will be with him in trouble, I will deliver him and honor him." (Psa 91:14-15 NIV)

Do you see that we have a part to play? We must love the Lord. We must trust Him. And we must be humble enough to realize that we need Him and call on His name. May we always recognize our need for a Savior and be willing to call on His Name.

Prayer: I call out to You when wicked men bring their abuse on me, when they are out to destroy me. You have allowed the trials in my life so I may gain wisdom; for You are my refuge and strength and I accept Your great love for me. In Jesus name, Amen.

Day 151

HIS GLORIOUS JUSTICE
Read: Psalm 92-101

Our hope lies in His glorious justice when He will give the wicked what they deserve. He rescues His people from evil and He protects their lives. Yes, this realization brings joy to our hearts and strength to our bones. Just knowing His great love helps us to go forth each new day. It helps us to continue to serve Him.

Psalm 101: 7-8a (NLT), "I will not allow deceivers to serve in my house, and liars will not stay in my presence. My daily task will be to ferret out the wicked." We must remain as pure as we are capable of and keep deception away only as we draw close to Him and surrender to Him. Staying away from wicked people, from people who lie and plan deception in their hearts is a good start.

Prayer: Hear my prayer O Lord, for You cherish justice and punish those who follow after evil. May I keep my eyes on You and You alone for I long to lead a blameless life. May I grow by Your River and gain wisdom from drinking Your waters. In Jesus name, Amen.

Day 152

GOD'S TESTING
Read: Psalm 102-106

In Psalm 105:19b (NLT), we read that "the Lord tested Joseph's character." I do not know about you, but this helps me to stop and think, to contemplate what Joseph went through and to realize that God was using each circumstance of his life to test Joseph's character. Is it any different with us, in today's world? God not only uses circumstances in our lives to test us but also to shape our character, to be more Christ-like.

He forgives, He heals, He frees us, He crowns us with love and gives tender mercies. He fills our life with good things, but he also gives righteousness and justice to all who are treated unfairly. (see Psa 103: 3-6) We are fortunate to have such a loving Father who cares so deeply for us. He hears our prayers and gives us what is best for us.

Prayer: May Your name be praised, O God, throughout the land. May repentance become a part of my daily life and may I fall on my knees before you often. Remind me of your power and may I fear You Lord, as I obey Your Word. Thank You Lord, for Your great love! In Jesus name, Amen.

Day 153

HE IS TRUSTWORTHY
Read: Psalm 107-114

When reading the Psalms, sometimes it is best just to pray His Words. Let us consider Psalm 111:7-8 (NLT):

"All He does is just and good, and all His commandments are trustworthy.

They are forever true, to be obeyed faithfully and with integrity."

Verse 10 continues, "Fear of the Lord is the foundation of true wisdom.

All who obey His commandments will grow in wisdom." (NLT)

Let us pray for wisdom each day and may we take His Words into our heart as He tells us to obey with faithfulness and integrity. Most importantly, He reminds us often that when we follow His Word and fear Him, we grow in wisdom. What more can we say but thank you Jesus for Your great love for us!

Prayer: Lord, from the earliest morning to the end of each day, I long for You and praise Your Holy Name. I thank You for Your love, and that Your hand is upon me, guiding me along the path to serve You ever deeper. In Jesus name, Amen.

Day 154

UNFAILING LOVE
Read: Psalm 115-118

When so many are looking to other things to fulfill their emptiness, may we remember that the Lord is all we need! What wisdom in Psalm 115:8 (NLT) "And those who make idols are just like them, as are all who trust in them." If you remember that in 2 Kings 17:15, we read that all who worship worthless idols themselves become worthless. We MUST be careful to whom we give our trust, who do we look to for answers? For many, it is money or another person, for some it is their possessions, what they own. For others, it is rebellion against their parents or society in general. Still for others, they insist that the answers are within themselves. What is your idol?

May it be that we always fear, totally respect, the Lord and understand that He is all we need. It is He who is faithful in all things and His love is our greatest need. We are called to walk daily in the Lord's presence and to live for Him. May we thank Him daily for His great presence in our lives as He cares for us with guidance that is beyond our understanding. He will give us victory as we look to only Him for all our needs, wants and desires!

> *Prayer: Lord, You gave me this day, may I find the joy and happiness that only comes from You. May I be ever attentive to all You have for me and grasp Your love and faithfulness to me. In Jesus name, Amen.*

Day 155

RESCUE ME!
Read: Psalm 119

I do not know about you, but oftentimes I need to be rescued from myself! From my thoughts, to wanting to get even, to feeling sorry for myself. Sometimes I need to be rescued from my behavior. In all my ways, I need a discerning mind and for God to listen to my prayers! His laws, commands and decrees are what I long to obey and yet, I fall so short. The Lord is my refuge and shield, keeping me protected from evil-minded people. I long for Him to surround me with His tender mercies! May each and every day be dedicated to Him so that I will be pleasing to Him.

What verses and words spoke to your heart as you read Psalm 119? Your list might be different from the above list. Isn't that what makes the Word of God so special, it speaks to each of us in a different way? It is convicting our hearts to serve Him better and if we have the Holy Spirit living in our lives, then He helps us each day to achieve what God has called us to do.

Prayer: O Lord, keep my ways from deceit; may Your Word always be before me to obey. Lord, give me a discerning heart so that I have understanding and will not be deceived by those smooth talkers who have no use for Your Word. Draw me ever closer to You! In Jesus name, Amen.

Day 156

HE HAS CUT ME FREE
Read: Psalm 120-131

Indeed, the Lord has cut me free from those ungodly people—people who controlled me, who abused me both by word and hand, people who only wanted something out of me to benefit themselves. But, He has cut me free and protected me, giving me a discerning heart to stay away from such users. He has cut me free from liars and evil people, He stands beside me, keeping watch over me.

To be set free from the oppression of evil people and waking me up to the fact that not all people are nice, not all people care about my welfare has been a big step. The Lord is the only one I can truly trust. He only wants what is best for me. When I awakened to this truth, I gained wisdom, but I know I must be careful each and every day to not fall back into such a filthy pit. I must keep my eyes on Him and Him alone. I must read His Word daily, devour it and make a choice to live by it. And, above all, I must be thankful, showing gratitude for all He has done for me!

Prayer: Lord, I choose to walk in Your ways for my help comes from You alone. Thank You for keeping me from wicked people, may they not rule over me. May I always keep a healthy fear of You Lord that I may walk in Your ways. In Jesus name, Amen.

Day 157

LEAD ME!
Read: Psalm 132-139

I am very much reminded of God's love, His watching over me and His guidance in my life as I read Psalm 139. The prayer that I have prayed for 33 years is a paraphrase from the Living Bible: "Search me, O God, and know my heart; test my thoughts. Point out anything You find in me that makes You sad and lead me along the path of everlasting life." (verses 23-24) Isn't that a wonderful prayer to petition the Lord with on a daily basis?

May we seek His face every moment of the day but also pray that we will have at least one friend who will encourage us to go before Him daily in repentance! We can read the Word of God daily, but it is such a blessing to have a person in our lives who reminds us what God has done for us and to point us into His arms!

Prayer: Your wisdom, O Lord, is beyond my understanding, yet You have compassion on even me. You show me my sin and I come before You in repentance. In Your grace You forgive me and take me in Your arms. You love me when no one else cares. In Jesus name, Amen.

Day 158

GOD IS MERCIFUL
Read: Psalm 140-145

The importance of prayer is the great reminder in today's reading. We must remember where we came from and be so thankful that He cares deeply for us and continues to love us and guide us. Oh, may we always listen to Him, read His Word daily and take it to heart by obeying.

When I am down, the evil one puts doubt in my mind and I think that no one cares, that I am alone in this big world. But then I read His Word, and realize that He is always with me, even when I do not feel Him, He cares for me and is there to guide me each step of the way. The Psalms help us with our feelings, putting into words the emotions that are so strong in our hearts. The Psalms helps us understand ourselves better.

Prayer: Lord, keep my heart pure! Lord, keep my ears and mind attentive to You! Keep my feet on firm ground that I may walk with You all the days of my life. In Jesus name, Amen.

Day 159

PRAISE THE LORD!
Read: Psalm 146-150

In each of the Psalms we read today, we see the Psalmist praising the Lord. It is good to read all the great things the Lord has done for the writer and see how he expresses his gratitude not only to the Lord but for those around us to know what the Lord has done.

In today's world, we seldom hear anyone giving God the glory, praise and gratitude He so deserves. Yes, God may use people in our lives, but we must realize that those blessings come directly from the Lord. We must also start taking the time to not only tell others of what God has done for us but to write these blessings out, so we can remind ourselves of His great love for us. Writing out, journaling, if you will, is of great importance because it is expressing our thankfulness and love to the Lord and a great reminder for each of us because we can easily forget what He has done for us. Today, write out one blessing or lesson the Lord has given you and save it and read it in a week, in a month, and in a year from now.

Prayer: I praise You Lord for Your great love! I praise You Lord for our protection. I praise You Lord for providing all I need. With my whole heart, I am thankful for Jesus and His sacrifice so that I may live for Him. In Jesus name, Amen.

Day 160

WISDOM
Read: Proverbs 1-4

Praying daily for wisdom is of the utmost importance. It is impossible to live a Godly life, to be pleasing to the Lord, to value knowledge and understanding that come from Godly wisdom. Wisdom is the key to knowing and doing what is right and leads us towards common sense. As we hold on to wisdom, with deep determination, we are given good judgment as well. Surely there is not much argument against wisdom! Then why? Why are people not praying for and seeking wisdom daily?

The Book of Proverbs has so much to offer. I have, at times, read it daily. Thirty-one Proverbs and 30 to 31 days in each month. It is an easy task to look at what the date is and go to that Proverb to be enlightened, gaining wisdom day by day. So much to learn in those 31 Proverbs and you can read them again and again and still learn something new. The important thing is to remain open to learning, be willing to accept new wisdom and set that wisdom into action. What is your choice? To continue to tell yourself that you do not have time to read the Bible, or take 15 to 30 minutes each day and start gaining the wisdom that only God can give you?

Prayer: Heavenly Father, I look to You and Your Word to gain common sense, and to live a life pleasing to You. May I stay away from fools, those morally deficient, who look to make themselves feel good at the expense of others. May I trust You with all my heart and follow You as You give my life purpose and meaning. In Jesus name, Amen.

Day 161

WARNINGS
Read: Proverbs 5-9

When we take the Proverbs to heart, heed the warnings, taking the corrections deep within our being and make a choice to live the Proverbs in our daily life, we have chosen to do a good thing. Stay away from adultery, be humble, work hard, keep His commands, do not let lust guide you, maintain high morals and good judgment and flee from pride and arrogance. Whew! We will work on these all the days of our life!

Although I have said this before, I think it bears repeating that we are to fear the Lord, for that is the beginning of true wisdom. Proverbs 9:12 (NIV) says, "If you are wise, your wisdom will reward you; if you are a mocker, you alone will suffer." We cannot necessarily understand why things happen a certain way, but we must trust God to know what is best for us.

Prayer: Lord, I long to store Your Words in my heart and mind so that I may obey willingly and immediately. I long for good judgment that I may have high moral standards. May I be always truthful, with a pure heart that stays away from evil. In Jesus name, Amen.

Day 162

DISCIPLINE OR STUPIDITY
Read: Proverbs 10-14

Proverbs 12: 1 says "Whoever loves discipline loves knowledge, but he who hates correction is stupid." (NIV) There are other Proverbs that say pretty much the same thing but this one is straight forward, no mincing words! It seems that everyone can understand it but yet, how often do we run across people who hate correction? Who, it seems, would rather be stupid instead of learning from discipline or modifying their behavior?

May we pray every day to be humble people who are willing to learn from correction and to love discipline (which truly means to train). May we be associated with wisdom, having truthful lips, a tongue that bring healing, being respectful, being level headed, having a discerning heart, being patient and finally, being a people who fear the Lord which brings life.

Prayer: Father in Heaven, Your Word is a soothing ointment to my soul! I long to be wise and walk with integrity so You will count me as righteous. May I promote peace and experience the joy of speaking truth. In Jesus name, Amen.

Day 163

GENTLENESS
Read: Proverbs 15-19

Both Proverbs and James tell us to watch our tongue, what comes out of our mouth (consistently) is what is in our heart. Either life or death comes from the tongue. We cannot have both one will prevail. Wisdom or foolishness?

This is a good check for ourselves and if we want to truly be good people, we need Jesus in our heart. We will not have to tell people how good we are, it will show in our words and in our behavior. It is making those choices to do what God's Word says, to love others so much that we put them first in our life. To be patient and stay away from quarrels and wicked people. Most of all to fear the Lord, respecting Him and His Word and trusting that even if we do not understand we will obey Him, doing what is right.

Prayer: Heavenly Father, I long for Your wisdom, that I may bring glory to You. My spirit has been crushed but Your Word is like medicine and sooths my pain, bringing joy to my heart. Keep me in Your perfect will. In Jesus name, Amen.

Day 164

BECOME LIKE THOSE YOU ARE AROUND
Read: Proverbs 20-23

Proverbs 22: 24–25 tell us, "Do not make friends with a hot-tempered man, do not associate with one easily angered, or you may learn his ways and get yourself ensnared." (NIV) These words are great advice, and this is a principle that should be followed, especially in youth when we develop habits that often last the rest of our lives.

I remember, when I was a child, my mother telling me not to associate with certain girls because they had a bad reputation. I truly did not understand what my mother was saying when she said that. I saw goodness in these girls and wanted to be their friend. But truly, my mother was right, and these girls soon moved on from my friendship. By hanging around them, becoming friends with them, I would have picked up their ways. "Do not be misled: Bad company corrupts good character." (1 Corinthians 15:33 NIV) So whether we are children or adults, we need to guard ourselves because we can become like those we hang around. Make good choices in friends, a life partner, and even becoming close to family members.

Prayer: Lord, may I strive to take the path most pleasing to You! When I fall short, when I sin, may I recognize it and repent and fall back into Your loving arms quickly. In Jesus name, Amen.

Day 165

FOOLS
Read: Proverbs 24-27

One of my prayers is to stay close to God and obey His Word but I also pray for wisdom. Today's reading has many warnings concerning a fool. He lacks judgment, he is deceptive, he is rebellious, he is not careful with the words he speaks, he does not like to be corrected, he is unfaithful to all, he says and does much that is inappropriate, not caring who he hurts, he is lazy, he can flatter but it is for his benefit and the list goes on.

The Proverbs are filled with wisdom for everyday living. We can read one Proverb a day and in a month's time, we have read them all. What a great guide for daily living, to strive towards pleasing God and bringing true love to our fellow man. When we miss a day, do not beat yourself up to the point that you give up this daily reading, just go to the day you are to be on and catch the day you missed next month.

Prayer: Heavenly Father, help me not to get discouraged in my Bible reading or my time with You. Keep me reading even on those days that I do not feel like it. When I fall behind, it is not the end! Help me to remember that you are a God full of grace! In Jesus name, Amen.

Day 166

FINAL INSTRUCTIONS
Read: Proverbs 28-31

These final chapters of Proverbs are full of wisdom and instructions on how to live. To maintain self-control in all our ways is of utmost importance. To not be prideful or angry, for a hot-tempered man is never far from sin (see Pro 29:22). We are to be kind to the poor and honest in all our dealings. We are to recognize our sin and confess it, we are to turn away and walk a different path. Proverbs 31 is often used to direct a woman's heart, but it starts out telling the man to not give way to too much alcohol and to judge fairly and defend the poor and needy.

The final words of wisdom are describing a woman of great character. She is trustworthy, compassionate, fears the Lord, has moral integrity, has a sense of humor and does not compromise. Proverbs closes with reminding the man to give his wife the affirmation she needs so she knows that he loves her.

Prayer: O Lord, I strive to walk before You in a pleasing manner, help me to love Your Word. Help me to obey Your Word! Help me to always have a heart for those who are hurting and to stay away from evil. May Your wisdom never depart from my mind and may I speak words that heal. In Jesus name, Amen.

Day 167

TWO
Read: Ecclesiastes 1-4

What a great reminder for each of us that we cannot travel through this life alone, we need another person. Sometimes this is a spouse but oftentimes it is a dear friend, someone who is there for us as well as us being there for them. And we must remember that there is a time for everything. Sometimes people come into our lives for just a short while, God's purpose for them is precise and then they move on but there are others who come into our lives and stay. This is not just for the purpose of us getting from them or them getting from us but probably more importantly, God has brought them into our lives to teach us to give, for true love is in giving of ourselves to that person.

May we pray each and every day that we are open and willing to learn from Godly wisdom and stay far away from what the world has to offer. Worldly knowledge will puff you up, making you think you are more important than you really are. Do you think that people are looking at you all the time, or talking about you? If so, your thinking is not God centered. Do you strive to make more and more money without thinking about those around you and what they really need? Are you looking to entertainment, always wanting to have more fun? This too is truly meaningless! Only God offers true value and it is in serving Him that we find true pleasure.

Prayer: Holy Father, help me to keep my eyes on You and my heart turned towards doing Your will. Help me to find companionship, comfort and protection from true friends. In Jesus name, Amen.

Day 168

INVESTING
Read: Ecclesiastes 5-8

Investing ourselves is not something we are taught. Whether it is our time, our talents or our wisdom, we are directed to use them wisely for His work. We are to work with what we have, not with what we do not have (or what we long for). Perhaps just being satisfied in what state you are in, not wishing you had something more, is what we need to learn

So often man does not have the answer to life's problems and does not even ask the right questions. Most look for laughter and a good time rather than toil and hard work. Have you ever heard the laughter of fools? Fools are all around us, luring us towards their ways. Run into the arms of God and dwell in His heart so you can learn that being a patient person is better than pride and that anger lives in the fool. (see Ecc 7:9)

Prayer: Father God, I look to You to be satisfied and for wisdom. May I consider my every thought and action to be pleasing to You at all times. For those times that I fall short and sin against You, may I be quick to acknowledge, confess and turn away from my evil behavior and turn back to You. In Jesus name, Amen.

Day 169

GOD'S JUDGMENT
Read: Ecclesiastes 9-12

Without God in our lives, we feel an emptiness deep within our soul. Ecclesiastes 12:13b speaks truth, "Fear God and keep His commandments, for this is the whole duty of man." (NIV) It is the summation of who man should be and yet, we look for satisfaction in other things. More money cannot fill that void. A bigger house cannot fill that void. Being in control of your own life (if that were truly possible) cannot fill that void. Only the pride of man, thinking that he can do it all, holds us back from turning our lives over to the one true God. Our Creator can fill that void that cries out for Him and Him only.

It is important to remember the last verse (Ecc 12:14), "For God will bring every deed into judgment, including every hidden thing, whether it is good or evil." (NIV) And never think that your actions are better than another, for we all have sinned and fall short of God's glory (see Rom 3:23). Perhaps this little list will help in some small way: 1) learn of God and obey Him, 2) do not assume nothing bad will happen, 3) rest in God during the bad, 4) as you rest, hold your course, 5) live boldly, a holy life, 6) enjoy your life with those around you and 7) when times are good, seek God even more. (I wrote that list in my Bible, I am not sure where it came from.)

Prayer: Without You Lord, life is empty, truly meaningless. I long to hold on to You and carry Your Word to all who will listen. Help me Lord to fulfill Your purpose for my life. In Jesus name, Amen.

Day 170

TRUE LOVE
Read: Song of Songs 1-4

The Song of Songs is a love story a love story between Christ and His church a love story between a man and his very special woman. Whatever the case may be, each time we read this book, we can learn a bit more about true love. A woman who is married but does not feel or know the love of her husband is very sad. (see Pro 30:21-13) The Song of Songs is an excellent example of how words of affirmation towards the one you love will strengthen the relationship. Not only are words important but putting those words into action speaks volumes. This book is a wonderful guide!

To have the security of His love, "His banner over me is love" (SS 2:4b NIV) brings adoration from her, "My lover is mine and I am His" (Song of Songs 2:16a NIV). Although I have not received this kind of love from a man, I have received it from my Lord. We cannot cry over what might have been but need to look to the One who can fulfill our deepest desire for love—Jesus. We are never alone, never forgotten and never unloved when we have Jesus in our lives. A personal relationship with Him brings joy.

Prayer: How I long for you, O Lord. You stole my heart and now my desire is to please You for You are mine and I am Yours. You cover me with Your great love, may I never let go. In Jesus name, Amen.

Day 171

MY FRIEND
Read: Song of Songs 5-8

Jesus...my Love, my Friend! Have you ever thought of Jesus in those terms? When He becomes your all in all, when your heart pounds for Him, when you realize His love for you is the deepest kind of love you will ever know, the kind of love of knowing that He longs for you and wants only you. Then you know the love of Jesus! Today's reading tells us that His desire is for you!

As a single woman, it took me a long time to finally accept His great love for me, to realize that His love satisfies beyond anything I have ever known or desired before . "I am my lover's and my lover is mine " (SS 6:3a NIV) Sometimes it is still hard to comprehend that He loves me so much. Even though I thought I knew Jesus for so many years, I still longed for love after my husband died. But now, I have the love of Jesus and it is enough! May you also be satisfied by Him and Him alone.

Prayer: At times, dear Lord, I am overwhelmed that You love me so much! You are my friend, my lover and my heart beats for You. I love You Lord! In Jesus name, Amen.

Day 172

REBELS
Read: Isaiah 1-3

As I read these first three chapters in Isaiah, it seems that it could be written to the United States right now, today. A rebellious nation who insists on rejecting God, full of evildoers (see Isa 1:4), rulers are thieves, many take advantage of widows and the fatherless (see Isa 1:23). May we fall on our faces and repent of the evil, may we stop doing wrong, and may be seek justice!

May our eyes be opened to truth the truth that God is calling us to. May we understand that He will bring punishment upon anyone who chooses to rebel and rejecting the Lord is a most horrendous offense to Him. We have become a harlot, turning from God and seeking out things to fill that void within us. May we recognize that He is our only hope, that we need Him and He is there, waiting for us to come to Him in repentance (that is confessing our sin, turning away from our sin and walking a new path). Yes, Isaiah is speaking to each of us, calling us to turn from our evil ways and following the path that God has called us to.

Prayer: Lord, help me to remember that Your great love brings responsibility on my part. Much of the world is turning away from You, in search of wealth, fame, peace and so much more. Forgive me for my past, forgive me for being silent. Help me to be bold in introducing You to those I know. In Jesus name, Amen.

Day 173

MILLENNIAL REIGN
Read: Isaiah 4-6

When Jesus returns those words seem to bring joy to most Christians. For those who have read the Bible and understand its content, it will be a glorious time, for He will be a shelter when it is hot and a refuge in the storm. But it seems that oftentimes we overlook that Isaiah spoke of such a time as in Isa 5:20 "Woe to those who call evil good and good evil, who put darkness for light and light for darkness, who put bitter for sweet and sweet for bitter." Verse 21 goes on "Woe to those who are wise in their own eyes and clever in their own sight." (NIV)

Further on in chapter 5, we read of the consequences of living in such evil. Their roots will decay and they will blow away like dust "for they have rejected the law of the Lord Almighty and spurned the word of the Holy One of Israel." (verse 24b NIV) But it is a fact that those left will give glory to God and praise Him. We must live a life that follows the Word of God. Oh yes, we fall short but strive to stay humble and always go to Him in repentance. For those of you who need to go to Him and ask forgiveness, do it immediately! Do not let pride hold you back from what God is calling you to do. Do not be calloused nor close your ears to the truth, set your mind on Him.

Prayer: Holy Father, keep me ever close to You that I may know that my guilt is taken away. May I be ever ready to go out and serve You and be healed. In Jesus name, Amen.

Day 174

HOPE
Read: Isaiah 7-9

We are reminded today that God gave hope to us in telling us about the birth of Jesus (see Isa 7:14-16 and again Isa 9:6) Then in chapter 8 we are reminded to fear God and not follow after the people. He is the holy one, we are to give reverence to Him and to follow only Him. So often men seek answers in evil (mediums and spiritualists) but they cannot give us answers, only God can. God's Word has the answers, if we will only read it and obey it, putting what we learn into practice.

Be careful to always be humble, to search out God at all times. Stay away from people with pride and arrogance of heart and be careful not to allow this evil to enter your heart. In the world today, there are ungodly people and much wickedness and many speak vileness (see Isa 9:17b). We must be careful of whom we follow, even if it is a pastor or a president, we must know the Word of God so deeply that we are aware when evil is spoken. The times are difficult, keep your eyes on Jesus!

Prayer: Lord, I am thankful for Your Word! You spoke of what was to come and it came to pass. You promised us Jesus and He came in the place of the sacrificial lamb because none of us can be perfect. We need a Savior to cover our sins. May I never give up or lose heart but hold on to Your promises. In Jesus name, Amen.

Day 175

WARNINGS
Read: Isaiah 10-13

The warnings of those who go against God are powerful! "Woe to those who make unjust laws, to those who issue oppressive decrees, to deprive the poor of their rights and withhold justice from the oppressed of my people, making widows their prey and robbing the fatherless." (Isa 10:1-2 NIV) It is a time of oppression towards Christians like never before. Yes, this is the beginning, it will become worse and it will reveal who really stands with Christ and those who will let go of Christ to please the evil oppressors.

The choice will reveal our true colors! We have always had a choice, and many appeared to choose Christ but then did not make a choice to be pleasing to Him. Instead, they chose to continue their lifestyle just as before. When confronted, they said things like, 'this is the way I am' rather than letting the Word of God transform them. They have taken advantage of the widow and the orphan, then saying it was her choice. They continue to victimize the very people that they take advantage of. Check yourself this very moment, make sure you are right with the Lord, and that you are following His Word.

Prayer: O Lord my God, help me not to follow evil and certainly not to look to myself. For my strength and wisdom are nothing and I long for You, for Your salvation is what I need. In Jesus name, Amen.

Day 176

PRIDE
Read: Isaiah 14-18

In the last days, those who have followed the Lord will experience the Lord's compassion. He will give them relief from suffering (see Isaiah 14:3). But to those who have worked against the Lord, it will be a different story. For those who have their priorities in the wrong place, who see money more important than relationships and who constantly tear others down so that they themselves might be built up, the Lord is against you. Even if it seems that you are experiencing success at the beginning, it will not last for God will take you down.

Over and over in these chapters, we see nations whose god is satan or even self, we are told how God is going to destroy them. Pride and conceit, whether a nation or an individual, those characteristics will take you down to the pit of hell. You had a choice and did not want to humble yourself. You decided that you were stronger than God and that you were going to fight against Him. You counted on yourself, the works of your own hands instead of looking to your Maker for help and learning how to be humble in all areas of your life. When the days are difficult, only God will bring comfort!

Prayer: Heavenly Father, keep my heart directed towards Your goodness and far away from evil. May my hands be used for good and my heart always be inclined towards helping others. May I be a witness and an instrument of our grace and great love. In Jesus name, Amen.

Day 177

EVIL MUST GO
Read: Isaiah 19-24

Over and over we read how God will bring judgment upon the nations of the earth, nations who seek evil rather than God. These people do not feel any sort of sorrow for what they have done or are doing, they party and celebrate day in and day out. The sin of the nations' come before the Lord this very day, it is only a matter of time before He brings judgment.

Yes, we read of the Lord's judgment upon the nations and forget that His same judgment is upon us today. If we choose to live a life of self-indulgence we will suffer the consequences. So, make a choice to serve God, to give of our most valuable assets wholeheartedly, to care and serve others and fulfill God's calling in our lives. We are blessed to have the Bible, so read it and do what it says it is not as easy as it sounds but at least work at it daily. We all fall short, but we should continue to improve in obeying God.

Prayer: Dearest Lord, I fall short! Please give me the strength and perseverance to follow Your Word. When I fail, help me to be wise enough to confess my sin and determine to walk in the path that brings goodness not cruelty, kindness not hatred and to be thankful that Jesus paid the price. In Jesus name, Amen.

Day 178

IN THAT DAY
Read: Isaiah 25-27

When we read "in that day" in Scripture, it is taking us to the end times the day of Christ's reign. Do we look forward to that time? Do we look forward to the time when "the Sovereign Lord will wipe away the tears from all faces; He will remove the disgrace of His people from all the earth." (Isa 25:8a NIV) Or do we long for "Your name and renown are the desire of our hearts. My soul yearns for You in the night; in the morning my spirit longs for You." (Isa 26:8b-9a NIV) Oh how sad when we read, "even in a land of uprightness they go on doing evil and regard not the majesty of the Lord." (Isa 26:10b NIV)

So often when we think of the Lord's return, we think all will be peaceful and full of happiness but according to today's reading, He has some business to take care of. The Lord will have a time when He must rid the earth of evil, even from among people who seem to call themselves His own. We must daily (hourly and even moment by moment) check ourselves to be sure we are pleasing to the Lord in every way. We must ask the Holy Spirit to show us our evil ways that we may make a conscience effort to change our behavior. We must go to Him often and repent, asking forgiveness for the sin we have committed but also have a desire to change, to be more pleasing to Him. When we belong to someone, we have a responsibility. We should long to please that person all the while knowing that they love us dearly, right where we are.

Prayer: O Precious Lord, I trust in You and long for the day when I see You face to face. I am so thankful for Your love and I strive daily to know You more intimately, so I may walk in Your truth to the end. In Jesus name, Amen.

Day 179

CHECK YOUR HEART
Read: Isaiah 28-32

Just as it was in Isaiah's day, some things never change. The heart of man can be so deceptive. "These people come near to me with their mouth and honor me with their lips, but their hearts are far from me. Their worship of me is made up only of rules taught by men." (Isa 29: 13 NIV) We need to check our own lives before we start judging or condemning others. Are we so rebellious that we are unwilling to listen to the Lord's direction? Are we reading His Word so we know what He expects from us?

So many look for peace and happiness but continue to search, trying many things. Isaiah 30:15 gives us the solution to our search, "In repentance and rest is your salvation, in quietness and trust is your strength, but you would have none of it." (NIV) What is your choice when the answer is right there at hand? Will you choose to live a self-centered life or a righteous life? Do you long for peace? The Lord is your answer and you can only come to Him through a repentant heart, a heart that allows your mouth to speak only truth. Repentance will bring a love to you like you have never known before, God's love. Repentance does not mean you will never sin again, it means you are forgiven and He is there to help you live a different life! Forgiveness is waiting but you must act, you must seek to live a new life a new life in Christ.

Prayer: Heavenly Father, may I stay close to You, reading Your Word daily and striving to obey so that I may know Your peace. May I always be humble enough to cry out for help through repentance, for You are my Rock and my Strength. In Jesus name, Amen.

Day 180

PRAYER
Read: Isaiah 33-37

In today's reading, from Isaiah's prayers to Hezekiah's prayer, we witness the power of prayer and the work of an Almighty God. May we pray, "Oh Lord, be gracious to us; we long for You. Be our strength every morning, our salvation in time of distress." (Isa 33:2 NIV) May we have the assurance and trust that "the Lord is exalted, for He dwells on high; He will fill Zion with justice and righteousness. He will be the sure foundation (stability) for your times, a rich store of salvation and wisdom and knowledge; the fear of the Lord is the key to this treasure." (Isa 33:5-6 NIV) We no longer pray with this sort of confidence and power what has happened? Has the Lord gotten weak? No, we have! We do not live or pray as a redeemed people whose God is stronger than all the evil around.

Throughout the Bible we have great examples of seeking God's face through prayer and Hezekiah's prayer (see Isaiah 37:16-20) is no different. Being reminded that God is over all the kingdoms of the earth is good for us to read and hear. Coming before the Lord and asking Him to help us should be humbling and a great reminder how much we need Him in our everyday lives. Now as we read the rest of the chapter, we see how God answers Hezekiah's prayer. Be assured that God longs to hear your prayers to Him, and that He is still a God who answers prayer.

Prayer: O God, You are my stability and my strength! Help me to walk in Your ways and to constantly hold on to You. Help me to walk in devotion to You as my faith grows ever stronger. In Jesus name, Amen.

Day 181

STRENGTH FROM GOD
Read: Isaiah 38-40

After having suffered with Chikungunya virus for months, it is an encouragement to read, "Surely it was for my benefit that I suffered such anguish. In Your love You kept me from the pit of destruction; You have put all my sins behind Your back." (Isa 38:17 NIV) In the midst of my pain and suffering, I prayed 'Oh God, You knew before I ever left for Tobago that I would get Chikungunya and You allowed me to serve You in a land of mosquitoes (it was rainy season). Lord God, use this for Your glory.' And just like Hezekiah, the Lord brought healing to my body. A process that took the frail person I had become, and slowly strengthened my muscles. Our God is ever faithful to keep His promises!

Yes, He renewed my strength (see 40:31)! For all the pain that I experienced, I know that God has used it for His glory and that I cannot always understand His purpose—but I know it is perfect. And I assure you, your suffering and hard times are to grow you. Keep your eyes on Jesus and ask Him what you are to learn. The blessings that come in the end are more than you can ever imagine. If you have accepted the precious gift that God has given to you and made a choice to live for Him and love Him deeply, you are on a beautiful journey. Look only to Him for your help as He guides you. Reading the Bible daily will give you so much insight and direction, it truly does have all the answers.

Prayer: Heavenly Father, may I seek You in all my decisions and may I faithfully walk with You in whole-hearted devotion. Keep me close to You at all times! In Jesus name, Amen.

Day 182

ONLY GOD
Read: Isaiah 41-45

This passage of Scripture is such a good reminder that only God is God. We must constantly check ourselves to be sure we hold nothing in His place. No thing or person should take His place. He is the only One who saves (see Isaiah 45: 22). He is righteous (see Isaiah 45:24) It is not always easy for us to comprehend what the Lord warns us about. In this day and age, we may not bow down to a block of wood. Instead, we may bow down to a person in our lives whom we deem as smarter (dare I say, smarter than God? Oh heavens no! We would never say that! But yet, we let that person rule us without asking questions. We definitely think this person is smarter than us.) We may bow down to beauty and keep trying all the latest trends or we grab on to our grandchildren to the point that is sickening to all around. Yes, we do have idols today.

But God is not in competition with anyone or anything. He has given His Word to us, so we can be guided. No one is as smart in guiding our lives as our Lord and Savior, Jesus. He is all knowing and looks out for us. He wants what is best for us. We have choices in life, we can look to shopping to fulfill our needs or we can look to God. His promises are there for us, but we must read them and believe: "When you pass through the waters, I will be with you; and when you pass through the rivers, they will not sweep over you. When you walk through the fire, you will not be burned; the flames will not set you ablaze." (Isa 43:2 NIV) He further comforts us, "Do not be afraid, for I am with you " (Isa 43:5a NIV) What is your choice today?

Prayer: Lord, may I always choose You for I know the depth of Your love for me. You created the earth and the heavens, and You formed me in my mother's womb, You have a purpose for me, give me the courage to do Your will. Give me the strength to continue that which You have called me to do. In Jesus name, Amen.

Day 183

REFINER
Read: Isaiah 46-50

Sometimes we are such a stubborn lot of people! We go our own way, insisting that we know better than the Lord. But He says, "See, I have refined you, though not as silver; I have tested you in the furnace of affliction." (Isa 48: 10 NIV) It is truly loving parents who discipline their children and it truly is a loving Heavenly Father who disciplines us, who takes us through those tough times to make us better. If we are listening, He is there to teach us what is best and directs us in the way we need to go (see Isa 48:17). Such hard lessons to learn but such a loving God!

"Who among you fears the Lord and obeys the word of his servant?" (Isa 50:10 NIV) Over and over throughout Scripture, we see that we are to fear the Lord. When we read something in Scripture a number of times, God is trying to get that lesson across to us. In recent years, some people say that we are not to fear the Lord, that He is a loving God and more like a close friend, so we are not to really fear Him. I think that train of thought goes against what the Word says and what we just read. No, on the contrary, we are to have a healthy fear and respect for God. Then we will listen and obey. Oh yes, the above Scripture also says to obey His words. Obeying is doing what God has called us to do according to Scripture. We cannot pick and choose or make up ideas that you think God told you but only obey His Word, the Holy Bible.

Prayer: Father God, my heart's desire is to be obedient to You, to read Your Word daily, comprehend it and do what You so plainly tell me. May I surrender my stubborn self-will to You. In Jesus name, Amen.

Day 184

COME TO HIM
Read: Isaiah 51-55

"Seek the Lord while He may be found; call on Him while He is near." (Isa 55:6 NIV) No matter what you have done, no matter what your past is, God is waiting for you with open arms! All we need to do is forsake our evil ways and turn to the Lord He freely forgives us. It truly is that simple. Sometimes others hold us back by reminding us of our past but most often it is us we keep playing our sin over and over in our mind. We do not think that God would ever forgive us. We think we must clean up our act before we can come before God. We think we must change, we must be better for God.

But He is right there for you. He loves you right where you are. He is ready to forgive you as long as your heart is ready to invite Him into your life. He knows it is a process, no one is perfect. But we have a different mindset when we decide to confess our sins to Him, one that wants to please God and serve Him. That is taking those steps toward Him and then taking His hand and walking the rest of your life with Him. He will not force Himself on you, this has to be a willing decision. Please know He loves you and is waiting.

Prayer: Lord God, I have been rejected by man, I do not fit in! But You have taken me in Your arms and willingly given Your life for me. Your love and forgiveness are too much for me to understand and yet, I accept it with gratitude. Jesus guide me each step of my life. In Jesus name, Amen.

Day 185

REVIVE THE SPIRIT
Read: Isaiah 56-59

True fasting must include humility and godliness as we serve the Lord with compassion for those who are lost. We need to share our food with the hungry and provide shelter for those who have none. We are never to neglect our responsibility to our family (see Isa 58:7) Do not fail to show mercy, be careful what comes out of your mouth and in judging others (see Isaiah 58:9b), instead meet the needs of the oppressed and feed the hungry and always look to the Lord for your guidance for He is our strength and will satisfy our every need. (see Isa 58:11)

As we are refreshed by our Lord, He will show us other people who need refreshing. As we are obedient to the Lord, to love the Lord and worship only Him, as we hold fast to His Word and seek Him in prayer, He will care for us and bless us to be there to help others through their difficult times. As we make Him our refuge, He will give us much. (see Isa 57:13b) But with being given much, much is required of us.

Prayer: Heavenly Father, sometimes I struggle to keep You central in my life. Forgive me! I long to be led by the Spirit, to allow You to give me the Words of Truth to speak to all I meet. I claim Your promises to bring all mankind to You. In Jesus name, Amen.

Day 186

HE LIFTED THEM
Read: Isaiah 60-64

When we make a choice to look to the Lord, to do what His Word says, to follow Him completely, He will show us compassion, He will shower upon us His splendor (see Isa 60:9c), and we will experience peace as well as righteousness (see Isa 60:17b). Can you imagine that "the Lord will take delight in you"? (Isa 62:4c NIV) or that "your God (will) rejoice over you"? (Isa 62:5b NIV) It is true!

"As a young man marries a maiden, so will your sons marry you; as a bridegroom rejoices over His bride, so will your God rejoice over you." (Isa 62:5 NIV) For those of us who have experienced abuse at the hands of the man who was supposed to protect us, this verse has great comfort. Instead of being beaten down with words that destroy, our Lord loves us deeply and finds great joy in us. What a comfort to know that our Lord feels this way about us when we have been brainwashed to believe otherwise. Cling to Him who loves you and esteems you; cling to Jesus!

Prayer: Father of all Creation, I am thankful that You look upon me with compassion and great kindness. That Your glory is upon me and too much for me to comprehend and yet, I accept Your comfort and love. My mourning shall flee as Your anointing oil covers me. In Jesus name, Amen.

Day 187

FAITHFUL PROMISE
Read: Isaiah 65-66

There will come a day when God will judge those who "did evil in My sight and chose what displeases Me." (Isa 65: 12b NIV) For those who choose salvation and put their trust in the Lord, He says, "My servants will eat, but you will go hungry; my servants will drink, but you will go thirsty; my servants will rejoice, but you will be put to shame." (Isa 65:13 NIV)

God has a plan, a promised future for us and depending on our choices today determines the judgment. "This is the one I esteem: he who is humble and contrite in spirit, and trembles at My Word." (Isa 66:2b NIV) Our esteem comes from God only, for any self-pride will take us down.

Prayer: Lord, I bow down before You and seek Your comfort. Keep me humble at all times so that I am not stubborn and seek evil. I long to be pleasing to You all the days of my life. In Jesus name, Amen.

Day 188

UNFAITHFUL PEOPLE
Read: Jeremiah 1-3

"Let us lie down in our shame, and let our disgrace cover us. We have sinned against the Lord our God, both we and our fathers; from our youth till this day we have not obeyed the Lord our God." (Jer 3:25 NIV) What a strong confession of the wrong the nation of Israel had committed but truly, each of us could make this same confession this very hour. Today's reading could be said of the United States, who has also forsaken the Lord. Such sad times we live in, but God has a plan.

"Your wickedness will punish you; your backsliding will rebuke you. Consider then and realize how evil and bitter it is for you when you forsake the Lord your God and have no awe for Me," declares the Lord, the Lord Almighty." (Jer 2:19 NIV) The sad part is many do not even feel shame for their backsliding and wickedness in today's world. We seem to have a professional group that have made shame evil and stated that people should not feel shame. We should feel the shame of going our own way, of not obeying the Lord, of looking to things such as money, possessions, of people meeting our inner needs and longings instead of God meeting those needs. "They followed worthless idols and became worthless themselves." (Jer 2:5b NIV)

We, as a nation, must wake up! We, as individual people, must wake up! We must repent, turn from our sin and turn to the Lord. We must make choices in our heart to serve Him, not ourselves. He is waiting

> *Prayer: O Heavenly Father, I am in awe that You had Your hand on me before I was born. That nothing has happened in my life that You did not ordain. You have used it all as training so that I will do Your will. You are my husband, my protector, to whom I run. In Jesus name, Amen.*

Day 189

WICKED AND DISHONEST PEOPLE
Read: Jeremiah 4-6

Jeremiah has been commissioned by the Lord (see Jer 1:6-8) to tell the Israelites to turn back to Him but they ignored these warnings. So now Jeremiah is telling the people what will happen to them because of their behavior and the consequences to their actions. And, so it is today, there are consequences to our behavior and many of us ignore the warnings that we find in the Bible. We want to focus on 'God is love' and 'He would never hurt us' but that philosophy is certainly not Scriptural. God is patient and brings warning after warning to His own, but He is also a God of judgment when all He sees is rebellion.

"Your own conduct and actions have brought this upon you." (Jer 4:18a NIV) But He called out to them and calls to us to turn from our evil and to fear Him, to obey His commands and to receive life. He longs to give us rest for our soul if we seek Him and make the choice to walk in His truth. What is in our heart? What is our choice? The goodness of God or the evil of this world?

Prayer: Heavenly Father, I choose to walk on the path that You have set before me. I want to hear You at all times, keep my heart ever bent on You. May I be ever quick to confess my sins and turn away from evil for I seek Your truth. In Jesus name, Amen.

Day 190

UNCIRCUMCISED IN HEART
Read: Jeremiah 7-9

As Jeremiah is warning the people of their evil behavior, God compares them to the nations, the nations who are uncircumcised. Circumcision was obedience as God made the covenant of circumcision with Abraham that all the males were to be circumcised. (see Genesis 17:9-10) And again when Moses' wife cut her son's foreskin and touched Moses feet (see Exodus 4:25-26). This foreskin formed a complete circle to depict that the promises of God are never broken. These promises come with rules to obey and the people of Israel had fallen so far away from obedience to the point that they sacrificed their own children to the foreign gods. God referred to their falling away and disobedience as uncircumcised and in other places as committing adultery.

A day is coming when those in the United States will experience His wrath because of our loathsome conduct, of doing what we want instead of obeying God's Word. We follow after sports that entertains us, movies and TV that are vile, shopping beyond our means, eating like gluttons, control and power of those around us the list could go on and on; we seek such gods instead of the one true God who calls us to "change your ways and your actions and deal with each other justly". (Jer 7:5 NIV) Satan uses every tool he can to draw us away from God. It is time to check ourselves, not our neighbor, friend or a relative, check ourselves against the Word of God. What false god have you been serving? It is time! Time to turn from evil and turn to God. Ask Him to forgive you of your sins and invite Him into your life.

Prayer: Dear Lord, I cry and am so sad because I fall so short; I fail to keep my eyes on You. Yet You test me once again that I may draw near to You with a repentant heart. Forgive me O Lord! May my mouth speak Your truth only and may my heart grow more faithful to You each day. In Jesus name, Amen.

Day 191

CORRECT ME, LORD
Read: Jeremiah 10-12

May Jeremiah's powerful prayer be found upon our lips, "I know, O Lord, that a man's life is not his own; it is not for man to direct his steps. Correct me, Lord, but only with justice—not in Your anger, lest You reduce me to nothing." (Jer 10:23-24 NIV) May we always remember that the Lord knows us and sees all we do. He tests even our thoughts! (see Jer 12:3)

The Lord wants us to turn from our evil ways and yes, we are all evil. He longs for us to obey Him, doing what is right. It seems that throughout history, we, as a people group, cycle from doing wrong, swing from evil deeds then to repentance and turning away from such behavior to doing good and obeying the Lord. I have seen this cycle in my own life as a Christian. I, at times, go my own way and do what I want to do rather than what I know God has called me to. We all do this. This call to repentance is for all of us. It is good to be reminded, through reading of the Word, that God is continually calling us back to Himself. He loves us, and His desire is for us to be with Him.

Prayer: Lord, You know me, You test me, You long for me to willingly obey You. May I let go of my selfish ways and do what You are calling me to. May I keep my eyes and my heart on You Lord. In Jesus name, Amen.

Day 192

FURTHER BACKSLIDING
Read: Jeremiah 13-16

The evil of people, the backsliding, seems to go on and on. Will it never end? Generation after generation the people follow their own evil hearts and have forsaken the Lord. Oh yes, we worship the gods of wood and stone. Why would we choose a piece of wood to worship instead of the one true God of the Universe? Even the prophets and priests give false testimony and do not direct the people to repentance and to the Lord. Such a sad state the world was (is) in!

We see today the exact same sins the Israelites committed. People looking to other means to get satisfaction when they should be seeking the Lord and doing what His Word tells us. "Hear and pay attention, do not be arrogant, for the Lord has spoken. Give glory to the Lord your God before He brings the darkness, before your feet stumble on the darkening hills. You hope for light, but He will turn it to thick darkness and change it to deep gloom." (Jer 13:15-16 NIV) Jeremiah gives the people warning after warning and yet, they do not listen. They close their ears and minds to truth and wallow in lies and their own hopes. What are we doing today?

Prayer: O Lord, forgive us for we have forsaken the One True God for our selfish, lustful desires and our detestable behavior. Lord, a change of heart starts with me. May I devour Your Word and know the joy that only comes from You. I long to be obedient to Your Word. In Jesus name, Amen.

Day 193

THE LORD SEARCHES THE HEART
Read: Jeremiah 17-21

Let us never forget, "I the Lord search the heart and examine the mind, to reward a man according to his conduct, according to what his deeds deserve." (Jer 17:10 NIV) Certainly God knows all about us but we must remember that He knows more about us than we know about ourselves. For, if we had the least understanding of our great God, we would be more careful concerning our behavior and our thoughts. The wickedness or goodness in our heart is shown in our speech and behavior. So often, rather than submitting to God, people defiantly continue to live as they want. Truly, it is the hardness within our own heart that causes us to feel worthless for hardness comes from sin.

"O Lord Almighty, You who examine the righteous and probe the heart and mind, let me see your vengeance upon them, for to You I have committed my cause." (Jer 20:12 NIV) Please know that when a people or a nation reject the Lord long enough, they will be rejected by Him. There are deep consequences when we turn away from the Maker of heaven and earth!

Prayer: Lord, like a warrior, You protect me from the enemy. May I know Your Word in my heart and may it be a consuming fire. Mold me to be more like You and that my ways will be pleasing to You. In Jesus name, Amen.

Day 194

ADULTERERS
Read: Jeremiah 22-25

The people of Israel were prone to make wrong choices in pleasing themselves and not listening to what the Lord was telling them. Worse yet, they had given themselves to false gods, things they thought would make them happy and listening to people who only said what they wanted to hear. The sad part is, are we any different today? Don't we look to people and things that will make us feel good, even if it is not the truth? Don't we look to empty nothings of this world for our happiness? We have the Bible and God has given us exactly what we need to know—true joy—but we need to first: read it and second: do it.

When we know the truth of God's Word, we need to lovingly give it. First to our family. The husband should love his wife so deeply that she has no doubt of his love for her. The wife will lift up her husband with great respect. Children are children and need Godly training covered in prayer. Then we reach out to our community, not in preaching and beating God's Word into people but in love and by our actions. When we sin, and we all do daily, we need to ask God to forgive us and continue to move forward, learning those valuable lessons. Oh, and we need to ask those around us to forgive us. It is all about choices.

Prayer: Father God, forgive me for I am not always obedient to Your Word. I struggle for I know what You ask of me but yet, I do not do it and I do what I should not do. Continue to work in me so that my heart will do what You have called me to do. In Jesus name, Amen.

Day 195

SEEK TRUTH
Read: Jeremiah 26-29

The Israelites were now in Babylon and Jeremiah sends a message of hope, that after 70 years they will come back to the Promised Land. "For I know the plans I have for you," declares the Lord, "plans to prosper you and not to harm you, plans to give you hope and a future." (Jer 29:11 NIV) We know a true prophet because what is predicted will come true (see Jer 28:9). Also, let us not forget for today's readers that what is prophesied must align with the Word of God.

We are to change our ways, to follow the Word of God, our words and actions should be obedient to what God has called us to. If we choose to do our own thing and go against the Lord, there will be consequences. Yes, God is love and we hear this often; how could He ever want to hurt us? But God is a God of judgment, evil will be wiped out destroyed one day. Repentance is of the utmost importance. It is only in our repenting, changing our behavior to be what God has called, that God will relent and not bring disaster on a people who have chosen sin over God. When we go against the Word and Its Author and do our own thing, the consequences are our own making, God did not bring it on us.

Prayer: Lord God, I want Your plans for my life to be my plans. May I always be wise enough to seek You in humility and keep in mind to obey You at all times. When I fall, may I immediately repent of my wrong thinking and abhorrent behavior. In Jesus name, Amen.

Day 196

HIS COVENANT
Read: Jeremiah 30-32

God compares the pain of childbirth to the pain of not living as the Lord has called us to live. He has given us rules to live by and yet, we turn our backs on Him. Seems that we oftentimes have to suffer before we will listen and obey. The pain of childbirth is great, so God says that the face of man will be oh, so pale from the pain of not living according to His laws.

May we wake up, may our eyes be opened and our minds aware that God has done so much from creation to now in forgiving mankind. May we grasp His wanting us to do the right thing so that He can bring us back to Himself. May we respond to the discipline He has had to use, and may we come before our Lord and Savior in humbleness and ask for forgiveness. May we turn from our wicked ways and decide to live a new life apart from pleasing ourselves. May we live a life pleasing to Him!

Prayer: With your loving-kindness Lord, You desire to draw me ever closer to You. May I respond to Your calling and discipline with open arms and a willing heart. In Jesus name, Amen.

Day 197

REFORM YOUR ACTIONS
Read: Jeremiah 33-36

The Word of the Lord is once again given to Jeremiah. The king and his attendants were not moved by the words read to them, Words from the Lord. In fact, the king burned those very words and was not even fearful of the Lord. If we are not taught to have a healthy fear (respect) for the Lord, most likely, we will not have a respect for authority, whether it is our parents or the law of the land. Also, the king showed anger by cutting the scroll and burning it. Oftentimes when people are confronted with the truth of their sin, they respond with anger or even violence.

God was calling these people to "turn from your wicked ways and reform your actions; do not follow other gods to serve them." (Jer 35:15b NIV) That is what our Lord wants each of us to do, to turn from evil, to turn from our wicked ways and certainly to follow and worship only Him. Whether we say God, the Lord or Jesus, they are one in the same and serving Him is worth all we think we have to give up. Does evil have a hold on you? If you cannot give up your ways and turn to Him, it does have a hold on you. Making that decision is not easy and you may fail along the way, but do not give up, keep turning to the Lord in repentance and He will give you the strength to follow Him.

Prayer: Heavenly Father, may my heart and mind be willing to always turn away from the sin that entangles me. May I be strong enough to walk away from enticing evil and humble enough to recognize when I am too weak to do so. May I grab on to You in true obedience. In Jesus name, Amen.

Day 198

JERUSALEM FALLS
Read: Jeremiah 37-40

Jeremiah went through so much because the people did not want to believe what he was saying. He continually warned the people that disaster was coming upon the city, and that the people needed to obey the Lord and repent of their evil ways. The people and the king responded by throwing Jeremiah in jail, another time they threw him down a well, and still another time he was put in chains in a courtyard. Jeremiah suffered as he obeyed the Lord and continued to give message after message that was not popular to the people.

In this modern day, when we are so much more civilized, we still find many people around the world who are suffering because of the message they give. The message that Jesus is Lord and offers salvation. Oftentimes, at the name of Jesus, people will lose their lives. Certainly, the hatred from the world, from satan, will bring destruction and suffering to many but just like Jeremiah, it is the call of Christ for us to tell many about Him. The days are short, we must do our part, no matter what the consequences if death, we will be with Jesus, if we continue to live, we must go forth and serve the Lord.

Prayer: Dear Lord, may I be obedient to You no matter how hard it gets! May I be slow to speak but quickly to know Your Word and ever hesitate to go against You. I trust in You, O Lord, I trust in You! In Jesus name, Amen.

Day 199

DISASTER
Read: Jeremiah 41-44

So often we make decisions without taking the Word of God into account. These same mistakes were made by the Israelites and have continued to this very day. Why do we think we know more than the Lord? They even went to Jeremiah and asked him to seek the Lord's will but when Jeremiah told them what the Lord had told him, they would not believe him. When Jeremiah pointed out that their women were worshipping other gods, they did not listen. "To this day they have not humbled themselves or shown reverence, nor have they followed My law and the decrees I set before you and your fathers." (Jer 44:10 NIV)

Are we any different than they? Do we go to church, listen to the preacher and then do exactly what we want rather than what the Word of God tells us? Is our primary goal to worship God? To please Him in all we do? Or is God getting ready to destroy a group of people who continue to live in their wicked actions and detestable practices? (see Jer 44:22 NIV) Do we even know what God has called us to do? Do we read the Bible daily, asking for insight to do what it says? Seek the Lord and Him only!

Prayer: Lord God, may I humble myself and show reverence to You by following Your Word. May I stay away from evil and may my heart be set on pleasing You in all I do. In Jesus name, Amen.

Day 200

PUNISHMENT FOR PRIDE AND ARROGANCE

Read: Jeremiah 45-48

Whether the message is to Egypt, Philistia, or Moab, it is the same. The people have turned away from the Lord and are serving themselves. When they do serve Him, they serve Him half-heartedly and with indifference. The Lord was not happy with such behavior then and He is not happy with this same behavior nowadays.

So many today call themselves Christian but they do not obey the Word of the Lord. They serve with little enthusiasm, in fact, they do not even go to church much of the time. They belong to organizations where they give of their time but when it comes to the Lord's work, they do not have time. They go to ballgames and yell their voices out but when it comes to the Lord's work, they do not have time. They go out with friends and drink and party late into the night but when it comes to the Lord's work, they do not have time. When are we going to take time to serve, to give of our time to the most important work there is?

Prayer: Precious Lord, forgive me for not coming before You with enthusiasm and a heart ready to serve. I turn my heart and mind over to You for I long for a right relationship with you, knowing it starts with reading the Word and obeying Your calling. In Jesus name, Amen.

Day 201

PRIDE OF HEART
Read: Jeremiah 49-50

When a person or people have an attitude of pride, they are a deceptive people, a people who do not look to the Lord for guidance. These people have been led astray, they are truly lost sheep but do not acknowledge their loss. They continually sin against the Lord for they think they have all the answers. They look to idols instead of the One True God.

The reading today is a warning from God. Just as pride and arrogance were signs of people wanting to go their own way, to do their own thing, it is the same today. It is of a people who think their ideas and their ways are better than what the Lord's laws and regulations are. The Bible is not an outdated book, it is for today. As we read the Bible, ask the Lord to show you how to apply His Word to your life each and every day. And know that our life will be better as we humble ourselves and obey Him.

Prayer: Father God, You are just and know what is best for me. Help me to stay close to You and to be humble enough that I listen to You through Your Word and through people You bring into my life. I long to be Your servant in all I do and say. In Jesus name, Amen.

Day 202

HE REPAYS IN FULL
Read: Jeremiah 51-52

As we finish Jeremiah today, we see that God will use those around us to repay us for our sin. Over and over Jeremiah warned the Israelites to turn from their evil ways and turn back to God but they would not listen. They went further and further into sin. "For the Lord is a God who gives just punishment; He always repays in full." (Jer 51:56b NLT) God gave them plenty of warning, of telling them to turn from their wicked ways, He is patient but know this, He will punish those who continue to sin, in due time. We see this fulfilled when Judah went into captivity and was taken away from the Promised Land. What a sad lesson to learn!

Can each of us learn this lesson before it is too late? Have we not done what we have wanted for way too long? Have we not worshipped other gods and now feel so worthless? Is not our worthlessness because we have forsaken the One True God, Creator of heaven and earth? Or must we be invaded by foreigners, have all our possessions taken from us and go into captivity? Wake up oh Christian, wake up before it is too late! Repent and turn from our evil ways, turn back to truth and serving the One who makes a difference. Turn to Jesus!

Prayer: Thank You dear Lord for caring so deeply for me. Even when I have turned away from You and have gone my own way, You were there, waiting for me when I felt such despair and finally confessed my sin. I realized it did me no good but only brought pain. You are the Healer and are ready to take me back. In Jesus name, Amen.

Day 203

HIS COMPASSIONS
Read: Lamentations 1-3:42

The sadness of Lamentations is great but in the middle of it all, we find hope. We find we must be careful of false prophets who give great hope but are full of lies for "they did not expose your sin". (Lam 2:14b NIV) Remember, it is of great benefit when our sins are exposed, and we take it to heart and repent, turning away from our sin and making a conscience choice to go a different direction. Hope comes as we let go of our old ways and turn to the Lord, surrendering our lives to Him. His compassion never fails but He will allow pain in our lives if we are not living for Him nor listening to Him. He will draw us to Himself one way or another.

"Let us examine our ways and test them, and let us return to the Lord. Let us lift up our hearts and our hands to God in heaven and say: We have sinned and rebelled and You have not forgiven." (Lam 3:40-42 NIV) As it was then, it is the same now. We must constantly look to the Lord for guidance and be ready to repent of our ways that are not pleasing to Him. He is truly our hope and He is there the moment we cry out to Him!

Prayer: Heavenly Father, Your love for me is beyond my comprehension and I lift my heart to You. I am thankful for Your compassion that never fails and Your faithfulness. May I always be willing to examine my ways and repent of my sin. In Jesus name, Amen.

REPENT

Read: Lamentations 3:43-5

Lamentations expresses the sorrow of Jeremiah for the Israelites. "The false prophets were politically motivated and could not see that disobedience to God was the root of the nations' troubles." (Bible Pathway Ministries, Aug 2011, p 58)

Isn't that the way it is today? We look to our political leaders to get us out of our financial woes instead of repenting and turning back to obedience according to the Bible. We find ourselves in the same position as many before us because we are either too proud or too stupid to turn to God. Of course, evil wants us to look to ourselves for the answers. Evil says you can do it yourself. Evil and rebellion will bring death, both spiritually and physically. We have a choice.

Prayer: O Lord, keep my heart open that I may recognize my sin and repent immediately. My heart longs to be pleasing to You, Lord. Keep my mind focused on Your Word so I do not sin against You. I call on You daily to refresh my heart and keep me close to You. In Jesus name, Amen.

Day 205

GET UP AND GO
Read: Ezekiel 1-3

In these first few chapters of Ezekiel, this priest is called by God to take an important message to the people of Israel. The living creatures showed him the glory of God, that they were prepared at all times to obey. That is exactly what God wanted Ezekiel to do, to obey.

Moreover, that is what God calls each of us to do, to obey Him and bring glory to His name. When He says to go, we go. The important thing to remember is when He calls us to serve Him, we are to be obedient. If we do not share what God has shown us, their blood will be on our shoulders. I do not know about you, but I cannot live like that. We must be obedient to God. I do not wish for anyone to go to hell because I was afraid to tell them to repent and turn from their evil. And yes, who am I that anyone would listen? I am a simple woman of prayer, knowing when He shows me what to say, I will go before Him in humble prayer before stepping out in obedience. Yes, that is what He calls each of us to do.

Prayer: Lord God of all creation, may I be prepared to obey You at all times. Lord, may I stay in Your Word, may my ears be attentive to what You want me to learn and may I have a willing heart to do Your will, full of the Holy Spirit. Through You, I can do all things. In Jesus name, Amen.

Day 206

MOURN AND TREMBLE
Read: Ezekiel 4-7

"I will deal with them according to their conduct, and by their own standards I will judge them. Then they will know that I am the Lord." (Eze 7:27b NIV) "How I have been grieved by their adulterous hearts, which have turned away from Me, and by their eyes, which have lusted after their idols. They will loathe themselves for the evil they have done and for all their detestable practices." (Eze 6:9 NIV)

As God used Ezekiel to warn the Israelites of their evil practices, please know that these warning are for today as well. God will deal with every person, especially those who call themselves 'Christian'. We grieve Him by our behavior, what we watch on TV and the Internet or other devices. If God considered these people adulterous, how much more today? Especially when we watch TV that is full of immoral behavior, a lack of integrity and we give excuse after excuse as to why it is acceptable to watch such filth. And pornography is everywhere, to the point that even pastors give excuses that such degradation is not sinful.

Yes indeed, we must turn from our sin for we will be judged by the Word of God. We look at others and make judgments but forget to look at ourselves. We measure others by our own standards rather than the Word of God. More importantly, we forget that God's grace is showered upon us daily but never pass that grace on to our fellow man who needs it so badly.

Prayer: Dear Lord, help me to have a compassionate heart towards those around me. Help me to show grace and love to the one who is hurting and to myself. Keep me from willful sin so it does not rule my life. Help me to be quick to ask forgiveness and be pleasing to You. In Jesus name, Amen.

Day 207

UNDIVIDED HEART
Read: Ezekiel 8-11

In the midst of something bad, God will give us a bright hope, a promise and it was no different for the Israelites. Prophet after Prophet was sent to the people to warn them of their evil ways, but they would not listen. Here, Ezekiel told the people to get rid of their idols and their detestable practices and turn back to the one true God, but they turned a deaf ear.

"They will return to it and remove all its vile images and detestable idols. I will give them an undivided heart and put a new spirit in them; I will remove from them their heart of stone and give them a heart of flesh. Then they will follow my decrees and be careful to keep my laws. They will be my people, and I will be their God. But as for those whose hearts are devoted to their vile images and detestable idols, I will bring down on their own heads what they have done, declares the Sovereign Lord. (Eze 11:18-21 NIV)

We today must be careful that we are not like the Israelites, worshiping our idols (football and other sports, our cars, our houses, our money, our position, our children and grandchildren) rather than our Sovereign Lord. Are we so wrapped up in our lives that we do not give the Lord ourselves, to serve Him and to bring glory to His name? Do we look at our words and actions and ask, "would this bring glory to my Father in Heaven?" It is time to turn from evil and do good. It is time to change those ways, to let go of self and to cling to Him.

Prayer: Father God, may I check myself daily and remove the vile idols from my life. May my heart be prone towards You Lord and may I willingly confess my failures to You and turn to pleasing only You. Thank You for caring so deeply for me and for being so patient with me. In Jesus name, Amen.

Day 208

REPENT! BE RELEASED FROM THAT LIE!
Read: Ezekiel 12-15

"Repent! Turn from your idols and renounce all your detestable practices!" (Eze 14:6b NIV) I once heard a pastor explain repentance as turning 180 degrees from your old way of life. To turn and walk away from the evil that you were involved in is dramatic indeed! But just as so many have good intentions of doing just that, they cannot seem to let go of the evil that has them bound. They live a life with one foot towards heaven and the other established in what they have known so well and continue to live mostly in that world.

Well, the Israelites were doing much the same thing when Ezekiel was telling them to turn from their wicked ways and turn back to God. The sad part today is that we do not hear pastors telling us to turn from our idols. Have you ever wondered why this is? Is it because they, like all of us, struggle with their own evil ways or they enjoy their life and don't want to give it up? Sometimes we benefit so much from those around us, living in evil, that we make a choice to not call them on their wrong living and just enjoy it. Ezekiel was an obedient prophet who repeated exactly what God wanted him to tell the people. Life was not easy for him.

Do we want to listen to the false prophets, who say sweet things, but will allow you to go to hell? Do we desire to continue in our rebellion rather than listen to the truth and make the changes that need to be made? May we turn from our evil ways so that our lives can be saved!

Prayer: Father, forgive me! Just like the Israelites of old, I cling to idols. Give me the strength to hold fast to You and to let go of my sins. In Jesus name, Amen.

Day 209

SUFFER FOR OWN SIN
Read: Ezekiel 16-18

We cannot always claim innocence saying that we did not know that we were sinning. We must take responsibility for our behavior. We cannot live like others, we must choose to be different, to live for the Lord and follow His Word. This is not a once in a while thing. We must read God's Word daily and determine to follow Him, to obey what He tells us to do.

It can be so easy to miss a day or two of Bible reading; of taking our eyes off of the One Who is caring for us. We see how Jerusalem fell into evil practices without even looking back evil is often enjoyable, and we want to please our flesh rather than please the Lord. Living a Godly life takes work on our part, to constantly live for Him, to be aware when we do sin and repent, to know that if we choose to live in sin, we will suffer the consequences for that sin. We cannot look to our neighbor and justify our behavior because he did it too. No, we will be punished and die in our sin or we will live a righteous life, keeping His laws and commandments.

Prayer: Father God, may I make choices that are pleasing to You. May I walk away from detestable practices and not be cruel and stay away from doing what is wrong. Lord, help me to stay on the upward path that brings You joy and walk according to Your Word. In Jesus name, Amen.

Day 210

BITTER GRIEF
Read: Ezekiel 19-21

It seems that Ezekiel has nothing good to say day in and day out. But the truth of God's Word is not always positive, nor does it always feel good. No, when a group of people make choices to turn away from God and His teachings and direction, God goes after them out of love. He will use those around the rebellious to warn them of their wicked ways, their lust for evil and vile images. From the beginning of time, man has tried to go their own way, not listening to God's direction. Yet, we ignore the truth of what happens each time we rebel.

Today's world is not any different. Instead of honoring God and serving Him, on Sundays, we have a new god: Sports. We see more dedication to the team we love than wanting to serve God and be obedient to Him. If you are feeling quite smug at this moment because you are not a big fan of any special team, let me ask you, what or who is your idol, that thing you cannot do without? We all have something! I see many grandparents setting their grandchildren up as idols and instead of being a good role model and teaching them God's Word, we let them get away with evil. Wake up people! Wake up and turn from your wicked ways! Wake up and turn to God!

Prayer: Heavenly Father, I have turned away from You and gone after my own self-interest. There are so many thoughts and interests that pull me away from You. Forgive me! In Jesus name, Amen.

Day 211

YOU WILL BE JUDGED
Read: Ezekiel 22-24

"Then confront them with their detestable practices, for they have committed adultery and blood is on their hands. They committed adultery with their idols; they even sacrificed their children, whom they bore to me, as food for them. They have also done this to me: At that same time they defiled my sanctuary and desecrated my Sabbaths. On the very day they sacrificed their children to their idols, they entered my sanctuary and desecrated it." (Eze 23:36b-39a NIV)

Oh the sadness of the above verses because, once again, this is exactly what the United States has been doing. Detestable practices: turning oneself over to idols, sacrificing their children (government schools and etc.), turning the churches over to the government (501C3). Ezekiel was met with closed ears. Will anyone listen? We are sacrificing our children to abortion for the sake of a woman's rights! Women make bad choices and when they end up pregnant, they then kill the baby, so they can continue their evil lifestyle. They have become their own idol always lusting for more. And the churches who have sold their souls to the government for tax exemption purposes are now told what they can preach and what they cannot. Getting a favor from the government will always come at a price!

"You will be judged according to your conduct and your actions, declares the Sovereign Lord." (Eze 24:14b NIV)

Prayer: Search me, O God, for You alone know my heart! Enlighten my mind with Your truth that I may turn away from the sins I commit. Fill my mind and my heart with remorse for my wrong doings and forgive me. May my sorrow for my behavior be a constant reminder to do Your will. In Jesus name, Amen.

Day 212

PROPHECY AGAINST THE NATIONS
Read: Ezekiel 25-28

Today's reading is such a great reminder that those who go against God and His people will suffer consequences. The nations surrounding Israel treated them cruelly and were sinning in many other ways and as a result, God destroyed them. It is hard to believe that with this said, Israel was taking much of the same path and would not change their ways. Whether it was Israel or the surrounding countries, we can see that God did not take kindly to pride nor those who thought they knew more than God. Even their wealth made them full of pride.

It is not any different today! God's people today have a changed heart and call themselves Christians. The persecution of the Israelites was real, and the persecution of Christians is real. There are those who want all Christians dead. These are not loving or kind people. No! In fact, they are quite ignorant for they do not take heed to God's Word. These passages that we read today are a warning to the countries around Israel but also should be a warning for those who oppose God's chosen (both Jews and Christians) today.

Prayer: Heavenly Father, please help me to be obedient to Your Word. Help me to take heed to Your warnings. Keep me from being prideful or arrogant and to always show humility by keeping my heart from evil. I long for Your will. In Jesus name, Amen.

Day 213

WHY?
Read: Ezekiel 29-32

It is hard for me to understand why those listening to Ezekiel would not heed his warnings. How could they turn a blind eye or a deaf ear? Why wouldn't they take what Ezekiel was saying and turn from their wicked ways? Of course, his own nation would not listen to him let alone the surrounding nations.

Yet, are we any different today? We have the Bible, the Word of God, telling us how to live and yet we live like heathens. There are some out there that are our modern-day prophets, who are warning the people to turn to God, to repent of the evil acts, to walk away from people who are leading them astray, yet, we do not listen. Do we enjoy our idols so much? Do we want to please ourselves so much? Are we so self-centered that we do not care for those around us? Sadly, most do not care about anyone but themselves. We insist on our rights. Our words are offensive to those around us and we do not care. We each need to check ourselves often, are we one of them?

Prayer: Dear Lord, May I not become complacent when reading Your Word or hearing the warnings of the nations. May I take to heart what I read and hear and strive to be obedient to what You are saying. Lord, my heart yearns to do Your will, keep me ever so close to You. In Jesus name, Amen.

Day 214

SHOWERS OF BLESSING
Read: Ezekiel 33-35

There is a second warning in today's reading concerning warning a man of his wicked ways. It is hoped that the warning will turn this man from his evil ways, so he will not die in his sin. By the same token, if a good man is banking on his good behavior and makes a choice to do evil, he will not be allowed to live and will die in his sin. When we know of a person who is living in sin, we are responsible to go to that person and tell them what will happen to them. This is in hopes that they will turn, repent and live.

"I will save My flock, and they will no longer be plundered."(Eze 34:22a NIV) I have written in my Bible for the word plundered: abused and destroyed. For those of us who have experienced abuse, it is a comfort to know that when we give our lives to the Lord, He cares for us in a way that cannot be explained. In my own life, I made some wrong choices as a Christian and experienced great abuse. It was by God's saving grace that I was able to get out of that situation and be safe. The longer I live the better choices I am making as I look to the Word of God more each day. It is my guide and refuge. When this happens, we experience showers of blessing that can only come from Him.

Prayer: O Lord, I am so thankful for Your love and guidance. I long to be ever obedient to Your Word and truly thankful for Your mercy towards me. When I was beaten down, You lifted me up. You cared for me when no one else was there. In Jesus name, Amen.

Day 215

GOD'S FAVOR
Read: Ezekiel 36-39

As we have seen through our reading today, the nation of Israel was not living as the Lord had declared. They had turned from the Lord and worshipped other gods, they had done things their own way and forsaken the Lord. Yet, He is now giving these same people hope, knowing that they will turn away from their wicked ways and He "will look on you with favor" (Eze 36:9b NIV) "I will give you a new heart and put a new spirit in you; I will remove from you your heart of stone and give you a heart of flesh." (Eze 36:26 NIV)

Even today when so many have fallen into doing their own thing, doing what is right in their own eyes, we must remember that God allows pain and suffering for a purpose. That is, to draw us closer to Him. But once again we are reminded that we must be careful to follow His decrees and laws. (see Eze 37:24) He longs to show Himself holy through us, His people, who have surrendered to Him. We are here to bring glory to Him, not for our own pleasure. We are here to bring His love to the people around us, not what we can get from those around us. He longs for us to open our hearts to Him and do what He has called each of us to do.

Prayer: Lord God, maker of heaven and earth, You alone care so deeply for me. You have cleansed my heart, allowing me to see my sin and shame, but have covered me in Your blood and given me a new purpose in life. I am ever grateful for Your forgiveness and through the blood of Christ, my sins are washed away as I turn to You. I am thankful for Your cleansing power! In Jesus name, Amen.

Day 216

GOD'S GLORY
Read: Ezekiel 40-44

Once again, we see that God is a God of specifics. He expected the people to follow these instructions before His glory would return. The people had committed spiritual adultery. They had turned to idols and had defiled God by their detestable practices. Even the priests!

And it is the same today as well. We see men who, in the eyes of the common people, are holy men but they live in luxury, worshiping their possessions more than they worship God. Spiritual adultery! These same holy men have the nerve to tell the common people to become more humble by giving up their meager income by giving more but are not willing to practice what they preach. God expects us all to follow His laws and decrees, all of us! There is not one set of rules or laws for one person and another for someone else, we are all the same in His eyes.

It is a sad day when a man, who is not as holy as he appears, is worshipped more by his fellow man than God is. It is a sad day when man looks to another sinful man for answers rather than the God of the Universe. The Bible is just as relevant today as when it was written. We must read it with the Holy Spirit's guidance. We must read it daily. We must read all of the Bible not just what feels good but the whole Bible, from cover to cover.

Prayer: Heavenly Father, I fall short daily. And each time I have to acknowledge my sin and ask Your forgiveness, but I also want to turn away from my unlovely behavior and strive towards a new life in Christ. I fall down but You pick me up with Your loving hands and willingly guide me once again. In Jesus name, Amen.

Day 217

ALIENS
Read: Ezekiel 45-48

As we finish the book of Ezekiel, God is ever faithful to give us a reminder of His rules and regulations. He sets boundaries for His chosen people, for their own good. He even gives direction on how to treat the alien as they settle among the Israelites. Concerning the alien, it must be understood that this outsider must also follow the rules of God, which were the rules of the land. Without following the directions that God has given, they are not willing to live among the Israelites but rather to conquer them.

And so, it is today. First, if we can look at ourselves as aliens that is, we are grafted into God's family, we also understand that we cannot go on living our old sinful lives once we ask the Lord to forgive our sin. We must work daily on learning our new life, our new regulations and directions so as to live peacefully with mankind. When we come into this foreign land of Christ followers, we choose to live differently, we choose to live like Christ. It is a choice we have to make do we want to continue to live our old life or do we want to live in a new land and become a better person?

So it is with the alien who comes from another country and makes a choice to live in a new land. They must follow the rules and laws of their new country. They must make a choice to leave their old ways behind and fit into this new land or go back to where they came from. Let go of your former ways and grasp what is being offered you with appreciation and gratitude.

Prayer: Dear Lord, as an alien coming into the land of the Lord, I strive to forget the past life that I once lived and to run towards the goal of Your high calling, as a citizen of a place I had not known before. My heart's desire is to be pleasing to You, my new leader! In Jesus name, Amen.

Day 218

DANIEL
Read: Daniel 1-3

The book of Daniel covers the entire 70 years of captivity and obedience is the central theme. Daniel was one of the first captives to get to Babylon, being, most likely, in his mid-teens. This book is also a reminder that Babylon looks inviting, with its entertainment and many over-indulgences, but, just as in Daniel's time, we too need to be aware of satan's hold.

Daniel realized that it was only through God's mighty hand that he would survive in Nebuchadnezzar's service. Daniel boldly told the king that he would interpret the dream he had but then went to his friends and asked them to pray. Daniel then gave God the glory in great thanksgiving before going to the king. As he stood before the king, Daniel acknowledged that no one was wise enough to be able to tell the king his dream, but that God had given him the dream and the interpretation.

When Daniel's three friends were told they had to worship an image of gold they boldly continued to worship the Lord God. They were willing to give up their lives rather than worship anything other than the One True God. This strong faith will be needed by Christians throughout the world as evil becomes more prevalent. Just know that you will want to keep the strength of Shadrach, Meshack and Abednego in your life and always look to God to make it through that fiery furnace.

Prayer: Father God, may I be willing to give up my life rather than renounce You. Lord, I pray that You will give me wisdom in dealing with those of this world and strength to do Your will. May I not be enticed or drawn to the pleasures of this world but be pulled to You in true obedience. In Jesus name, Amen.

Day 219

FAITHFUL PROMISE
Read: Daniel 4-6

"And those who walk in pride He is able to humble." (Dan 4:37b NIV)

In today's reading, we see that Daniel is under the rule of three different kings: Nebuchadnezzar, Belshazzar and Darius. Amazingly, not every king experienced Daniel's God and proclaimed God's glory. "Now I, Nebuchadnezzar, praise and exalt and glorify the King of heaven, because everything He does is right, and all His ways are just." (Dan 4:37a NIV) Darius wrote "that in every part of my kingdom people must fear and reverence the God of Daniel." (Dan 6:26a NIV) Belshazzar, on the other hand, worshipped "the gods of silver and gold, of bronze, iron, wood and stone, which cannot see or hear or understand." (Dan 5:23b NIV) But right after Daniel told him the meaning of the inscription that was written on the wall, "that very night Belshazzar, king of the Babylonians, was slain," (Dan 5:30 NIV).

Just the example of these three men would be enough for some to keep their eyes on the Creator of the universe. But, so often, we hear people say, "it is just a story, a fairytale", concerning the Bible and the stories within. Trust me, the whole Bible is true. The whole Bible is the Word of God given to man that we may learn from the past and apply it to our lives today. Jesus is our Savior who made a choice to die for our sins that we may live for Him.

Prayer: Heavenly Father, may I recognize all the days of my life that You are God. All that You do is right and just. May I always walk in humility with a thankful heart. In Jesus name, Amen.

Day 220

INSIGHTS
Read: Daniel 7-9

I could talk about the visions Daniel saw, as many others have done but I want to focus on Daniel's prayer. It is a prayer that we could pray even today. How many of us plead with the Lord? How many of us go before the Lord in fasting? Praying for our nation, not just personal wants? "We have sinned and done wrong. We have been wicked and have rebelled; we have turned away from Your commands and laws. We have not listened to your servants." (Dan 9:5-6a NIV) Lord forgive us! Most importantly, may we learn a lesson from our evil behavior and repent, turning away from such behavior.

May we grasp that our evil behavior is what has brought consequences upon our nation and us personally. He is a righteous God! He will allow us to suffer until we finally turn back to Him, not because we are tired of suffering but because our hearts are heavy for not being obedient to our Lord. It is only because of His great mercy (see Daniel 9:18) that we can ask His forgiveness. And it is for His sake that He will act, at just the right time, to save a few who have been faithful.

Prayer: Forgive me, O Lord! I have been like generations before me who were not obedient to you, doing what I wanted and not looking to you. I confess my sins to you and want to live a different life. I am Yours Lord! In Jesus name, Amen.

Day 221

VICTORY
Read: Daniel 10-12

"Set your mind to gain understanding and to humble yourself before your God" (Dan 10:12b NIV). These are such encouraging words as God also says to Daniel that He heard Daniel's words. We must remember that when we are going through a hard time, a trial so to speak, God is there giving us strength. Times are going to get much harder not because God has lost control but because He wants to strengthen us and bring fulfillment to His Word.

"Some of the wise will stumble, so that they may be refined, purified and made spotless until the time of the end, for it will still come at the appointed time." (Dan 11:35 NIV) Refined, purified and made spotless that is what He desires for each of us who have repented and are living a life for Him. It repeats almost the same words in Daniel 12:10 but it goes on to say "Many will be purified, made spotless and refined, but the wicked will continue to be wicked. None of the wicked will understand, but those who are wise will understand." (NIV) Do not lose heart my friend! Stay close to the Word, Who is God. Pray for strength for each new day and know that He will give it to you.

Prayer: Thank you, Lord, for loving me so deeply as to allow me to go through refining, making me ever more pleasing to You. You strengthen me in Your Word daily, giving me peace that passes all understanding. In Jesus name, Amen.

Day 222

NO FAITH, NO KNOWLEDGE
Read: Hosea 1-4

Israel, like many in the United States, said they knew the Lord but their behavior showed something different. We today do not acknowledge God and there is cursing, lying and murder along with stealing and adultery throughout the land. So many wipe their mouths and say "I've done nothing wrong. (Pro 30:20b NIV) We are truly "a people without understanding will come to ruin!" (Hos 4:14b NIV)

The book of Hosea is about a Godly man who loved an adulterous woman. His love for her was strong and persistent, he never gave up on her. This is an example of the love that God has for us. We say we love the Lord but then we seek entertainment and long for that more than our longings for the Lord. We seek financial gain and say we will use the money to further God's work. We seek a relationship that is more exciting than the one we are now in and say surely God wants us to be happy. We give a thousand excuses, all pointing to show that we do not think God is enough, or that it is too hard to follow Him. But we must remember "my people are destroyed from lack of knowledge." (Hos 4:6b NIV) We must seek only God, listen and please Him and forsake those things that pull us away from Him.

Prayer: Dear Heavenly Father, I thank you for your faithfulness in loving me even when I have gone my own way. You have pulled me back into a right relationship with You. You have cared for me even when rejected by those around me. You saw my worth beyond my actions. I am so very thankful for You! In Jesus name, Amen.

Day 223

RETURN TO THE LORD
Read: Hosea 5-9

My heart is heavy within me! Israel turned away from the Lord, seeking other fulfillment rather than God, Who guided them and protected them. They turned away from all that is true to seek lies. In fact, they even got to the point where they would not acknowledge the Lord. God, in His great mercy, loved them and wanted them back; but they had to admit their guilt and turn away from their sin and seek Him earnestly. (see Hosea 5:15)

Now, I ask you, is it any different in the United States today? As a nation, we were formed as a land that God provided. One Nation under God. But as time has gone by, we have forgotten God. We have sought after pleasures instead of sacrificing for the common good of the people. We have broken the laws of the Bible and our land and have become arrogant, sometimes flashing our sin around. Our leaders "have sunk deep into corruption," (Hos 9:9a NIV) and have all forms of wickedness added to the list of sins they have committed. We, as a nation, are not any different than Israel, we see history repeat itself, for we have not learned from the sins of our forefathers. We are descendants of Adam, and there are lessons to be learned. It is time we opened our eyes, ears, and hearts to learn from Him and repent!

Prayer: Dear Lord, only You can bring healing and acceptance when we confess our sin to You. You give mercy to us when we acknowledge You. You long for us to give up our wickedness and idols so that we can reap the harvest of love as we seek only You. I long for You Lord! In Jesus name, Amen.

Day 224

WHO IS WISE?
Read: Hosea 10-14

Can we truly comprehend God's great love for us? Even as the chosen people, Israel, rebelled, refusing to repent, and God calls them with great compassion. And at this moment, He is calling each of us, to turn from our rebellion and turn to Him. "Who is wise? He will realize these things. Who is discerning? He will understand them. The ways of the Lord are right; the righteous walk in them, but the rebellious stumble in them." (Hos 14:9 NIV)

Over and over we do our own thing, doing what we think is right and finding out it is so wrong! We seek our own wisdom or that of someone who is wicked and continue to go our own way. We feel worthless because all that we seek is worthless. And even so, with all our rebellion, God says, "I will heal their waywardness and love them freely, for my anger has turned away from them." (Hos 14:4 NIV) His forgiveness is beyond our comprehension! He is waiting, waiting for you and me to come to Him on bended knee, humble and asking forgiveness. We must repent, recognize our sin for what it is, and turn away from our evil ways. Each and every day, coming to the One who loves us and forgives our sins is the only answer to true peace.

Prayer: Oh Lord, may I turn from my wicked ways, filling those ways with only You. May I walk in Your righteousness so that I will be pleasing to You. But when I sin, may I be quick to recognize it and confess it, so I may walk closer to You. In Jesus name, Amen.

Day 225

A CALL TO REPENTANCE
Read: Joel 1-3

If we are serious about repenting of our sinful ways, Joel 1 tells us how to prepare, that is, how to listen to what the Lord is showing you. We should come to Him in mourning for what we have done. To fast and cry out to the Lord! And as He reveals our sins to us, we will go before Him in humble confession to turn away from those sins and to live a life pleasing to the One who cares so deeply for us.

Only then can we receive the blessings that He has for us. "Be glad, O people of Zion, rejoice in the Lord your God," (Joel 2:23a NIV). He also promises, "I will repay you for the years the locust have eaten" (Joel 2:25a NIV). And we see promises for the future when they proclaim 'in that day'. If some do not believe that God loves Israel, they have never read Joel! "The Lord dwells in Zion!" (Joel 3:21b NIV)

Prayer: Lord, You say in Your Word, that all "who call on the name of the Lord will be saved" (Joel 2:32a NIV) so I call out to You right now and ask You to come into my life and help me to live a more pleasing life than I have in the past. May each new day be a time of drawing closer to You. In Jesus name, Amen.

Day 226

MAINTAIN JUSTICE
Read: Amos 1-5

Amos was like you and I, a common laborer, a shepherd and a keeper of fig trees. (see Am 1:1 and 7:14) He warns Israel and the surrounding nations of the coming judgment. Did they listen? Did they repent and turn to the Lord? No! They rejected the law of the Lord and did not keep His decrees and yet, they thought they would not experience judgment! Could not our country experience this same judgment because we have turned away from the Lord? Do we value marriage between a man and a woman, walking together as one? Do we believe the lies of the masses who say that a baby within the womb is nothing but a mass of cells, calling it a fetus, rather than a life created by God?

The United States needs to repent of their evil ways. God is calling us the same way as He called Israel all those years ago, before they went into captivity, "Seek good, not evil, that you may live. Then the Lord God Almighty will be with you, just as you say He is. Hate evil, love good; maintain justice in the courts." (Am 5:14-15a NIV) A day of judgment is coming and it will not be a pretty sight. Repent now and turn from your evil ways and habits, read His Word daily and do what it says.

Prayer: Dear Lord, may I walk hand in hand with You, may I understand that it is a privilege to serve You but with that comes responsibility. May I be obedient to what You are calling me to do. In Jesus name, Amen.

Day 227

PRINCIPLE OF RIGHT AND WRONG
Read: Amos 6-9 and Obadiah

"The days are coming," declares the Sovereign Lord, "when I will send a famine through the land—not a famine of food or a thirst for water, but a famine of hearing the words of the Lord." (Am 8:11 NIV) Just as the Israelites had fallen so far away from the Lord, we too are experiencing this famine in the United States. Not only is the government telling our pastors what to say, not allowing the Word of God to be heard but we have many who do not want to hear the Word. They have closed their ears to the truth of the Gospel.

Then as we read the shortest book of the Old Testament, Obadiah continues to speak truth to the Israelites. Again, these truths are for today as well as then. "The pride of your heart has deceived you " (Ob 3a NIV) and don't we know when we get to this point that we are not willing to listen to anything that goes against what we are doing? "As you have done, it will be done to you; your deeds will return upon your own head." (Oba 15b NIV). This is a principle that we should be reminded of daily. Perhaps then we will listen to the Lord and treat people as He has called us to do. God directs us, but we often do not listen, and if we did hear, we are not obedient. Let us determine to do what God is calling us to do. To step out in faith and let our behavior show that we belong to the One True God.

Prayer: Heavenly Father, may I not have pride in my heart but humility in all my thoughts, words and actions towards those around me. May I always remember that what I do to others will return to me. In Jesus name, Amen.

Day 228

PERSONAL OBEDIENCE
Read: Jonah 1-4

When Jonah made the decision to go against the Lord, he boarded a ship headed the opposite direction as Nineveh. Even though a strong wind brought a storm, he felt peace of mind and went to his room and slept. This should always remind us that having peace of mind in a situation does not indicate God's will is at hand. When we are going against God's calling it will never lead to a pleasant ending!

Jonah's repentant prayer and seeking God's forgiveness, once he was in the fish, is what saved him. He needed an attitude adjustment in the worst way and being swallowed by a giant fish was just what it took. We read, "Those who cling to worthless idols forfeit the grace that could be theirs." (Jonah 2:8 NIV) Looking to our own desires rather than doing God's will is worthless! Pleasing ourselves only leads to surrendering God's grace, which leads to low self-worth.

As it was in Jonah's day, so it is today. We have people looking to all sorts of God's creations for their happiness but turning their backs on God. They do not read the Bible. They do not pray. And they certainly will not go to church and seek a relationship with fellow believers. Their hearts have become hardened and they must seek after one more pleasure in order to be happy. Happiness is not in the things that God has created. True happiness is in a relationship with God, to repent and humble yourself and decide to live for Him. Maybe a fish will not swallow you, but I ask you, how miserable do you need to be before you will repent and turn to Him?

Prayer: Lord God, I am thankful for Your discipline. May I not go by my feelings as to the direction I am to go. May I look totally to Your Word and pray for proper direction and be obedient to what You tell me to do, in daily reading Your Word. In Jesus name, Amen.

Day 229

THE LORD'S REQUIREMENTS
Read: Micah 1-7

"He has showed you, O man, what is good. And what does the Lord require of you? To act justly and to love mercy and to walk humbly with your God." (Mic 6:8 NIV) This seems so simple yet such a great feat! God has shown us what is good and has given us the Bible to guide us each step of the way. To be merciful to those around us and to always be humble. Easy enough but much harder to live.

As time goes on and we get ever closer to those last days that we have read about today, there are warnings that should alert each of us. "For a son dishonors his father, a daughter rises up against her mother, a daughter-in-law against her mother-in-law—a man's enemies are the members of his own household." (Mic 7:6 NIV) Yes, we have seen this in today's society. There is a lack of respect for older people, especially among family members. Why would we act in such disrespect to those who raised us? Who only have our best interest at heart?

The time is coming when "my enemy will see it and will be covered with shame, she who said to me "Where is the Lord your God?" My eyes will see her downfall;" (Mic 7:10a NIV). If our dear Lord can show such great mercy for us, we must show mercy for those who have been cruel to us, abused us and been hateful to us. We forgive but set a boundary, not allowing them to continue treating us with such evil. We have read over and over those same boundaries the Lord has set for His people. As we grow in Him, we gain a new strength, not of hate but of love for mankind. For love sets boundaries and that sets us free.

Prayer: Thank you Lord, for loving me and drawing me ever closer to You and setting boundaries of love. Help me daily to show love and mercy to those around me. In Jesus name, Amen.

Day 230

HE IS OUR STRENGTH
Read: Nahum 1 - Habakkuk 3

We must always remember, "The Lord is slow to anger and great in power; The Lord will not leave the guilty unpunished." (Na 1:3a NIV) During those times when life does not seem 'fair', remember that there is a purpose for what is happening, and the Lord is always in control. He may allow unpleasant things to occur as in Job's situation, but there is always a purpose that will make us better people and glorify God in the end.

May we cling to, "The Sovereign Lord is my strength; He makes my feet like the feet of a deer, He enables me to go on the heights." (Hab 3:19 NIV) This reminds us in the middle of calamity that our faith must be in the One True God, trusting that He knows what is best and what is needed. Only faith in Him can give you the strength to carry on when life seems hopeless.

Prayer: Lord, You are my refuge at all times, during the hard times, when it is easy to call out to You and in the good times, when I may need reminding how much I need You. Thank You for Your encouraging Word each and every day. In Jesus name, Amen.

Day 231

LOOK TO THE LORD
Read: Zephaniah 1-3

Zephaniah was a contemporary of Jeremiah and was the great, great grandson of King Hezekiah. He brought warnings to the people to turn to the Lord and serve only Him, but he also gave hope for a future time.

The day is coming when only the meek and humble, who trust in the Lord, will be here as God brings full restoration. Those that call on the Lord and serve only Him, He will purify their lips. Those who are corrupt and eager to destroy, who oppress and are rebellious and those who are disobedient, He will take out. This is very clear as to who God will protect and who God will take out in the end.

Sometimes it does not seem right that the evil ones should prosper and seem to get away with so much but, mark the words of Zephaniah, only the righteous, those who seek humility and listen to His commands, will survive. All this may not be in a way that we can even comprehend today. But know that our actions, our beliefs, and Who we listen to does make a difference. Seek God and read His Word daily, determined to obey Him.

Prayer: Heavenly Father, may I speak only truth and walk in integrity, for I desire to please You. May I humbly do Your will that I would bring glory to You. May I accept Your correction for I trust in You. In Jesus name, Amen.

Day 232

ENCOURAGEMENT AND HOPE
Read: Haggai 1 - Zechariah 3

Haggai was the first prophet to speak for God after the return of the Israelites from Babylonia. His contemporaries were Ezra, Nehemiah, Esther and Zechariah. Both Haggai and Zechariah give encouragement and hope to the people. And today we should grab onto that hope, "Be strong and work. For I am with you, declares the Lord Almighty My Spirit remains among you. Do not fear." (Hag 2:4-5 NIV) And finally, "I have chosen you," (Hag 2:23b NIV). So when God calls us to do something, remember, He has chosen us and will give us the strength to carry out what He intended for us to do. And He will bless you. (see Hag 2: 19)

When we examine Zechariah 1:6 we are reminded that repentance and confession are of utmost importance as we serve our Lord. Further reading, it also reminds us of God's great love and forgiveness because He then promises, "I Myself will be a wall of fire around it" (Zec 2:5 NIV) and "whoever touches you touches the apple of His eye". (Zec 2:8b NIV) We should honor Him with our actions and our words!

> *Prayer: As I wait before You Lord, I think about my behavior and contemplate how I can be more pleasing to you. Those we love, we want to please. I love you Lord, and give you my heart, my very life, to serve You. In Jesus name, Amen.*

Day 233

TRUE JUSTICE
Read: Zechariah 3-7

"This is what the Lord Almighty says: 'Administer true justice; show mercy and compassion to one another. Do not oppress the widow or the fatherless, the alien or the poor. In your hearts do not think evil of each other." (Zec 7:9-10 NIV) If a man should marry a widow and be abusive to her and take her land and other possessions from her dead husband, will not God administer true justice? This man is not good, he has not obeyed God. He may do things to look good to those around him, but his heart is bent on evil. By the way, the same applies to women who take advantage of marrying widowers for their money.

There are such people who are full of greed and only care about what they can get from another person in this world today. But as we read today's selection, we can see there have been evil people like this since the beginning of time. But God has said "for whoever touches you touches the apple of His eye " (Zec 2:8b NIV) Such people who take advantage of others only live for today, they forget that God will judge them, and justice will be administered. And yet, such men and women come to the widow (or widower) proclaiming their great love. Beware, dear one, they are full of lies! Stay close to God and His Word, follow the Spirit, and obey His Word moment by moment. Evil lurks and wants to take the Godly down, but God is greater and when we live with Him guiding us, striving to obey, evil can only win for a time He wins in the end.

Prayer: Lord, so many of us have experienced abuse at the hand of someone who claimed to love us. That is what we longed for, true love, but got only hatred. May Your healing power sooth the hearts and minds of those hurting, who experienced evil at the hand of someone who claimed to love them. You, Lord, are the husband we need, You care for us and protect us. In Jesus name, Amen.

Day 234

REFINING
Read: Zechariah 8-14

"These are the things you are to do: Speak the truth to each other and render true and sound judgment in your courts; do not plot evil against your neighbor, and do not love to swear falsely. I hate all this, declares the Lord." (Zec 8:16-17 NIV) I long for the day when truth will be spoken, and justice will prevail but in today's reading, we learn that the Lord hates this injustice. He hates deceitful people, lying people and people who speak falsely. If we got rid of this behavior that God hates, the world would be a much better place.

Because of His great compassion, He will one day restore peace, honesty and integrity. As we come to Him in repentance, He will cleanse us from our sin and impurity. He will refine us like silver and test us like gold. He will answer when we call on Him. That glorious day is certainly something to look forward to, but it does not prevent us from doing what is right and just right now. To repent and start leading a new life in Christ. We are to show those around us our new life by humbly going to all we have hurt, offended, crushed to make things right. What a great first step.

Prayer: Lord, I long for truth and peace sprinkled through love. Because of my love and devotion to You, Lord, I long to please You. Refine me that I may be righteous in Your eyes. In Jesus name, Amen.

Day 235

MY MESSENGER
Read: Malachi 1-4

Today we come to the end of the Old Testament. Malachi means 'my messenger', a final Word from God to His people. Sadly, this final message is full of ways the Israelites were not faithful. From not offering clean sacrifices to not honoring Him, the priest set the example. The men broke faith with their wives as if divorce was not bad enough, they went one step further by covering their wives with violence. God hates abuse! But do know that justice will come, abuse not repented of will have dire consequences. God also told them that they were robbing Him. In their arrogance, they questioned Him, "How do we rob you?" (Mal 3:8b NIV) The Lord replied that they were under a curse because they robbed Him in their tithes and offerings.

There are some pretty powerful allegations in the above paragraph and in today's reading but let me ask you, are these allegations not true today as well? Men are still abusing their wives and children and acting like they have done no wrong. They are unfaithful! And today, in the United States, which is still a wealthy country, people hold back money that they should be giving to the Lord. They live beyond their means and give the excuse that they must pay their bills or that they give in other ways.

Return to God in true repentance! Turn the arrogance of your heart over to Him and take on the garment of humility. Serve others, do good to your family, especially care for your wife. Protect her and provide for her like never before. Give to God with a happy heart the tithes and offerings due Him and watch Him take care of you.

Prayer: Forgive me Lord, for I have sinned against You! May I revere Your name and be pleasing in your sight. Continue to show me where I need to change and give me the desire to cleanse the evil from my life. In Jesus name, Amen.

Day 236

A NEW WAY
Read: Matthew 1-3

Matthew starts out with an (incomplete) genealogy of Jesus. I have always felt these lists of forefathers are a reminder that God is orderly and that we need to know our history. The book of Matthew is written to the Jews, establishing that Jesus is the fulfillment of prophecy concerning the Messiah King, it has 7 parables and records 23 miracles.

We are introduced to Joseph, the husband of Mary. What a man! Not once or even twice but three times he is visited by an angel: 1) after finding out Mary is pregnant, the angel tells Joseph to not be afraid to take Mary as his wife; 2) after the visit from the Magi, an angel of the Lord came to Joseph in a dream and told him to take Mary and Jesus and go to Egypt; 3) after Herod's death, the angel came to Joseph and told him to take Mary and Jesus back to Israel. And what did Joseph do? He obeyed. It does not say that he got up and prayed about what the angel told him to do, it says he did what the angel told him.

When we are walking with God, in close relationship, being a Christ follower means we will do what He calls us to do. We see this with John the Baptist as well. He obeyed by calling people to repentance and told them they must produce fruit. When we meet the Savior, we can talk about Him and how He has changed our lives, or we can demonstrate this changed life. If people cannot see a difference in your behavior, maybe we need to check our relationship and commitment to the One who has called us.

Prayer: Dear Lord, You have called me to not be a part of the religious establishment but to follow You. Help me to produce fruit daily and to be a witness to glorify You so as to draw people to You. May I always give You my best and not become discouraged. Keep evil away from me. In Jesus name, Amen.

Day 237

SEEK HIM
Read: Matthew 4-6

We start out today's reading with Jesus being tempted by satan. After a 40 day fast, Jesus was hungry and satan tempted Him in His most vulnerable area. But satan did not stop there, He tested Jesus' loyalty to God. "Jesus said to him, "Away from Me, satan! For it is written: 'Worship the Lord your God and serve Him only.'" (Matt 4:10 NIV) When we are tempted and not sure how to get away from the temptation, these words that Jesus spoke are perfect.

Another area where we can defeat satan is by loving our enemies. That does not mean that we need to let them in our lives. No, we need to be wise and follow Jesus, "But I tell you: Love your enemies and pray for those who persecute you." (Matt 5:44 NIV) There is the key, through prayer, we can learn to love those who have hurt us. This is not saying that we condone what they did to us, certainly not! We ask God to help us to forgive them through Him and use wisdom in setting boundaries. Always forgive but you do not need to let an abusive person back in your life unless they repent of their sin and are walking in a repentant life.

With so much to learn in today's reading, I can only highlight what God has laid upon my heart. "But seek first His kingdom and His righteousness, and all these things will be given to you as well." (Matt 6:33 NIV) God showed me this verse early in my Christian walk and I always seem to come back to it, no matter what the situation. As we seek Him and strive to be pleasing to Him, He will care for us. No need to worry, knowing that He cares for the animals and the beauty all around us, He will take care of us even more!

Prayer: Heavenly Father, thank You for Your loving care to make sure I have enough to eat and a roof over my head. Give me strength when the enemy approaches to condemn or to tempt me. You are my treasure, and my desire is for only You! In Jesus name, Amen.

Day 238

PRACTICE MAKES PERFECT
Read: Matthew 7-9

Many non-Christians will quote the first verse in today's reading, "Do not judge." Far be it that they would truly know the whole verse as well as verse two which might help with their argument, "or you too will be judged. For in the same way you judge others, you will be judged, and with the measure you use, it will be measured to you." (Matt 7:1-2 NIV) To apply these verses to our lives, it might be easiest to start practicing compassion for those who are hurting, or to give mercy to those who seem to be such great sinners, in our own eyes. We must remember that we once were the same as them.

This same thought goes along with bearing good fruit. There are so many who talk a good talk but never put their words into action. In fact, sometimes these same people can look good to the church, flashing their money around or even doing great deeds at the church but at home, they do not help their spouse nor do the children know that parent as more than a glorified gift giver. No indeed, they can be abusive with their words and even physically harsh and later justify their behavior or with false repentance, make a show of how sorry they are.

So, let each of us make a daily check on our own lives. Is the fruit we bear good or bad? Is it being obedient to God's Word or for our own egos? Do we daily humble ourselves before our family and friends and ask forgiveness for our rudeness, or insisting on having our own way, or that insensitive remark? This is not a one-time occasion and practice, no indeed, much practice, will bring out perfection. But perfection will not come anytime soon.

Prayer: Lord Jesus, as I read Your Word, help me to put these Words into practice and that I would bear only good fruit. May I always be a willing worker in whatever area You call me, with a compassionate heart. In Jesus name, Amen.

Day 239

DO GOD'S WILL
Read: Matthew 10-12

"The good man brings good things out of the good stored up in him, and the evil man brings evil things out of the evil stored up in him." (Matt 12:35 NIV) If you are like me, you try to find good in all people and the ones that are cruel and abusive, you make excuses for them. That was the old me, I have learned to set boundaries and using Scripture, have learned that I can only help them so much. If they are not willing to learn from God's Word and repent and change their evil behavior, then I must not have them in my life for the evil comes from deep within and I am only enabling them if I continue to make excuses for their behavior.

God is calling us to give Him our burdens and unload those worries because as we grow in Him, we gain rest and peace. Oftentimes the well-educated never understand what the Lord can do for them, they think their education has all the answers. But He has given so much to the children and those who trust Him, most importantly He gives them peace beyond understanding. We should pray for wisdom, asking God to help us change our actions as we gain His wisdom.

As we grow in His grace, we will have such a desire to serve Him and mankind. Preaching, healing the sick, drive out evil, giving of ourselves and expecting nothing in return. But for those receiving from Him and His servants, remember that "the worker is worth his keep". (Matt 10:10 NIV)

Prayer: Lord, You have called each of us to a different part of Your ministry. Help me to accept the job You have for me and not look to others and wish I could do that job instead. Help me Lord, to keep my priorities in order and to serve You daily. In Jesus name, Amen.

Day 240

PLANTING
Read: Matthew 13-15

We must hide God's Word in our hearts, but it is not enough to memorize Scripture. We must yield a crop for Jesus, that is, we must become doers of the Word. We must be careful not to let other interests get in the way of what God has called us to do. We must stay focused on the mission that God has called us to. The extent of our fruitfulness depends on how thoroughly we weed out our material, social, political and other interests so we can produce a crop for Jesus.

"But the things that come out of the mouth come from the heart, and these make a man unclean. For out of the heart come evil thoughts, murder, adultery, sexual immorality, theft, false testimony, slander. These are what make a man unclean ". (Matt 15:18-19 NIV) Again, in today's reading we find that the heart is exposed by what a man says and does. We can tell the kind of person someone is by their speech and their behavior. Time reveals this.

Prayer: Father, Your Word is planted a little more each day into my heart, my mind, my very being. May it take root and produce an abundant crop. May Your Word touch areas in my life that have not yielded to You, and may I surrender all the more to You. In Jesus name, Amen.

Day 241

KINGDOM OF HEAVEN
Read: Matthew 16-18

"If anyone would come after me, he must deny himself and take up his cross and follow me. For whoever wants to save his life will lose it, but whoever loses his life for Me will find it. What good will it be for a man if he gains the whole world, yet forfeits his soul?" (Matt 16:24b-26a NIV) I think this verse can be quite confusing for some of us. What exactly does it mean to lose your life? Is it death? Or something a little more complicated? Through the years, I have come to understand that letting go of my old self and embracing the life that Christ has called me to is losing my old life but gaining true life.

As we know, we cannot take any possessions with us when we die and oftentimes, the family fights over possessions of their loved one. As we let go of things, and cling to Christ, some will reject us. They were only nice to us because of what they thought they could get out of us. So sad! Others will love us not for what we can give them but because their heart is full of love.

May each of us be like little children in humbling ourselves before the King, as well as each other. It is a hard journey to let go of the power we find so important. Let go, humbling ourselves so that we can deny ourselves and one day find we have made it to the kingdom of heaven.

Prayer: Lord Jesus, may I be reminded often to check my forgiveness bank. Have I forgiven like You have forgiven me? Have I humbled myself and asked another to forgive me? Have I changed my behavior, so I will not hurt that person in the same way? Am I brave enough to confront someone who sins against me? Give me strength Lord! In Jesus name, Amen.

Day 242

WITH GOD
Read: Matthew 19-21

Are we like the rich ruler who is not willing to give up all we have to follow Jesus? For some it is not that we are super rich, but we are not willing to give up what little we have to serve Him. Sometimes God uses a spouse to illustrate this fact, what are you willing to give up to please the one you are married to? I have known people who were not willing to live in a certain area for their loved one or a husband who was not willing to shave his beard for his wife.

Those not willing to give something so simple up for the one they love goes on to show the great examples of the greed of mankind. How much more or how little is God asking you to give up to serve Him? Are you willing? Are these things possible with God's help? There must be a willingness in our heart to serve God in whatever capacity that He is calling us to do. Even if our heart is a little bit willing, God will give us a new desire to do the impossible to give up what we are holding so tightly and to give us even something greater.

"Whoever wants to become great among you must be your servant, and whoever wants to be first must be your slave—just as the Son of Man did not come to be served, but to serve, and to give His life as a ransom for many." (Matt 20:26b-28 NIV)

Prayer: Heavenly Father, may I die more to self and be willing to do Your will, to go where You are calling me, stepping out in faith when I do not know what to say or do. You give me the strength and the words. In Jesus name, Amen.

Day 243

PRODUCE FRUIT
Read: Matthew 22-24

In today's reading, there is so much to share. As I prayed, I asked God to guide me into what He wants me to write about. It does not mean it is the most important, but it does mean that God has led me to this area. Producing fruit seems to be the direction He is leading me. First, the parables point us to learning from them; that is to repent and believe in Him.

Once repentance happens, we are to change our ways. Turn from our old thinking and seek God's ways, to change our heart to be like Him. We learn that we must serve others, not to have those around us tell us how great we are, but with a heart truly caring for others. This starts at home with caring for our wife or husband and children and then moves to outside the home. We must love everyone and lead them to Christ and care for all who are in need.

"On the outside you appear to people as righteous but on the inside, you are full of hypocrisy and wickedness." (Matt 23:28 NIV) We all want to look good to others but be sure that our motives are pure and be sure that one day we will stand before God and He will know the goodness within. Sometimes when we do this check, we will have to go back in our past and make things right with certain people that we have taken advantage of and used or hurt. Do this before it is too late!

Prayer: Lord, my heart's desire is to stand firm to the end. Help me to not neglect justice, mercy or faithfulness and may I be as clean on the inside as I appear on the outside. Help me to serve people in humble obedience. In Jesus name, Amen.

Day 244

OPPORTUNITIES
Read: Matthew 25-28

Throughout our lives, God gives us opportunities to serve Him through the abilities He gives us, or through financial blessings, or by bringing special people into our lives. As we read the parable of the talents, we need to realize that neglecting these opportunities bring irreversible consequences. The parable calls the man with one talent a "worthless servant" (see Matt 25:30). He was worthless because when given the opportunity to serve, he was only looking out for himself. That is the way many today are when they do not appreciate the husband or wife God has given them, they are abusive to them or are not willing to work alongside them for God's Kingdom. There are those who have come into large sums of money only to waste it on themselves and not realize that God expects them to invest it, so it can be used to further the Kingdom of God. Time after time, people are given opportunities, but they are only concerned about themselves.

There are those who call themselves Christian, who may have even gone through the motions of salvation but have never chosen to do the work that God has ordained them to do. Ephesians 2: 8-10 helps us to understand: "For it is by grace you have been saved, through faith—and this not from yourselves, it is the gift of God—not by works, so that no one can boast. For we are God's workmanship, created in Christ Jesus to do good works, which God prepared in advanced for us to do." (NIV) Yes, God has prepared work for each of us to do but He is not going to force us to do it. It is of our own free will that He has given us, that we should desire to serve Him. Have you answered that call?

Prayer: Lord Jesus, my life is Yours! My desire is to serve You wherever You send me. Give me the words and love for all to make disciples as I travel among the nations. May I obey Your every Word! In Jesus name, Amen.

Day 245

EVER HEARING, NEVER UNDERSTANDING
Read: Mark 1-4

Although Mark was not one of the 12 apostles, this book is written to the gentile readers, unlike Matthew which was written to the Jews. We do not see some things explained in detail here in Mark because gentiles would not understand.

The parable of the farmer sowing seed is explained to help us understand why some who hear the Word of God, seem so on fire and serve God in any capacity they can. They do not just read the Word and wish they could do something for God but get out there and do whatever is presented to them. Others are pulled away by their own desires, perhaps for wealth or having more or to be better than their neighbor. They worry about all that is going on around them and this makes them forget about the Word of God and they are not able to produce. Pity the person who hears the Word but just really is not interested. Satan has messed with their mind to the point that they do not see the Word is relevant in their lives.

We each will produce fruit in different ways. We each have different gifts given to us by the Father to fulfill the need at hand. One gift is not better than the next. They are all needed! Be content with what God has given you, get busy and see what you are called to do and do it!

Prayer: Heavenly Father, may I consider Your Word daily and use the gift You have given me. May I soak up Your Word as dry soil needs the spring rains. Help me to memorize Your Word that I may hide it in my heart. In Jesus name, Amen.

Day 246

WHAT MAKES YOU UNCLEAN?
Read: Mark 5-8

Isaiah 29:13 was quoted by Jesus: "These people honor me with their lips, but their hearts are far from me. They worship me in vain; their teachings are but rules taught by men." (Mark 7:6-7 NIV)

The people were so into traditions and yet, they did not recognize that the Son of God was right there among them. He healed people, he fed people, he shared deep wisdom with them, however, they did not seem to understand.

Then Jesus stated a truth that is for all time, not just to those people: "What comes out of a man is what makes him 'unclean'. For from within, out of men's hearts, come evil thoughts, sexual immorality, theft, murder, adultery, greed, malice, deceit, lewdness, envy, slander, arrogance and folly. All these evils come from inside and make a man 'unclean.'" (Mark 7:20-23 NIV)

I tell you that not one of us can look at this list and say that we are innocent of committing such evil. Yes, each of us has evil inside! That is why is it so important to ask Jesus to reside in our hearts and for us to read the Word, find friends who are like-minded, practice daily to walk (that is to behave and talk) in this newness of life. From the day we accept Christ as our Savior until the day we die, we will need to work on having a clean heart.

Prayer: Lord God, may I not look to man for my help but only to Jesus. May I spend time with You daily in Your Word and have a longing to do Your will because of my love for You. In Jesus name, Amen.

Day 247

BE A SERVANT
Read: Mark 9-11

As we left yesterday's reading, we were called to deny ourselves and to lose our lives, for we can only be saved by God. (see Mark 8:34-35) To be a servant of all (see Mark 9:35) takes on new meaning when we make that decision to give up worldly possessions, to make a choice to be last and to become like a child. But just exactly what does all this mean? Some live with very little but are very loud in letting you know this fact. They seem to work hard at making you feel guilty for not giving up everything. They want you to be as miserable as they are.

Is this illustration truly what God is talking about? Perhaps there are some who are given much so as to share they usually have the gift of giving. We cannot make that decision for another person and certainly cannot guilt them into it. But those who have this special gift usually are not showy about what they have or what they give they are being used of God in this way.

As we draw closer and closer to Him through His Word, we develop a desire to obey, to please Him and Him only. He gives each of us special gifts. Some will want to give, others are teachers, still others are very good at leading, but in their hearts, they have no desire to be first. Their desire is to serve God. They do not look at what they have or do not have. They have also forgiven and moved on in serving the Lord.

Prayer: Heavenly Father, help me to be a servant. Help me to remember that You are all I need, not friend or family but a servant's heart. Forgive me when I put myself before You and help me to forgive those who hurt me. I long to be Your pleasing servant. In Jesus name, Amen.

Day 248

BROKE DOWN AND WEPT
Read: Mark 12-14

When we love someone, first of all we care so deeply for them that we are willing to protect them. We see this with mothers and how they protect their children. We should see this between a husband and wife. Jesus gave the greatest commandment: "Love the Lord your God with all your heart and with all your soul and with all your mind and with all your strength. The second is this: Love your neighbor as yourself. There is no commandment greater than these." (Mark 12:30-31 NIV) This commandment is plain, there should be no question how we are to treat others.

Oftentimes, we have good intentions as we go into a relationship, but we do not love deeply enough to fulfill the above commandment. We are still in love with another or we are so angry that we cannot love at all. But certainly, if you confess this to Jesus and have a desire to change and do the right thing, your heart will change.

We see just exactly how our response should be when Peter realizes that he denied Jesus. Oh, you say that not all people are the same? But please know, throughout Scripture we see sorrow and brokenness when a person recognizes his sin, and this is no different with Peter. "And he broke down and wept." (Mark 14:72b NIV) When we sin, we should feel such remorse for our behavior that we are brought to tears. These are tears of regret for treating a person we claimed to love so despicable. This is realizing how wrong we were and how we have hurt them so deeply. We confess our sin to God and then we go and ask forgiveness. But remember, we are to turn from our sin and live a different life.

Prayer: Dear Lord, may I always break down and cry when I have broken Your heart, when I have sinned against You. May I be close enough to You that I seek forgiveness immediately from You first but also from that loved one that I have offended. In Jesus name, Amen.

Day 249

CRUELTY
Read: Mark 15-16

Jesus remained silent with the accusations being thrown at him. The people in this crowd wanted him crucified. The soldiers were abusive to him, hitting him, mocking him, spitting on him. Even when he was dying on the cross, people hurled insults at Him (see Mark 15:29). Doesn't this make you wonder why?

He did miracles in healing the sick, raising the dead, telling all about the Kingdom of God. He also was a man of convictions, as he called those cheating the people to account, and He revealed the hypocrisy of the religious leaders. He told parable after parable to guide the people into leading a better life. Yet, all this is forgotten when the leaders wanted to get rid of Him, to kill Him.

Were the people then any different than people today? We are willing to stand behind a cause until we must speak up for truth and justice. Then we return to our homes exclaiming that things can be done without making such a fuss. Of course, Jesus had to die so that each of us might live but we are to live lives that are honoring to Him. Some will be called to be mothers and fathers, some will be called to be preachers, some will be called to be activists and warn the people of evil. Our role will change through the years, we may start out teaching our children how to grow up with integrity of heart and strong character, only later to become active in our community or nations politics or go to a foreign country and love a people that we have never known, showing them Jesus.

> *Prayer: Heavenly Father, may I always be willing to do Your will. May I not love another person more than You. May I be willing to travel to a foreign land for You. May I be willing to give my very life for You. May I be a servant, wherever You call me. In Jesus name, Amen.*

Day 250

DO NOT BE AFRAID
Read: Luke 1-2

Luke, an educated man, was a doctor and investigated in detail the birth of John and Jesus. In the book of Luke, we see the humanity of Christ, who was fully man and yet fully divine. We also see three visits from Gabriel in these two chapters, who, when he appeared, always said, "Do not be afraid".

Are you hungry for the things of God? Is there such a hunger that only God can satisfy? In today's reading, we find people who wanted to be satisfied by God: Zechariah, Elizabeth, Mary, Joseph, Simeon and Anna. I pray that we can have even a small portion of their faith and that our faith will grow ever stronger.

May we not be afraid to step out in faith to serve God in the way He is calling. May we not listen to other voices around us who will try to discourage us. May we gain strength with each new day to be pleasing to Him. Do not be afraid, for He is with you!

Prayer: Lord, I hunger for You, for only You can fill that void deep inside my soul. The Scriptures say that Your mercy is for those who fear You, who revere You. Oh my Lord, I fall at Your feet and surrender my will to You. May Your will be done! In Jesus name, Amen.

Day 251

CHANGE YOUR BEHAVIOR
Read: Luke 3-4

John the Baptist was filled with the Holy Spirit and he was calling people to repentance, telling them to "produce fruit in keeping with repentance." (Luke 3:8a NIV) We also find in James 2: 26 where it says, "As the body without the spirit is dead, so faith without deeds is dead."(NIV) It is only through our behavior can we show whom me belong. If we claim to be a Christian but our behavior is the same as before we were saved, we are a liar, we do not belong to Christ.

John goes on when asked "what should we do then?" (Luke 3:12b NIV) His answer is life changing! He told them not to use their power or position to steal (see Luke 3:13) and he went further to explain that they should not use their position to manipulate the people (see Luke 3:14). So I ask, you claim to be a Christian today, yet, you do not show the love of Christ by doing right? You have stolen and yet do not think you need to repay? You continue to use people? You pretend you are married but live on the Internet looking at pornography and do not provide for your wife?

Wake up! Repent! You may fool many around you, but you do not fool God. You will have to answer for such behavior to Him on the Day of Judgment. Make things right with those you have used, with those you have stolen from. Humble yourself before the Lord and before man.

Prayer: Heavenly Father, may I have a willing heart towards doing what You have called me to. For doing what is right in Your eyes! May I be humble enough to come to You in repentance and be willing to live my life according to Your Word. May I surrender to You my will and produce fruit that is pleasing to You. In Jesus name, Amen.

Day 252

DO GOOD
Read: Luke 5-6

"The good man brings good things out of the good stored up in his heart, and the evil man brings evil things out of the evil stored up in his heart. For out of the overflow of his heart his mouth speaks." (Luke 6:45 NIV) Have you ever met someone who is so brutally honest or sarcastic that they don't seem to care who they hurt with their words or actions? And their excuse for being so cruel is that at least they are honest? Or that is just the way they are. Yes indeed, they seem to be that tree which bears evil fruit stored up within.

Jesus goes on in His teaching to tell us that whoever hears His words and puts them to practice, belongs to Him. He has built a good foundation. But the man who hears the Word of God and does not put it into practice, is a man who makes a choice not to have a good foundation, and his behavior will reflect his decision.

Choices, we all must make choices in our lives. We do not have to be around people who continue to make bad choices, letting evil spew out of their mouth and heart. At some point, we need to walk away from this sort of hate. This sort of person does not care about anyone around them, they do not guard their heart or mind. Forgive them but do not allow yourself to be assaulted by such a person.

Prayer: Father God, I long to bear good fruit and I ask that You cleanse my heart from evil. Show me Lord, the areas of my life that are not pleasing to You and help me to change, to truly become a new person because of You. In Jesus name, Amen.

Day 253

PERSEVERE
Read: Luke 7-8

In today's reading, I am struck by the number of people who had big faith. First, the dear woman who anointed Jesus with expensive perfume, then the man who had the many demons cast out of him, and the woman who had a bleeding problem and finally let us not forget Jairus. All of these were common, ordinary people. Certainly not the religious group who had all the training and were well read.

So, today, some are like those who did not even want to hear the Word of God, yet others listen but their hearts are cold, hardened, they would rather turn away. Of course, there are those who get excited when they hear the Word of God but do not take the time to learn anymore, they soon fall away. There are others who hear the Word but are busy with life, work and family and they truly have no desire to mature in Christ.

Finally we do see some seed that falls on good ground, that is, people who have a desire to serve the Lord, to learn as much as they can and obey, and to persevere through those hard times and to produce a crop. You and I have choices, which do we want to produce? Are we willing to persevere so as to bring others to Christ? Are we willing to show kindness and give up our selfishness? Are we willing to humble ourselves by going to those we have hurt and admit our evil towards them and apologize? Are we willing to step out in faith and persevere to the end?

Prayer: O Lord, I long to serve You and to grow daily in my walk with You. May I do what You are telling me in Your Word. I have done much and need Your forgiveness, help me to never condemn others but to love them where they are and share what You have done for me. In Jesus name, Amen.

Day 254

DENY SELF
Read: Luke 9-10

Luke has an intellectual way of conveying God's message to us and yet he realized that he must come to Jesus like a child, innocent and believing. He also realized something much deeper, that we must "take up his cross daily and follow me. For whoever wants to save his life will lose it, but whoever loses his life for me will save it." (Luke 9:23b-24 NIV) Following Jesus is not an easy task if you are serious about being a Christian. We must daily search our heart and seek to please only Jesus. Beware when criticism or condemnation comes your way!

The most condemnation will come from the evil one, the one who wants to see us fail on our journey and he uses even those who are supposed to care about us, to help with that condemnation. We may not always understand but need to pray that we are childlike enough to receive wisdom from the Father. Most importantly, may we learn to put into practice those things which He is showing us. This takes an active willingness on our part to be pleasing to Him and He will use us and send us out. May we love our neighbor as much as we love ourselves and seek guidance from a trusted Christian friend and mentor.

Prayer: Dear Jesus, only You can heal the pain that is deep within my heart and in my head. You care about my healing but expect me to go out and share Your Word by loving those who are also hurting and feeling so unloved. I am to accept those who have a stained past and show compassion that only can come from Jesus and is so needed. In Jesus name, Amen.

Day 255

WHERE IS YOUR TREASURE?
Read: Luke 11-13

Be on your guard! So many are full of hypocrisy! Can you judge yourself? Are you full of greed and yet point the finger at others? Are you ready to give all up to serve Him? Are you like those religious leaders who did not even care for their own family? But yet put on a show of how they served God? "For where your treasure is, there your heart will be also." (Luke 12:34 NIV) You claim that your heart is with the Lord, but you do not obey His Word? You pick out certain verses that make it look like you are some great man, but He will say, "I don't know you or where you come from. Away from me, all you evildoers!" (Luke 13:27 NIV)

Yes, this is a lot to think about our hearts are evil, our minds fool us. Sometimes we need a person who is close and honest with us, as to where we fall short and need to repent. We need to be open to what they say and willing to see ourselves as we truly are because then we can repent of such behavior and lead a richer life, closer to the Father. He does come to divide us the good from the evil. Even within our own body, we need to purge out wrong thinking and wrong behavior. Walking the path with Jesus is not easy, it is a lifetime of working on becoming a better person. Through pain, persecution and dying to self; putting others first. That is where our treasure is.

Prayer: Father, without the Holy Spirit to guide me, all my efforts are in vain. But with You all things are possible. I willingly follow You, help me to see myself as You see me and be willing to change those things which are not pleasing to You. In Jesus name, Amen.

Day 256

BEING TRUSTWORTHY
Read: Luke 14-16

Was the younger son who insisted on receiving his inheritance trustworthy? It does not seem so, but it was exactly what he needed (or the events that followed) to bring him to a place where he would learn a valuable lesson. Yes, through the pain and humiliation of being so poor that even the hog slop looked good, brought this man to a new awareness. He needed to humble himself before the Father, he came home confessing his wrongs to his Father and had a willingness to change his behavior. He came in with honesty, did not make any excuses but took responsibility for what he had done. He recognized that he had "sinned against heaven and against you. I am no longer worthy " (Luke 15:21 NIV)

Such repentance is an important part of our daily walk with Christ. As we read our Bible each day, we need to be humble enough to see the lessons He wants us to learn. We need to remember that we cannot serve two masters whether money, or perhaps material possessions? Or, are you serving yourself? Willing to take from others what does not belong to you so you can have a better life but not willing to give of yourself? Remember, "you are the ones who justify yourselves in the eyes of men, but God knows your hearts." (Luke 16:15a NIV) Are you trustworthy?

Prayer: Precious Heavenly Father, sometimes I am like the son who wanted to take his inheritance and run to another country. Please forgive me! I must face my problems straight on and take them to You in prayer. In Jesus name, Amen.

Day 257

LOOK FORWARD
Read: Luke 17-18

God has wonderful plans for us! But, did you know that you have a big say in letting those plans come to completion? First, we must let go forgiving those who have brutally hurt us or even hurt us in some small away. Sure, it is a process but each time that unforgiving spirit rears its ugly head, you make the choice whether to dwell on the hurt and pain or to give it to God and forgive the incident. It goes further, when we do not forgive, we also hold on to so much more. But Jesus said, "Whoever tries to keep his life will lose it, and whoever loses his life will preserve it." (Luke 17:33 NIV) Yes, all those memories and possessions of the past cannot compare to what God has for us if we let go and look forward. Look to what He is calling us to.

That seems to be a pretty tall order, but it will bring fulfillment to our lives. God takes care of situations and people in our lives much better than we can. It is by faith that we trust God, that we let go of the past and let God do the changing. We can never change another person, we can only work on ourselves. On this day and the rest of my life, I will ask, What shall I believe, confess and pray? And then apply it in my life. For, all that I have and all that I am is because of God's mercy and love!

Prayer: Lord Jesus, have mercy on me! When no person cared about me, You were there! When I feel so alone, You are there! May I look forward to the joys that lie ahead and not hold on to the pain of the past. In Jesus name, Amen.

Day 258

LENGTHY PRAYERS
Read: Luke 19-20

We must guard ourselves, we must show self-control, and constantly check ourselves to be sure that we are not trying to impress those around us. Are we wanting people to look at us or to Christ? There are plenty of people who call themselves "Christian" but use their status to take advantage of other people. Sure, there are many so-called pastors who use guilt and shame so you will give them money, but we also see individuals who get money from others (usually widows or older people) for their own benefit. Luke 20:47 says "Yet they shamelessly cheat widows out of their property and then pretend to be pious by making long prayers in public." (NLT)

It seems that widows are a target for many a con-man where they give large amounts of money to someone whom they have thought they could trust, only to find out they were being used, taken advantage of. They are left with nothing and are crushed because they trusted that person. But the rest of Luke 20:47 says, "Because of this, they will be severely punished." Family and friends should be there to protect the widow when their husbands have been taken from them. There is responsibility of close relatives to care for the widows. If you are a widow who has been taken advantage of, or if you know of one, remember that God will certainly punish those evil doers.

Prayer: Holy Father, may my actions and my words be pleasing to You and be a part of my professing to belong to You. May I care for the widow and the orphan as you direct us to do. May I multiply the gifts You have given me to bring glory to You. In Jesus name, Amen.

Day 259

SIGNS
Read: Luke 21-22

From the poor widow to Jesus before the council of the elders, today's reading is filled with so much wisdom. Giving from your heart, knowing that God will care for you is a lesson that we must learn daily. But when Jesus said, "Watch out that you are not deceived." (Luke 21:8 NIV), we must take these lessons and learn from them. We must not live a life of fear but trust that God has everything in control and He will care for us. The catch is, where is your heart? Are you reading the Word daily, repenting, practicing what His Word says? Are you trusting that He will care for you? That He "will give you words and wisdom that none of your adversaries will be able to resist or contradict."? (Luke 21:15 NIV)

We know the final result will be Jesus' victory but getting there may not be as easy as being raptured and not having to deal with the evil that is to come, that is, the evil that is already among us. We must "Watch out! Don't let your hearts be dulled by carousing and drunkenness, and by the worries of this life. Don't let that day catch you unaware, like a trap." (Luke 21:34-35a NLT) We will have people in our lives that are just like Judas, they will betray us. We need to keep our focus on Jesus and what He is wanting us to do then do it. Make things right with those whom we have hurt. Care for the lost and certainly do not be lead away by the desires of our own heart. Satan will use even our closest friends and family to take our eyes off of the only One who can save us from what is to come.

Prayer: Lord Jesus, may I always be a servant that stands firm with You! May I be careful to guard my heart and always be prepared for Your return. May I repent of my sin and not fall into temptation. In Jesus name, Amen.

Day 260

UNDERSTAND
Read: Luke 23-24

Sometimes it is hard to understand why Jesus had to die such a violent death, but He was obedient to the Father. Sin needed a blood sacrifice so that we could continue in fellowship with God. The blood from sheep just covered that sin but the blood of Jesus, the Christ, paid the price for all our sin. I have never known anyone else to love me and you so much as to die for us.

The victory came on the third day when the tomb was empty and even though He had told them of the event that would happen before his death, they did not believe because they did not understand. We see this again with the two that were on the road, how slow they were to recognize our Lord and to grasp what had been told by the prophets had been fulfilled.

Finally he came to the disciples but they thought He was a ghost, so he reminded them that what had happened was fulfillment of what was written long ago. "Then He opened their minds so they could understand the Scriptures." (Luke 24:45 NIV) He also reminded them that repentance and forgiveness must be preached to all the nations and that is where our job continues. We must understand, by asking the Holy Spirit to open our mind so that we can understand the Word and share Jesus' love and truth wherever God sends us.

Prayer: Lord God, where You send me, I will go. I ask that You open my mind to understanding the Scriptures daily. Your Word is peace, Your Word has power, help me to be obedient today. Help me to gain strength in sharing Your Word. In Jesus name, Amen.

Day 261

TRUTH REVEALS JESUS, WHO IS LIGHT
Read: John 1-3

With Jesus, people wanted to see miracles but what they saw was truth. Jesus exposed the evil men in the temple courts. They were out to make a profit for themselves selling below standard sacrifices. They did not care what God required, but they took advantage of the people who needed to buy a sacrifice by selling them an animal that was not perfect, without defect. Although many knew of this practice, it was Jesus who spoke up, who exposed these con-artist with the light of the truth. Right there in the Temple court, people did not have respect for what was sacred, and Jesus booted them out.

We find on these pages that God loves us so much that He sent Jesus to save us all. Our job is to believe the truth, accept His love and turn away from evil. When Jesus told Nicodemus that he must be born again, or born from above, there was responsibility on his part. Today we have that same responsibility and choice, we can turn away from our old ways, giving no excuses, and turn to the truth of His Word and obey.

> Prayer: Jesus, I love you! You are light and truth and I want to walk in the light and live by Your truth. I put my faith in Jesus and want to study the Scriptures until the day You call me home. In Jesus name, Amen.

Day 262

WORKING
Read: John 4-6

If Jesus could do nothing by Himself but did the work of His Father (see 5:17-24), this is our example. We have a record of the work of Christ and when we are one with Him, we will do His work as well. As we follow Jesus, we realize that we can do nothing by ourselves but only through His power and that work is liberating for each of us.

So, we will do good works, not because it saves us or makes us look better in God's eyes. Not at all! When we have a personal relationship with Jesus, we have such a desire to imitate Him that it is a pleasure to serve Him and those around us. But, always remember, we are called to care for our family first before we go off to help others. If you are blessed with a husband or wife, He expects us to provide and protect and support them first. When two become one, they care for each other. Only as we fulfill that obligation, can we reach out to others.

Prayer: Lord, I long for the living water and a relationship with You. Because of my love for You, I long to please You. Amazingly, I need You in order to do Your will, to show You and those around me, my great love for You. In Jesus name, Amen.

Day 263

TRUTH WILL SET YOU FREE
Read: John 7-9

"Jesus said, "If you hold to My teaching, you are really my disciples. Then you will know the truth, and the truth will set you free." (John 8:31b-32 NIV) Jesus taught the words that His Father gave him, but some did not understand the truth that was in God's revelation. Why is this? When we are not filled with the Spirit of God, or when we reject Him, we are not able to understand the Word. It seems meaningless to us. So, if you know of someone who says they cannot read the Bible because they cannot understand it, you know they have not been filled with the Spirit that will give them understanding when reading the Word.

The truth is that the Bible is our guide, it helps us live our daily lives and directs us in how to treat other people not just our words but our actions too. When we comprehend this depth of His love for us, His guidance in every area of our life, we can then understand that His truth does truly set us free. We are set free because we hold to His teaching, His Word is there for us to obey, to do the will of the Father and we are pleasing to Him.

Through our obedience, we obtain true happiness. So, with us turning our lives over to Him, we are rewarded in a different way, and that is satisfaction in knowing we are doing the right thing. It is not for ourselves but for those we care about, our acts of kindness show to those around us but especially our loved ones, even though we do not do so for attention. So, it comes back to when we look to ourselves, we fail and the world says we lack self-confidence, but our desire should be to please God and He will give us the desires of our heart, and His confidence will shine through beyond worldly comprehension.

Prayer: Lord, Your truth has set me free and because of that, I must do what You have sent me to do obey Your Word. Not my will but Your will be done! In Jesus name, Amen.

Day 264

HE IS OUR SHEPHERD
Read: John 10-12

Sheep are trusting little critters. Isn't it amazing that God would compare us to sheep? With sheep, there is not safety in numbers, but a shepherd is always needed. Unfortunately in our modern age, many people think they do not need a shepherd, they can handle life on their own. But in doing so, they are not happy people. We truly need the guidance that only Jesus can provide, to know how to live and how to treat people. He is a shepherd that cares deeply for us!

When Jesus was talking about eternal life, He explained, "He who believe in me will live, even though he dies; and whoever lives and believes in Me will never die." (John 11b:25-26 NIV) Because of the miracle of bringing Lazarus back to life, many believed. Today we do not have these miracles, or should I say, we often do not recognize these miracles because there is not one man who performs them. God uses ordinary people who do His will without recognition. Many call themselves Christians but not all are. Those who do the Father's will are listening to the Shepherd, always willing to give of themselves in obedience to His Word.

Prayer: Jesus, I hear Your Word and I read Your Word. In my heart, I desire to obey but I often go my own way, meeting my own fleshly desires. Help me to obey You and to put to death the sins that entice me. In Jesus name, Amen.

Day 265

A TRUE SERVANT LEADER
Read: John 13-15

Over and over we read that those who belong to Jesus will obey Him. "If you love Me, you will obey what I command." (John 14:15 NIV) "Whoever has My commands and obeys them, he is the one who loves Me." (John14:21a NIV) "Jesus replied, "If anyone loves Me, he will obey My teaching He who does not love Me will not obey My teaching." (John 14:23a and 24 NIV) This teaching cannot be any clearer and yet many walk around claiming to belong to Him yet cannot even obey the least of His commands. Jesus was obedient to the Father and we are to imitate Him.

As we desire to do the will of the Father, with Jesus as our example, we will experience pruning for He longs for us to be more fruitful. And again, He tells us, "If you obey My commands, you will remain in My love, just as I have obeyed my Father's commands and remain in His love." (John 15:10 NIV) We must obey, through much practice, to do His will, with the help of the Holy Spirit. So, if we are saying that we have tried and cannot do it or if we fall back on our former way of life and say that is the way we are, perhaps we need to check our true identity. Are we a pretender or truly a Christ follower?

"Greater love has no one than this, that he lay down his life for his friends. You are my friends if you do what I command." (John 15:13-14 NIV)

Prayer: Lord Jesus, I long for Your peace and to obey Your commands, showing that I am Yours by my behavior. May I reflect Your perfect love. In Jesus name, Amen.

Day 266

TRUTH
Read: John 16-18

When Jesus, the Christ, was before Pilate, he said, "Everyone on the side of truth listens to Me." (John 18:37b NIV) Truth must have been very important to Jesus because as He prayed for his disciples, He asked God to "sanctify them by the truth; Your Word is truth." (John 17:17 NIV)

We can know that truth is of great importance, but it seems there are some who do not understand this, nor do they grasp that truth comes only from God. As Jesus was preparing the disciples for the future, He explained to them that when He left them, the Father would send the Holy Spirit or Counselor. It is His work even today that sets some apart from others because some are professing to belong to Christ but are not willing to listen to the Counselor. Here again, we see the word of truth as Jesus refers to the Counselor, "But when He, the Spirit of truth comes, He will guide you into all truth." (John 16:13a NIV)

You see, we can discern who belongs to Christ for they will hear His voice, and the Holy Spirit is here to guide us to all truth. The Holy Spirit quickens our spirit to obey the Word, to confess our wrongs to one another and to Him and seek forgiveness. The Holy Spirit is here to remind us of the direction the Father wants us to go so that we may give all glory to God the Father. When a person asks Jesus to come into their life, the Holy Spirit becomes the Teacher who explains the Word to us, so people will see a changed life. Have you made this decision? Can people see a different person in you today?

Prayer: Heavenly Father, may Your Spirit guide me through the truth of Your Word. Protect me as I do Your will in this world. May Your love for me bathe me so that I am known as Yours. In Jesus name, Amen.

Day 267

IMMEDIATELY OBEY
Read: John 19-21

When Jesus appeared to Peter and his fishing brothers, they were out all night and had not caught a single fish. Jesus called out to them and told them to put the net on the right side of the boat and without questioning Him, they obeyed immediately, even though they did not realize that it was Jesus speaking to them.

Oftentimes, God uses people around us to lead us into action. But the important thing to remember is that we always have the choice to do what the person suggests, or we can go our own way. We should always be sure that what is being suggested aligns with the Word of God and that is why it is so important to read and know what the Bible says. Also, we have the Holy Spirit living in us so there are times that we just know that God has directed us to go a certain direction. The men fishing could have said they needed to pray about throwing that net to the right or they could have simply gone with this suggestion. They made the right choice.

We have choices. Are we just going to tell those around us of our great love for Jesus or are we going to show them? And how do we show them? By doing what the Bible says we are to do and by meeting that other person's needs. That is true love. By being obedient to God's Word we must act upon that Word. We must feed and meet the needs of our family. We are to have compassion for those in need and who are hurting. Our love is nothing if we do not act upon it!

Prayer: Lord, what are You calling me to do? May I recognize Your voice and do what You are telling me. May selfishness be put aside, and may I follow You. In Jesus name, Amen.

Day 268

LISTEN CAREFULLY
Read: Acts 1-2

Before Jesus is taken to heaven, He reminded those around Him to expect the super-natural power of the Holy Spirit. (see Acts 1:5 & 8) And, just yesterday, we read in John 20:22, "receive the Holy Spirit". (NIV) So, they waited patiently for the Holy Spirit. Then, on the day of Pentecost, there was a large crowd gathered and "all of them were filled with the Holy Spirit and began to speak in other tongues as the Spirit enabled them." (Acts 2:4 NIV) We also see this in Numbers 11:25, where God allowed the Holy Spirit to rest on a group of men and they prophesied.

After Jesus gave His life for us, this precious gift of the Holy Spirit is given to each person who repents and makes the choice to live a new life in Christ. We see the super-natural power of the Holy Spirit when we see changed lives. It does not have to be dramatic. Let the Holy Spirit convict and work in your heart.

The Holy Spirit will change us, but again, we have the free will to accept His instructions or to reject it. As Peter is talking to the crowd, he says several times to listen carefully and to "save yourselves from this corrupt generation." (Acts 2:40b NIV) When the people heard him, "they were cut to the heart" (Acts 2:37 NIV) and asked Peter what they should do. "Repent, and be baptized and you will receive the gift of the Holy Spirit." (Acts 2:38a & b NIV) Repent, listen to the Holy Spirit and obey God's word.

Prayer: Heavenly Father, daily I sin in thought or deed or both but, as I come to You with a repentant heart, You give me more grace that I may grasp Your Word even with more clarity. I am responsible for my actions, help me to listen to the Holy Spirit better. In Jesus name, Amen.

Day 269

PROCLAIMING THE GOOD NEWS
Read: Acts 3-5

Filled with the Holy Spirit, the apostles were equipped to teach those they met about Jesus. They felt the resistance of the religious officials and experienced beatings from those who wanted to stop them, but they counted it an honor to suffer for Christ. Isn't it amazing that in the United States, people are being taught by so called religious leaders that once they accept Christ, they will be blessed and not experience suffering? In fact, some even teach that if you suffer, you have sin in your life or you are not a Christ follower. Scripturally we see this sort of teaching is a lie from the pit of hell. Many throughout history have suffered because they have been Christ followers and many throughout the world today still suffer.

What else is false teaching today? All religions are the same. False! You must give all you have to the church. False unless God directs you to do so. You must confess your sins to a special man. False. The Holy Spirit does not work today as it did in the early church. False. Or the lie that people use, "this is the way I am, I cannot change". False!

Indeed, when we accept Jesus into our lives, in all sincerity, we have read that the Holy Spirit comes to dwell in us. He directs us, pointing out wrongs but it still is our choice to change that behavior. Once we determine that we are willing to obey through the power of the Holy Spirit, He will walk with us. We are expected to pray constantly (see 1 Thessalonians 5:17) and confess our sins to Jesus (see 1 John 1:9). There is no other way than Jesus and He is the Truth that will set you free.

Prayer: Lord God, may I never grow weary of telling others about Jesus. May I speak boldly with the power of the Holy Spirit and remain humble as You use me. In Jesus name, Amen.

Day 270

REPENT OF WICKEDNESS
Read: Acts 6-8

We see in today's reading the importance of the body of Christ taking care of widows. So in today's society, we must remember that it is not the government's job to care for the widows and those in need, but it is the body of Christ's job. In that time, Stephan was one of the men chosen for such a task. Isn't it amazing that some found fault with him and finally stoned him? During that stoning, we must note that Saul was right there and that he was part of the persecution that broke out against the Christians.

We can see that even Simon, who practiced sorcery, wanted what the apostles had. He wanted to get it the quick way by paying money, not repenting of his bitterness and wicked heart. And so it is today. We must work on our heart, constantly checking it to make sure we are not holding any hatred or bitterness and to obey what God has called each of us to.

Philip was a man who obeyed. He went the way that the Lord directed and met the Ethiopian eunuch who was searching the Scriptures but could not understand. Philip, being led by the Spirit, explained the passage to him, leading him to Jesus. Right away, with great obedience and listening to the Holy Spirit, the eunuch wanted to be baptized. They immediately went down to the water and "when they came up out of the water, the Spirit of the Lord suddenly took Philip away, and the eunuch did not see him again, but went on his way rejoicing." (Acts 8: 39 NIV) May we make the choice to be led by the Spirit and rejoice in all we have in Christ Jesus.

Prayer: Lord, You have shown me in Your Word, how to handle persecution and those who are arrogant and even the joy of your Word. May all bitterness that I could hold be far from me as I confess and hand over such feelings to You. May I rejoice in Jesus with thankfulness. In Jesus name, Amen.

Day 271

GENTILES RECEIVE GIFT
Read: Acts 9-11

Peter learned a valuable lesson in today's reading. Even though the Jews had been a chosen people, now that Jesus had come and given His life, this gift of salvation was for the gentiles too. And as Peter was speaking the truth of the Word to the gentiles, they received the Holy Spirit as was evidenced with speaking in other languages and praising God. With this Peter also baptized these people in water.

At around the same time, Saul experienced a life-changing event. Remember Saul? He persecuted Christians and was there when Stephen was stoned. He met the Lord on his way to Damascus. He had planned on putting the Christians in prison but instead, he was set free from his own prison. So remember when you think you are not good enough, God uses all who are willing to turn their lives around, all who are humble enough to take a different path than the one they have been living.

What is your purpose as a Christian? We each have a gift that has been given to us by God, and we are to use that gift to further the Kingdom of God. Check your heart, seek God, repent daily of what is not pleasing to God, and step out in faith as you complete the calling He has for you. If He can use Saul, He can change and use you just be willing and do what He has called you to.

Prayer: Lord Jesus, You have called me, and I am going forward to do Your will. May I remain in Your Word and keep my mind and my heart fixed on You in true obedience. In Jesus name, Amen.

Day 272

PREACHING
Read: Acts 12-14

Living a Christ centered life is not easy because people around us see that we are different. They either do not like what we are saying, since it is convicting to them, or they are so evil they cannot accept the goodness of Christ. And so it was with the apostles. Peter was put in prison, but an angel walked him out the front gates, right past the guards. That could only have been a miracle of God!

By chapter 13, Saul, whose name was now changed to Paul, and Barnabas are sent out to preach "a message of encouragement" (Acts 13:15b NIV). What a message of hope they were bringing: "But the One whom God raised from the dead did not see decay." (Acts 13:37 NIV) Because of Jesus being raised from the dead, "the forgiveness of sins is proclaimed to you. Through Him everyone who believes is justified from everything you could not be justified from by the Law of Moses." (Acts 13:38b-39 NIV) What encouragement!

With all this reassurance, there were some who hated Paul and Barnabas and stirred up trouble which made them leave this area. This did not discourage Paul and Barnabas for they went to the next town and boldly proclaimed the Gospel. Please remember, "we must go through many hardships to enter the Kingdom of God." (Acts 14:22b NIV) We must commit ourselves to prayer and fasting and put our trust in the Lord. He will guide us, but it may not always be easy nonetheless be encouraged, He always has a purpose.

Prayer: Heavenly Father, may I have the strength to serve You. I have endured abuse and hardship as part of my training to speak more boldly and to bring honor to Your name. May I worship only You! In Jesus name, Amen.

Day 273

SHARP DISAGREEMENT
Read: Acts: 15-16

Today we find people who tell us that in order to be a Christian, we must do certain things. This notion did not start recently, no indeed, we see it during the time that Paul was on his missionary journey. Some were saying that men must be circumcised in order to be saved. Not only did this bring a sharp disagreement but it was cause for Paul and Barnabas to head for Jerusalem to see what the apostles and elders had to say about this.

After a considerable time of discussion, it was decided that "God, who knows the heart, showed that He accepted them by giving the Holy Spirit to them, just as He did to us." (Acts 15:8 NIV) Furthermore, they decided that they did not want to "make it difficult for the Gentiles who are turning to God. Instead we should write to them, telling them to abstain from food polluted by idols, from sexual immorality, from the meat of strangled animals and from blood." (Acts 15:19B-20 NIV) Pure and simple.

Later on, we see that Paul and Barnabas have a sharp disagreement over whether John Mark should travel with them. So, Barnabas took Mark and went one direction and Paul took Silas and went another direction. God used this sharp disagreement for His good as more people heard the Gospel. In our lives, we do not always understand why disagreements happen, but we must remember that God will use such times for His glory as we are willing to do what God wants and not dwell on what might have been with this friend.

Prayer: Lord, may I be willing to preach Your Word wherever You send me. Thank You for Your grace that brings salvation. Help me to grow daily in Your Word and give me a heart to be obedient to what I read. In Jesus name, Amen.

Day 274

EXAMINATION
Read: Acts 17-19

We can learn a valuable lesson from the people in Berea, who seemed to be more willing to listen to what Paul had to say. Not only did they listen to Paul's message of hope, they searched the Scriptures daily to see if Paul and Silas were teaching what was written. Truth is important to most of us. But, even so, often times we blindly believe and do not check to make sure that what is being said is true.

May we take a lesson from the Bereans and be known for our noble character. May we be known for our integrity of what we say is also what we do. May our words be true and honest for when they are checked out, no one can find fault with what we have said or how we are behaving.

May it be as with Paul that God leads us to speak the truth about Him without fear, knowing that He is with us. May we boldly live a life of integrity and love so differently from the world that people will want to be around us, and they will ask why we act the way we do. Then we can tell them about Jesus that we were once like the world, but Jesus came into our lives and we wanted to live a different life. We desire to give of ourselves and proclaim God's love when He sent Jesus, who was obedient unto death so that we might live.

Prayer: Heavenly Father, give me boldness to speak the truth of Your Word so that those who hear will believe and receive the Holy Spirit. May I only speak Your truth. In Jesus name, Amen.

Day 275

BE ON GUARD
Read: Acts 20-22

May we live our lives like Paul, who said, "I consider my life worth nothing to me, if only I may finish the race and complete the task the Lord Jesus has given me—the task of testifying to the gospel of God's grace." (Acts 20:24 NIV) Perhaps that is the reason he could endure stoning, being beaten, and rejection for he was serving God and being given his strength from the Lord. Not only did Paul encourage those around him but he warned them to be on their guard.

Sometimes we do not understand why we go through hardships, or through times of pain but know this, the Lord will use it for His glory. Just like Paul, who endured much adversity, we must realize that God has a purpose for everything that happens in our lives. We may not understand it at the time or we may never understand it in this lifetime, but it is not necessarily a need for us to know. The important thing is that we can praise God through it all.

Prayer: Lord, May I have the strength to endure those sufferings that You allow in my life. May they give me strength and insight that I may glorify You in all circumstances. Remind me to look to You in all situations. In Jesus name, Amen.

Day 276

TAKE COURAGE
Read: Acts 23-25

When Paul was being held in prison, being accused of all sort of lies because the people wanted him dead, God shows up and says, "Take courage!" (Acts 23:11 NIV) Immediately after that, Paul finds out that the Jews are not only planning on killing him, but 40 men have declared not to eat or drink until Paul is dead. That is serious!

In God's protection, Paul is taken to Caesarea, to Governor Felix. He stands trial before Felix. Paul makes his own defense, "I worship the God of our fathers as a follower of the Way, which they call a sect." (Acts 24:14a NIV) and "I strive always to keep my conscience clear before God and man." (Acts 24:16 NIV). When it is realized that there really is nothing to hold Paul, Felix wants to send Paul back to appear before those who want him dead. At this Paul appeals to Caesar.

When we are accused without cause or proof of wrong-doing, we must remember that God is teaching us and those around us a lesson. We must let God work for He has a better plan!

Prayer: Father God, May I maintain the self-control that Paul displayed when being falsely accused. May I look to You in all situations and know that You will care for me, give me the words to say. In Jesus name, Amen.

Day 277

PROVE YOUR REPENTANCE
Read: Acts 26-28

It was quite a journey just to get to Rome, but Paul proved to be true to his word and cared for those whom he traveled with. He lived in a rented house for two years once arriving in Rome. During this time, people came to see him and "boldly and without hindrance he preached the kingdom of God and taught about the Lord Jesus Christ." (Acts 28:31 NIV)

Even when Paul was taken to Rome, God's favor was upon him so that he could continue to preach the Good News of Christ. He was consistent for when he was before King Agrippa, he shared the reason he had been taken captive, "I preached that they should repent and turn to God and prove their repentance by their deeds." (Acts 26:20b NIV) But God used this time of imprisonment for Paul to witness to even more people that may have never heard the Good News otherwise.

And so it is today. If you know Jesus and serve Him as your Lord and Savior, God expects you to share that Good News with those you meet. Sometimes it is not with words, sometimes it is through kindness and a caring heart for the people who hurt. God uses all circumstances for us to meet the needs of those around us. What are you doing today? Are you ministering to your family, being the family member who is willing to help? Are you in the work force and the honest one with integrity that your superiors know they can count on? God calls each of us to a different work, are you willing to obey and be bold?

Prayer: Use me, O Lord, to touch those around me. May I prove to those close to me that my life has changed because I have given my life to You. May I draw ever closer to You and long to do Your will. In Jesus name, Amen.

Day 278

DEPRAVED MINDS
Read: Romans 1-2

Paul jumps right into the frying pan as he addresses sin and explains how it takes a downward spiral by those "who suppress the truth by their wickedness". (Rom 1:18b NIV) He also points out "they know God's justice requires that those who do these things deserve to die, yet they do them anyway. Worse yet, they encourage others to do them too." (Rom 1:32 NLT)

That is exactly what has happened to the people of the United States. Founded on religious freedom, we are now forced to hide our Christian beliefs because they may offend someone. Yet, the wicked ways of society are now forced upon all through decisions made by the Supreme Court, the lawmakers who are unfamiliar with God's Word of truth. Anyone reading Romans 1, can see the depraved thinking of our government, who seems to want to bring in all manner of depravity as acceptable behavior.

"For merely listening to the law doesn't make us right with God. It is obeying the law that make us right in His sight." (Rom 2:13 NLT) So, once again we read that it is not just saying that you are a Christian and continue living your life as before, but we must follow the Word of God, obeying because our hearts desire to do so. We can say that we love, but they are only words unless we act upon those words. That's what makes it believable. Paul points out that God's Word will be written on our hearts and we will obey those Words.

Prayer: Heavenly Father, I am thankful for Your patience as You lead me towards repentance and circumcision of my heart. Help me to stand daily for the truth of Your Word and not be led astray by the evil of this world. In Jesus name, Amen.

Day 279

REJOICE IN SUFFERINGS
Read: Romans 3-5

Beware of the teaching that everything will be a bed of roses when you accept Christ into your life! Throughout Scripture, we find that not only did Christ suffer but his disciples suffered and many throughout history have suffered for proclaiming Christ as their Savior.

The road to joy and peace is filled with a path through Christ Jesus, which will lead us to more faith in receiving His grace and along the way we will suffer. What hope is there in anything beyond our serving Jesus? And I remind you, "because we know that suffering produces perseverance; perseverance, character; and character, hope." (Rom 5:3-4 NIV) With such hope we find people of strong Godly character, full of compassion and a love that springs to action.

Faith without works is not faith at all and the same can be said about love. Do not claim to love unless you are willing to put that love into action. And what does such love look like? Jesus, He came to earth in love and gave His life in love and during His lifetime, His actions were love. To a woman, love means meeting her physical and emotional needs. On the other hand, a man needs respect. Love is not dominating another person but setting them free. Just as God gives each of us free-will, not harnessing us but allowing us to make a decision to follow Him or to go our own way. True love is caring so deeply for another person that it allows each of us to be with the other.

Prayer: Lord, help me to remember that You are always faithful. Even when I am weak and lack the faith, You are there to pick me up. Forgive me! I am thankful that I am redeemed by the blood of Jesus the Christ. Thank You for Your great love. In Jesus name, Amen.

Day 280

SLAVES
Read: Romans 6-7

I would say that most of us would not think of ourselves as slaves for we think we are masters of our own lives. But, today's reading totally proves that thought as fiction. Believe me, I have read this passage numerous times but only today am I grasping the depth of being a slave to what we allow to rule our lives. And, if we believe that we are ruling our own destiny, think again!

If we have truly accepted Christ, delivered from spiritual death and satan's control (a slave to sin) and are now empowered by the Holy Spirit to overcome sin and live a new life in Christ (a willing slave for truth), we are saved from the bondages of sin. To willingly become a slave for Jesus, the Christ, we "offer the parts of your body to Him as instruments of righteousness. For sin shall not be your master, because you are not under law, but under grace." (Rom 6:13b-14 NIV) Yes, we have a choice to use our body to obey His teachings, to do that which is righteous rather than pleasing self and choosing wickedness.

Daily we must make that choice to offer ourselves for doing good. The evil one will dangle sensuality in our face, which comes in all forms, but only will bring pleasure to self. Paul shares deeply how he struggled with his sinful nature even in the midst of wanting to do good. But as we offer ourselves to Jesus, and truly seek His will (and we know it is His will when it aligns with Scripture), our choice of whom we will serve becomes easier. How miserable I was before I chose to serve Christ, for He is my only hope! Funny thing is, often we don't even know that we are miserable!

Prayer: O Lord, I walk in the newness of life because I have been buried with Christ Jesus. I am thankful that Jesus was obedient to death so that I may live. I was miserable without Christ and now walk highly favored in my new life. In Jesus name, Amen.

Day 281

WHAT WE BECOME
Read: Romans 8-9

Being controlled starts with what we put in our mind and what we dwell on. "The mind of sinful man is death, but the mind controlled by the Spirit is life and peace; the sinful mind is hostile to God. It does not submit to God's law, nor can it do so. Those controlled by the sinful nature cannot please God." (Rom 8:6-8 NIV) So often we hear people who claim to be Christian make excuses for their actions, "this is the way I have always been, I can't change." But according to our Scripture reading today, we can change and will change when Christ becomes the center of our lives. Not just in word but in how we live. Is there peace in our lives? Do we strive to make things right with people? Or do we intrude in people's lives whom we have offended, telling them how good we are now? If we have to tell someone how good we are or how much we have changed, we probably have not changed.

When we turn our lives over to Christ, turning away from our former ways, we experience a battle. Do you think evil will give up that easily? No, we must fight daily to keep our eyes on Jesus and to focus our minds on His Word. As Christ followers, it is not only the behavior we no longer do but it is who we become in Him for we become more like Christ the longer we serve Him.

"The Spirit Himself testifies with our spirit that we are God's children if indeed we share in His sufferings in order that we may also share in His glory." (Rom 8:16 & 17b NIV) Have you ever met a person and you just clicked with them? That is probably because you have the same Spirit. Hold on to that sort of friendship and work to make it blossom.

Prayer: Dear Lord, daily I draw closer to You as I read Your Word and set my mind on being controlled moment by moment by Your life and peace. You search my heart and daily purify me so that I become more like You. In Jesus name, Amen.

Day 282

MY HEART'S DESIRE
Read: Romans 10-11

As a mother, grandmother and a great-grandmother, my heart's desire is that each generation will know Christ, that is, to serve Him with fervor and to live for Him. It is a matter of trust, to trust the One who can make all the difference in the world. I must let Him work in their lives. Then each of us must yield our will to Him, to ask Christ to come in and dwell in our heart. At that point, we make an effort to follow Him. Oh yes, there are times when we let our flesh take over but then we go back to following Christ.

Yes, it is His grace given to each of us, that we accept this free gift from our Lord. No matter how hard you try, you cannot be good enough for Him. He is calling you to Himself because He loves you, not for what you have done. He certainly does not want you to clean yourself up before coming to Him. No indeed! He has this gift for you, but you must take it. You must make that choice to grab hold of Him or to turn away. He wants us right where we are. He is there to help us become whom He desires us to be. What a gift is waiting for you! Are you humble enough to accept it?

Prayer: Lord God, I confess to You that I have not even thought of You at times. I fall short. I trust You Lord, that You Jesus are Lord. I long to follow You. Please forgive my sins, when I have hurt others but also when I should obey and do not. Thank You Jesus for Your kindness to me. I want to live a new life each and every day. In Jesus name, Amen.

Day 283

GROWING IN CHRIST
Read: Romans 12-13

Once we have given our lives to Christ, our desires change. I must go back to Rom 6:13, "Do not offer the parts of your body to sin, as instruments of wickedness, but rather offer yourselves to God, as those who have been brought from death to life; and offer the parts of your body to Him as instruments of righteousness." (NIV) This is the only way that we can be "holy and pleasing to God..." (Rom 12:1 NIV). But, how can we no longer be pulled by the attractive ways of the world? It is only possible if we make an effort to "be transformed by the renewing of your mind." (Rom 12:2 NIV).

God reminds Paul (and each of us) that it is only "by grace given" (see Rom 12:3) to each of us that we can fulfill further instructions. Through honest evaluation, we can ask God to change what is not pleasing to Him. We must realize that God has put us here for a purpose, not to live separately from the world but to join with others to further His purpose for our lives.

This could possibly be one of the reasons that Christianity has a bad name, many who come to Christ continue to cling to the evil in their lives. Often other Christians do not confront this person because they will see their own hypocrisy and unwillingness to change so they keep quiet. But Paul set the example and has shown us that it is possible to change our behavior, by knowing and doing what the Word of God says. Are you reading the Bible daily? Are you putting those words and thoughts into practice?

Prayer: Dear Heavenly Father, I long to be pleasing to You in all that I say and do. Help me to use my gift to bring glory to You. Remind me daily that You are in control and even when I do not understand, You have a purpose for what is happening. In Jesus name, Amen.

Day 284

ENDURANCE AND ENCOURAGEMENT
Read: Romans 14-16

As we finish reading Romans, Paul calls us to unity. He tells us not to be offensive to others and to respect those who live differently than we do. Snide remarks or making another person feel they do not have as much faith because they do not eat certain foods, or do not celebrate certain holidays is wrong. We are judging our fellow believer, acting like we are better than they are. Remember, "each of us will give an account of himself to God." (Rom 14:12 NIV)

We are to build one another up, for we know this pleases God. Accepting one another does not mean that you have to allow someone who has been hurtful back into your life. No, you set boundaries to protect yourself when a person claims be in Christ but continues to behave as before. I say it like this because it is easy to understand when a non-Christian is violent, and you close the door on such a relationship. The Christian who continues to be abusive is bearing fruit that is not conducive to Scripture. Pray, look to Scripture for your answers and let God lead you.

Through endurance and encouragement we move forward by reading the Word daily, looking as our hope to grows in Him. May God give you discernment to know whether the words we are hearing are truthful, and wisdom in knowing good from evil. "Believe and obey Him—to the only wise God be glory forever through Jesus Christ! Amen." (Rom 16:26b-27 NIV)

Prayer: Lord God, give me discernment so as not to be deceived by smooth words that feel like velvet to the ears. Help me not to pass judgment on those who live differently than what You have called me to and certainly not be a stumbling block. May I live righteously with peace and joy, truly a gift from the Holy Spirit. In Jesus name, Amen.

Day 285

GOD IS FAITHFUL
Read: 1 Corinthians 1-3

To think that when we, just ordinary people, come to Christ, we are set apart (sanctified) to be holy. In fact, the word sanctification is all about our growing process in Christ. When we first come to Him, we struggle a lot with our flesh, who is calling us back to our old life. But thanks be to God, Who longs for us to grow ever deeper in Him, to become more Christ-like and to be holy, He is patient.

Does He pick those who are so well educated? Those who have not known many struggles in their life? Does He want only those who have it all together (and who does—but some think they do)? No, of course not! Scripture says that He chooses the weak and foolish of this world, He chose those who are truly down and out, the addict, the prostitute, the murderer, the thief, the abuser all caught in their despised acts. He chose them because they would be thankful for His gift of salvation and love. He chose them because they could not point out their great education or how they have led a pure life. He chose them because it is a miracle that they now lead a different life, serving Christ in all they do.

Do those who have hurt others and are now serving Christ have no responsibility towards the people they used and abused in their past? Aww, yes, they do. Scripture (see Matt 5:23-24) points out that if someone has something against you, you are to go to that person and make things right before coming before the Lord. Concerning those who are married, 1 Pet 3:7 points out that a husband is to see his wife as a valuable and precious gem, being considerate of her "so that nothing will hinder your prayers." (NIV) Growing in Christ is a choice. What is your decision?

Prayer: Dear Lord, I long for a right relationship with You, to be pleasing to You. I long for Your wisdom and Spiritual truth to fill my mind and heart so that I may go to those I have wronged and make things right. I want more of You! In Jesus name, Amen.

Day 286

REBUKE WITH HOPE
Read: 1 Corinthians 4-6

So often I hear Christians say that they are not to judge but right here in 1 Corinthians 5: 12 Paul says, "What business is it of mine to judge those outside the church? Are you not to judge those inside?"(NIV) It seems that the Corinthian church was allowing a man who was sexually immoral to fellowship with them, and they had accepted him. But, if this man claims to be a believer, then the congregation has a responsibility to correct him but if he is not willing to listen, they need to "expel the wicked man from among you." (1 Cor 5:13b NIV)

This may seem harsh, but Paul does point out that "a little yeast works through the whole batch of dough" (Gal 5:9 NIV). And earlier in Matt 18: 15-20, Jesus explains what to do when a brother sins against you. Now that they have accepted him into the fellowship, accepted his detestable behavior, there is only one thing they can do to clean up the congregation.

Paul goes on "flee from sexual immorality. All other sins a man commits are outside his body, but he who sins sexually sins against his own body." (1 Cor 6:18 NIV) When a repenting person comes before our Lord with this understanding, he turns away from this immoral lifestyle with humble realization, "do you not know that your body is a temple of the Holy Spirit, who is in you, whom you have received from God? You are not your own; you were bought at a price. Therefore honor God with your body." (1 Cor 6:19-20 NIV) Oh, the freedom gained when we confess our sin and turn away from such behavior!

Prayer: Lord, please give me self-control so that I may glorify You. Help me to stay pure before You and stay away from those sins that draw me back to evil. In Jesus name, Amen.

Day 287

BE CAREFUL
Read: 1 Corinthians 7-9

Paul gives words of wisdom, both from himself and from the Lord in today's reading. He says it is better not to marry but also gives instruction for the man and woman who does marry: "But a married man is concerned about the affairs of this world—how he can please his wife—and his interests are divided." (1 Cor 7:33-34a NIV) And likewise, a married woman "is concerned about the affairs of this world—how she can please her husband." (1 Cor 7:34b NIV) These are instructions on how a husband and wife to be devoted to one another.

It also seems in this modern day, people are so intolerant of one another, everyone is insisting on their own rights or they are offended by others. Here Paul points out that whether you eat meat sacrificed to idols, or you abstain from such food, you must take the other person into consideration and not insist on your own way. Although Paul was meeting the needs of the people spiritually, he did not take money from them and he worked to pay his own way. He did not insist on his right to be paid. Likewise, we can learn from his example and not insist on our own way.

Whether in marriage or any other relationship, we are to always consider the other person first before ourselves. If each person would consider the other before themselves, the world would certainly be a much kinder place and we would find more love being spread around.

Prayer: Heavenly Father, You are all knowing and all powerful. You created heaven and earth but most importantly, You created each of us to bring glory to You. Lord, I give my life to You to be ruled by the King of kings. In Jesus name, Amen.

Day 288

EXAMPLES
Read: 1 Corinthians 10-11

Paul points out that we can learn so much from the Old Testament (he uses examples from writings that we now know as the Old Testament). He reminds us that these examples are there so that we will not set our hearts on doing evil. Do not be idolaters or overeat or drink to excess. Sexual immorality is so accepted in many parts of the world today, but as Christ followers, let's strive for a different lifestyle. Paul adds this one last instruction: "So, if you think you are standing firm, be careful that you don't fall!" (1 Cor 10:12 NIV)

I remember some years ago hearing a man declare that he would never commit adultery. This poor man lived under the illusion that he was a good person and that he would never sin in such a way. The sad truth was he was committing adultery every day with pornography controlling his life. I use this as an example of how evil can pull a veil over your mind to make you believe that you are the good one and so condemn those around you. We all have this tendency to point out someone who is acting worse than we are. Truth is, we are to examine ourselves with God's Word. This type of examination will convict us to repentance asking the Lord to help us to live a life pleasing to Him.

When we pretend to live a life for Christ but continue to sin in whatever way our weakness leads us, thinking that others do not know or see our hypocrisy, we are only fooling ourselves. When we humbly confess our sins to those around us, especially our immediate family, they are usually more than willing to pray for us and with us and to walk along side of us. Pride keeps us from doing this very thing.

Prayer: Lord Jesus, may I examine myself daily, using Your Word as my guide so that I may be pleasing to You. Remind me often that not all things that are permissible are beneficial to me. Help me to see the good of others and to be firm in serving You. In Jesus name, Amen.

Day 289

DESIRE THE GREATER GIFTS
Read: 1 Corinthians 12-13

Finding the body of Christ, the church, can take some time as we search to find out just where we fit in. Does their doctrine and our doctrine go hand in hand and is our gift needed? Some churches just want an extra worker bee but are not interested in whether our gift can be used. That is why it is very important to find out what your spiritual gift is. For years I thought my gift was mercy but when I took a spiritual gifts test, I found out that it was exhortation. Once I understood my spiritual gift, I was able to work in a whole different way within the body. I might add, we need a body who is respectful and actually sees you as an asset to the church.

Paul goes on to explain and list more gifts, or at least lists the gifts in a little different manner (see 1 Cor 12:31). We are reminded that we can have the gifts but without love, we are ineffective in ministering those gifts and it is worthless to God. It is not about desiring the faith to move a mountain or have so much wisdom to know all the mysteries of the world, but we are to possess and give Godly love, otherwise we are truly nothing. True Godly love is patient and kind and does not envy or boast. It certainly is not proud or rude or self-seeking. True Godly love protects the other person, always trusts and hopes and perseveres. True Godly love is wanting and giving of ourselves to the other person and not getting anything in return. We must seek Godly love daily, moment by moment, to attain such a great gift as to love in this manner.

Prayer: Lord Jesus, I am nothing without You! But with You and the body of Christ, we can do Your work. Lord, may I never try doing things on my own but only through Your power can I make a difference for the Kingdom. May I grasp and use the greatest gift love! In Jesus name, Amen.

Day 290

MORE INSTRUCTIONS
Read: 1 Corinthians 14-16

Paul continues with instructions concerning spiritual gifts "Follow the way of love and eagerly desire spiritual gifts." (1 Cor 14:1a NIV) Remember, this love is selfless, always putting the other person first. This is the kind of love needed to administer the spiritual gifts pouring out of self to nurture the other person. In all, this sort of love creates a trust between two people that goes deep. When things are done as God has ordered, there is trust and deep love.

"But everything should be done in a fitting and orderly way." (1 Cor 14:40 NIV) When we follow God's instructions, we find that it brings healing to the soul and when things are done in an orderly way according to His Word, situations are more peaceful. Where someone has sown hatred and discord, there is a lack of trust and certainly no love. We must remember "do not be misled: Bad company corrupts good character." (1 Cor 15:33) So, although we can pray for corrupt people, we need to be cautious to not get involved in their activity. We do not want to become like them.

"Be on your guard; stand firm in the faith; be men of courage; be strong. Do everything in love." (1 Cor 16: 13-14 NIV) Walk cautiously among the wicked, be of good courage, looking to Christ for your strength.

Prayer: Precious Heavenly Father, I am forever grateful for Your love. I thank you for the gifts You have given me and ask that You lead me to use these gifts to serve You and others. In Jesus name, Amen.

Day 291

PATIENT ENDURANCE
Read: 2 Corinthians 1-3

For those who have gone through trials of many kinds and know the Lord, we can testify that God is our comfort in the midst of the trial. He allows us to experience such trials because it "produces in you patient endurance of the same sufferings we suffer." Remember this, "just as you share in our sufferings, so also you share in our comfort." (2 Cor 1:6b & 7b NIV) And through it all, we learn to look to God all the more for our guidance, strength and comfort.

It amazes me that so many do not see this love and comfort from the Lord, but they are like those who have a veil over their mind, eyes and heart. They are dull and not open or understanding God's purpose for suffering and hardships. These may even be people who call themselves Christian but have never experienced the freedom that only comes in the Spirit of the Lord. It is time! Time to let go of self-indulges, tear away that film, that veil that keeps you from understanding God's Word because you are afraid to let the Holy Spirit into your life and rule your heart and mind. It is time to be set free!

Prayer: O Father God, I do not want to rely on anyone but You! Deepen my relationship with those who are obedient to You. For, where you are, there is freedom to grow. In Jesus name, Amen.

Day 292

BE SEPARATE
Read: 2 Corinthians 4-6

As believers, we get rid of our old, shameful ways that were used for deception and even distorting the Word of God. Unbelievers are blinded, their minds have a veil over them so they cannot comprehend the Gospel of Christ. This passage today encourages us not to lose heart but to "fix our eyes not on what is seen, but on what is unseen. For what is seen is temporary, but what is unseen is eternal." (2 Cor 4:18 NIV)

With this in mind, we, who are in Christ, know that "it is God who has made us for this very purpose and has given us the Spirit as a deposit, guaranteeing what is to come." (2 Cor 5:5 NIV) We were created for a purpose and must know that there will be people that will try to distract us from the goal that God has created us for. But our objective must be to please Him and be reminded that we will appear before His judgment seat and will receive our reward in due time.

Furthermore, we are instructed, "do not be yoked together with unbelievers. For what do righteousness and wickedness have in common? Or what fellowship can light have with darkness?" (2 Cor 6:14 NIV) This is good instruction for marriage as well as friendship and certainly in business. Be careful to be separated from this world so that you can live a life for Christ and fulfill the purpose that He has called you.

Prayer: Father God, daily I need to be reconciled to You for I long to please You. May I constantly be reminded that I have nothing in this world around me and my hope lies in You alone. In Jesus name, Amen.

Day 293

OBEDIENT TO CHRIST
Read: 2 Corinthians 7-10

We start out today's reading with instructions that will help us be obedient to Christ: "let us purify ourselves from everything that contaminates body and spirit, perfecting holiness out of reverence for God." (2 Cor 7:1 NIV) How do we purify ourselves? We never measure ourselves with ourselves. "When they measure themselves by themselves and compare themselves with themselves, they are not wise." (2 Cor 10:12b NIV) Be careful to not look at who you once were and say you are better now than back then. We never measure ourselves with someone else. Be careful not to say you are better than that guy over there. Our first step to holiness is setting ourselves apart from what we know will take us away from the Lord and His work. Finally, we should always have a healthy fear of God, knowing that without Him, we fall so short.

Paul further encourages the Corinthians towards being generous. I cannot highlight this principle enough! For, although it sounds like he just wants to get money from them, it goes far beyond just giving money. It is a heart softening tool but also a tool that measures where you are in your walk with Christ. If you say you love Jesus but live beyond your means or hoard your money and do not take care for your family or do not give towards the work that Christ has called some to do, your heart is hard. Giving is a choice, caring for those you say you love is a choice, giving to the body of Christ is a choice and giving to missionaries is a choice. If you are eager to help, then meet the needs of the people not just your own desires.

Prayer: Heavenly Father, You comfort those who are hurting and bring healing to my soul. May I not disappoint You in my giving and to supply the needs of those You have brought into my life. May I sow a bountiful harvest to bring many to You. In Jesus name, Amen.

Day 294

EXAMINE YOURSELVES
Read: 2 Corinthians 11-13

Just like today, the Corinthians struggled with being pulled away from the teachings of the Gospel. It is proof that the evil one wants to keep us distracted, luring us away from the truth, telling us partial truths, and clouding our mind so as to not be presented to our Lord as pure. We need to check that we are not being deceived by the teachings on all sides. Make sure that our mind and heart are pleasing Jesus, and Him alone. Examine ourselves to make sure we are not enslaved by people or things around us.

"I fear there may be quarreling, jealousy, outbursts of anger, factions, slander, gossip, arrogance and disorder. I am afraid that when I come again my God will humble me before you, and I will be grieved over many who have sinned earlier and have not repented of the impurity, sexual sin and debauchery in which they have indulged." (2 Cor 12:20b-21 NIV) Paul cared so much for the Corinthians that he was writing them the importance of self-examination along with repentance, which is, turning away from such sin. And so it is today, we need to know that those same sins are out there, and we can be pulled into these same snares if we are not focused on Jesus.

Paul's closing to the Corinthians is just as meaningful today as it was to then, "aim for perfection, listen to my appeal, be of one mind, live in peace." (2 Cor 13:11a NIV) May we humbly seek Him and long daily to please Jesus above all else.

Prayer: O Lord, I seek You daily and yet, I fall short, my sin is always before me. I strive to be pleasing to You and yet, my flesh is weak. I see and understand my wrongs and come to You in repentance, to turn away from my actions, only to realize there is yet one more part of myself that needs to be crucified. Thank You for Your great love. In Jesus name, Amen.

Day 295

SET APART
Read: Galatians 1-3

Paul reminds us in today's reading how he was set apart by God, to introduce the Son of God to the Gentiles. He reminds us "that a man is not justified by observing the law, but by faith in Jesus Christ." (Gal 2:16 NIV) The law was provided so that we may know sin but only Jesus provides forgiveness of sin. Knowledge of the law helps us to realize that we cannot obey those Ten Commandments, no matter how hard we try, we fail. This realization then leads us to Christ, Who paid the price for our sin once and for all. Our part is to believe that Jesus came for each of us and through Christ "we might be justified by faith." (Gal 3:24b NIV)

When we accept that understanding of Christ coming to earth to take our sin upon Himself, we, like Paul, take that first step in serving Him and living a life for Christ. We can see in Paul's life, how he suffered greatly because he turned from the Jewish faith and accepted Christ as his Savior. Paul points out that Peter, at one point was a hypocrite in his teaching (see Gal 2:13), and there will be times in our walk with Jesus that we may take a wrong turn also being hypocritical. Just as Peter was trying to tell the people that they had to be circumcised in order to be a Christian, may we pray that we have a friend who cares so deeply for the Lord, that we will be set straight and brought back to the Godly path in love.

Prayer: Heavenly Father, draw me ever closer to You. As a true believer and follower of the work Jesus did for me, test me daily of my sincerity to serve You and may I be quick to repent when I sin. In Jesus name, Amen.

Day 296

DO NOT BE DECEIVED
Read: Galatians 4-6

God's Word is truth! "Those who live only to satisfy their own sinful nature will harvest decay and death from that sinful nature." (Gal 6:8a NLT) We might ask what act of the sinful nature would include? Galatians 5:19b-21a tells us, "sexual immorality, impurity, lustful pleasures, idolatry, sorcery, hostility quarreling, jealousy, outbursts of anger, selfish ambition, dissension, division, envy, drunkenness, wild parties, and other sins like these." (NLT) Please take note the end of verse 21: "I warn you, as I did before, that those who live like this will not inherit the kingdom of God." (NIV)

In the middle of reminding the Galatians that God sees it all, that God cannot be deceived, Paul goes on to encourage us, "those who live to please the Spirit will harvest everlasting life from the Spirit." (Gal 6: 8b NLT) And again, we find a list that tell us just exactly what the results are as we live a life obedient to His Word: "but the Holy Spirit produces this kind of fruit in our lives: love, joy peace, patience, kindness, goodness, faithfulness, gentleness and self-control." (Gal 5:22-23 NLT)

We can deceive ourselves into thinking we are good people, but God has given us a list to check ourselves. Daily we can make the choice to live under slavery to the law or we can live free in Christ. We can cling to the past and the evil that was there, or we can move towards the light of Jesus. Paul is encouraging the Galatians to move towards Jesus and to let go of their past. The past was binding, full of rules. Christ is freeing, teaching us to love beyond anything we have ever experienced. Our faith is expressed through our love. (see Gal 5:6b)

Prayer: Lord Jesus, help me to love like You love and to live my life producing fruit with the help of the Holy Spirit. May I continually be alert to follow the Spirit's leading and put to death the desires of my sinful nature. In Jesus name, Amen.

Day 297

CHRIST ALONE
Read: Ephesians 1-3

Our flesh carries the values and attitudes of the world around us. If we are honest, we will admit that even after we have accepted Christ into our lives, we find ourselves "gratifying the cravings of our sinful nature and following its desires and thoughts." (Eph 2:3 NIV) Just like the first Christians, we can be selfish and only want to please our flesh. But God gave us the gift of Christ Jesus, Who gave His life so that we might be made clean.

It is not by following the Ten Commandments, or being a good person, or giving. No, not at all! God created us in our mother's womb (see Psalm 139), and He had a purpose for us from the moment we were conceived. When we live our lives to please Christ, we have a deep desire to fulfill that purpose. We are saved by grace as we long to serve our Lord the rest of our days. There are times when we get off the path and revert back to pleasing our selfish nature. What must we do? Confess our selfishness, turn away from such behavior and get our eyes and heart back on task. That is, using our gift of service to meet the needs of those around us.

When our desires are His desires, our prayers are answered. When the depth of our being is "established in love" we "have power, together with all the saints, to grasp how wide and long and high and deep is the love of Christ, and to know this love that surpasses knowledge—that you may be filled to the measure of all the fullness of God." (Eph 3:17-19 NIV) You can say that you love, but the love that is needed is Christ's love. Selfless love is needed.

Prayer: Lord, it is hard for me to understand that You love me so much and have called me to a higher purpose than just pleasing myself. I am a Holy Temple for You and my desire is to serve You as You have called me. Daily help me to listen. In Jesus name, Amen.

Day 298

BE IMITATORS OF GOD
Read: Ephesians 4-6

We are reminded in today's reading to renew our mind with the Word. We are taught "that you must no longer live as the Gentiles do, in the futility of their thinking. They are darkened in their understanding and separated from the life of God because of the ignorance that is in them due to the hardening of their hearts. Having lost all sensitivity, they have given themselves over to sensuality so as to indulge in every kind of impurity, with a continual lust for more." (Eph 4:17-19 NIV) With this passage, we better understand the person who is not a Christ follower, who seems to be filled with greed.

Paul encourages us "to put off your old self, which is being corrupted by its deceitful desires; to be made new in the attitude of your minds; and to put on the new self, created to be like God in true righteousness and holiness." (Eph 4:22b-24 NIV) How are we made new? How do we change that attitude and turn our mind away from being dark in our understanding? How can we become imitators of God?

Surrendering our lives to Christ is the first step. From that point on it is a daily, sometimes minute by minute process to retrain our mind and behavior to be more Christ-like. Reading the Bible daily, studying the Scriptures but most importantly, obeying the Word. It is a process, but progress does not happen without us putting effort into it and praying that God will give us the strength to change. Who is your accountability partner?

Prayer: Dear Heavenly Father, I do not want to live my life as I once did, pleasing only myself. Instead, I give my life to You to be used by You, following Christ's example. Give me strength to walk in life anew, throwing off the evil I lived. May I live in the Lord and walk in His strength daily. In Jesus name, Amen.

Day 299

LIVE HUMBLY
Read: Philippians 1-4

Paul starts out his letter to the Philippians with prayer and thanksgiving. We can learn so much about how to treat others from this precious book. Being joyful for others in our life is a great start and seeing them as equals. As we live humbly before the Lord, we value others before ourselves. Christ is our example for He relinquished His glory and His rights to come to earth for one purpose, us sinners.

"I want to know Christ and the power of His resurrection and the fellowship of sharing in His sufferings " (Phil 3:10 NIV) Wait, did we read that correctly? Share in His sufferings?? It seems that we want to know the blessings that God has for us but start to blame our sufferings on others, especially satan. We give satan the credit when it is part of our growing process. Often our sufferings are from our own doing because of our selfish heart, we act too quickly and suffer. But have we known the sufferings that Christ experienced? Around the world, there is a new wave of persecution towards those who serve Christ. We must know this part of Christ's life, not just the blessings.

Paul tells us that he has had little at times and at other times, he has had much but the key is to be content in Christ and it is He Who gives us strength, not wealth. See (Phil 4:11b-12a). Paul finishes this letter by reminding them that God does meet all our needs, but it is credited to each of us when we give. Giving is important!

Prayer: O Lord, the joy of the book of Philippians! May I learn to go through the times of suffering with the same joy as when I receive blessings. May I be ever stronger in telling others about Jesus in true love that can only come from the Father. In Jesus name, Amen.

Day 300

HOLY LIVING
Read: Colossians 1-4

"See to it that you complete the work you have received in the Lord." (Col 4:17 NIV) And what work is that? Seems that many Christians today have no idea what God has called them to or they know but choose not to do the work, using excuse after excuse of why they are not doing what the Father has called them to do. As we seek God's face, through the reading of the Word, prayer, fasting and thankfulness, the Holy Spirit will guide you and you will know what you have been called to do.

"So put to death the sinful, earthly things lurking within you. Have nothing to do with sexual immorality, impurity, lust and evil desires. Don't be greedy, for a greedy person is an idolater, worshiping the things of this world." (Col 3:5 NLT) Here, once again, is another list of the works of the flesh, in which we are to "rid yourselves of all such things as these: anger, rage, malice, slander and filthy language from our lips. Do not lie to each other since you have taken off your old self with its practices and have put on the new self, which is being renewed in knowledge in the image of its Creator. (Col 3:8-10 NIV)

Our faith looks up to heaven, to our Creator, true love looks to those around us and hope looks forward, to what God has in store. If we are following the Scriptures, we only want what is best for the other person and we take the proper steps to reaching the goal that God has called us to.

Prayer: Holy Father, may I follow You completely, not only reading Your Word but doing what You have called me to do. Give me strength for each new day and strip away my old nature and fill me with Your love and power. In Jesus name, Amen.

Day 301

BE BLAMELESS
Read: 1 Thessalonians 1-5

We, as Christ followers, are set apart by God and He is helping us to remain blameless, that is to behave in ways that are pleasing to Him. He is faithful as we seek Him in all that we do and say! (see 1 Thess 5:23-24) As we read the letters of Paul, we can no longer say that we do not know what God wants from us. No indeed, here Paul tells the Thessalonians to "avoid sexual immorality; that each of you should learn to control his own body in a way that is holy and honorable, not in passionate lust like the heathen, who do not know God; and that in this matter no one should wrong his brother or take advantage of him." (1 Thess 4: 3b-6a NIV)

As Paul greets the Thessalonians, he reminds them that genuine love always expresses itself in action, that of putting the other person's needs before your own. He also reminds us that people are always watching for outward evidence of who we are and Whom we belong. Truly, sincere faith in God the Father and believing that Jesus came to set us free, will always yield in a changed life. If those who have known us the longest do not see a change in our behavior, maybe we need to check ourselves for we are to "test everything. Hold on to the good. Avoid every kind of evil." (1 Thess 5:21-22 NIV)

If we think we only have to please God but continue to live the same way with those around us or the way we lived before, we are not pleasing God at all. When we let go of pleasing ourselves and putting the other person's needs before our own as Christ demonstrated, we start on the journey of living a life that is pleasing to our Lord and Savior. What do you choose this day?

Prayer: My Precious Lord, I choose Christ and ask that my old ways be crucified, be put to death. May all who knew me see such a change so drastic that it draws them into Your arms. Thank you, Lord, for pulling me ever closer to You. In Jesus name, Amen.

Day 302

PERSEVERANCE AND FAITH
Read: 2 Thessalonians 1-3

Persecution of Christians has taken place since the death of Christ, somewhere in the world. Here Paul encourages the Thessalonians "among God's churches we boast about your perseverance and faith in all the persecutions and trials you are enduring." (2 Thess 1:4 NIV) We are reminded that God will bring justice on those who are troubling us (see 2 Thess 1:6 and Rom 12:19). Hard times will come into each of our lives, but God will use these times to strengthen us and for us to draw closer to Him.

The purpose of this strengthening is because a time is coming when the evil one will do everything he can to draw us away from the Lord and into his evil clutches. He will do "all kinds of counterfeit miracles, signs and wonders, and in every sort of evil that deceives those who are perishing." (2 Thess 2: 9b-10a NIV) Paul further encourages that in such a time, we need to "stand firm and hold to the teachings we passed on to you, whether by word of mouth or by letter." (2 Thess 2:15 NIV)

Finally, we are reminded to "keep away from every brother who is idle and does not live according to the teaching you received from us." (2 Thess 3:6b NIV) There are people to this day that want to live off someone else, taking advantage of their generosity and love. There are people who expect you to meet their desires and buy whatever brings a fancy to them. No indeed, Paul tells us to stay away from such people and says, "if a man will not work, he shall not eat." (2 Thess 3:10b NIV) Keep persevering, my friend and seek His face daily through the Word and prayer.

Prayer: Father God, I am thankful for the Word as it teaches me what You want me to do to be pleasing to You. To work hard because You are my Joy. To flee from those who do not follow Your Word for they want to pull me away from You. To do good and obey the Word. Thank You for Your peace. In Jesus name, Amen.

Day 303

KEEP YOURSELF PURE
Read: 1 Timothy 1-6

The advice that Paul gives to Timothy should be for each of us, "so run from all these evil things. Pursue righteousness and a godly life, along with faith, love, perseverance, and gentleness." (1 Tim 6:11 NLT) Just before this statement, Paul was talking about the love of money being the root of all kinds of evil (see 1 Tim 6:10), instructing Timothy to stay away from this eagerness to have lots of money. This is not saying that money is evil, but if our focus is on getting rich, then we have taken our focus off of Christ.

We are encouraged to do good deeds and to give freely to those who are in need. That includes caring for the widows and their children and especially our immediate family. (see 1 Tim 5:8b) Those who do not provide for their immediate family have turned away from their faith in God and are "worse than an unbeliever." (1 Tim 5:8c NIV) Amazingly, even a nonbeliever will have a desire to provide for his wife and children. Paul points out that if this is true for the nonbeliever, how much more should a Christ follower want to give the best for his family?

Finally, Timothy is urged to stay away from "unhealthy interest in controversies and quarrels about words that result in envy, strife, malicious talk, evil suspicions and constant friction between men of corrupt mind, who have been robbed of the truth and who think that godliness is a means to financial gain." (1 Tim 6:4-5 NIV) Are we looking out for the good of the other person? Do the words we use edify the other person? What is our intent when we start to argue with another person?

Prayer: Heavenly Father, cleanse my heart that I may stay away from all sorts of foolishness and may I always be pleasing to You. May I learn the lessons that You have put in my path and be a reliable witness for You. In Jesus name, Amen.

Day 304

BE PREPARED
Read: 2 Timothy 1-4

In this last letter, Paul writes to his dear, Spiritual son, Timothy. "So do not be ashamed to testify about our Lord, or ashamed of me His prisoner. But join with me in suffering for the gospel by the power of God," (2 Tim 1:8 NIV) We are to be prepared to tell others about Christ, no matter if we are rejected or at some point, suffering.

As we tell others about our precious hope in Christ, we must "turn away from wickedness" (2 Tim 2:19b NIV) and check ourselves to make sure our outward conduct is agreeable with our inward decision. So many may speak about Christ, but they refuse to let Christ transform their lives. They continue to hold on to their past, not allowing Christ to work in them, creating new creatures. We are to be prepared to show love to those around us with patience and Godly instructions. You be the judge of yourself, which are you? Perhaps ask your spouse or a dear friend if you are living a changed life.

But, remember "the time will come when men will not put up with sound doctrine. Instead, to suit their own desires, they will gather around them a great number of teachers to say what their itching ears want to hear. They will turn their ears away from the truth and turn aside to myths." (2 Tim 4:3-4 NIV) As we speak God's truth and give the hope that can only come from Christ, we will come against those who will oppose us, and who will ridicule us, but we are to stand firm. We are to love them even when they are cruel. Life in Christ is more than a good feeling, it is work to be done, no matter what the cost.

> *Prayer: Holy Father, I often fall short of my calling and ask Your forgiveness. Give me strength for each new day so I may fulfill the purpose for which You have called me. In different situations, give me the words to speak, love and the patience to show such love. In Jesus name, Amen.*

Day 305

ENCOURAGE AND REBUKE
Read: Titus and Philemon

Yet another day and Paul writes about how we should behave as Christians. We are reminded that Jesus the Christ gave Himself to set us free and, in that freedom, we are set apart to serve Him. In both Titus and Philemon, the principle theme is our behavior, showing others what we believe.

Putting our faith into practice tells those around us that we are changed individuals. "But avoid foolish controversies and genealogies and arguments and quarrels about the law, because these are unprofitable and useless. Warn a divisive person once, then warn him a second time. After that, have nothing to do with him. You can be sure that such a man is warped and sinful; he is self-condemned." (Titus 3:10-11 NIV) According to "Explore the Bible", "a divisive person is perverted, who is twisted mentally, morally and spiritually. By his own stubborn willfulness and refusal to accept counsel, a divisive person contributes to his own condemnation." (1&2 Timothy, Titus; Lifeway Church Resources. p112)

Not only is Paul encouraging Titus to help the people of Crete to change their lives, Paul calls each of us today to check ourselves as to where our behavior is. Better yet, find someone who will walk alongside you to grow in Christ. We have a list in Titus 2 that gives us the guidelines, but we do not see this taught much in the modern U.S. churches, thus another reason we must read the Word for ourselves. Remember, God's mercy is the only thing that keeps us from eternal damnation. We may be able to fool another person, but we never fool God.

Prayer: O Lord, may I live to please You and daily strive to meet the standards You have set before me in Your Word. May I grasp with boldness the authority to lovingly direct all to You, so we may live in peace and humility with one another. In Jesus name, Amen.

Day 306

DO NOT HARDEN YOUR HEARTS
Read: Hebrews 1-4

If we do not believe that God created the heavens and the earth, it will be hard to believe in His Son, Who came to earth as a baby and grew to be a man Who took our sins upon Himself. "Because He Himself suffered when He was tempted, He is able to help those who are being tempted." (Heb 2:18 NIV) Yes, when we are going through the trials that this evil world can throw our way, we must be grounded in the Word of God to know that Jesus also suffered, that He was tempted in every way, just as we are, and He can carry us through as long as we keep our thoughts and eyes on Him. (see Heb 3:1 and 12:12:2)

We are to encourage one another towards growing in Christ. Share answers to prayers and share what Jesus has done for you or is doing for you this very moment. It is in salvation that we find rest. Peace, as we listen and obey. "For the Word of God is living and active. Sharper than any double-edged sword, it penetrates even to dividing soul and spirit, joints and marrow; it judges the thoughts and attitudes of the heart." (Heb 4:12 NIV) We need to hold firm to what we believe and profess and know that we can always go before our Lord "with confidence, so that we may receive mercy and find grace to help us in our time of need." (Heb 4:16 NIV)

Prayer: Heavenly Father, I long for Your grace and mercy, clinging to the hope that is only in You. May I never tire reading Your Word of Truth and keep my mind clear to Your truth. Help me to encourage others with the truth of the Word. In Jesus name, Amen.

Day 307

MATURE IN CHRIST
Read: Hebrews 5-8

We all know people that use the saying, 'I may grow old, but I do not have to grow up'. In today's reading, God is calling people to maturity. He even says, "you are slow to learn" (Heb 5:11b NIV) and rebukes the people because they have chosen to not grow up. They only want to drink the milk of the Word and remain as children. God is calling all of us to maturity, we start out as babes, but it is truly not natural to want to remain in that state. God designed us to have a desire to grow up, to look to the next stage in life with anticipation. But throughout history, evil has pulled people away from maturing in Christ and to enjoy being a child, to never grow up.

We desire to mature because as Hebrews 5:14 explains, "But solid food is for the mature, who by constant use have trained themselves to distinguish good from evil." (NIV) It seems that some want to force evil on all the population. They have rejected the Word of God and no longer know what is good and what is evil, there is only one way to cure such a dilemma and it starts with one person at a time reading the Word.

There are those who say they cannot understand God's Word. By now, we should understand that when the Holy Spirit comes to dwell within us, we are given understanding as we read the Bible in our heart language. The unusual thing about the Bible is that we can read it again and again and the Holy Spirit will quicken our heart and our mind so that our eyes are opened even more to the truths each time we read it. We will become aware of insights we never saw before, no matter how many times you read it.

Prayer: Lord, may I continue to work for You and have a longing to mature in You. I want to know good from evil. May I never grow lazy in my quest to bring Your Word to all people. May I work to the fullest to sow the seeds of Christ in those who have a fertile heart, who are ready to receive. In Jesus name, Amen.

Day 308

DRAW NEAR TO GOD
Read: Hebrews 9-11

"And let us consider how we may spur one another on toward love and good deeds. Let us not give up meeting together, as some are in the habit of doing, but let us encourage one another—". (Heb 10:24-25a) Do you see the reason we are to meet together? Do you better understand why so many people meet at their local bar? Or others meet for coffee each morning? We all need that fellowship. God is the Creator of this principle. He wanted fellowship with Adam and Eve and through the ages, He longs for fellowship with each of us. He also understood that man needed fellowship with each other. We need each other to be encouraged. We are to be there for those who are hurting, to carry some of the pain and heartache. We need each other!

As we meet together, we also need to share God's Word with one another, to be encouraged by Hebrews 11. Reading each name and being reminded of their hardships Abel, Job, Noah, Abraham, Jacob, Joseph, Moses, Stephen, Paul. Just to name a few. All strangers on this earth but looking forward to their heavenly home and making the choice to live for God.

We too, have to make the same choices. So, go out and find a church body that is an encouragement to you, one that preaches the Word, and is not afraid to tell you when you sin and to encourage you along the way. We all need fellowship. We all need Jesus.

Prayer: Heavenly Father, I need that encouragement that you talk about. I need fellowship on a daily basis but yet, have a hard time finding it here on this earth. I walk with You, hand in hand, but I sometimes need a person in the flesh that I can trust and who will not use my weaknesses against me. Lord, bring me a true friend. In Jesus name, Amen.

Day 309

LIVE IN PEACE
Read: Hebrews 12-13

"Bear with my words of exhortation". (Heb 13:22a NIV) There always seems to be at least one Esau in our lives. That is the person who wants to live for themselves, living a godless life but then wants to be blessed. These people are not truly repentant, they just go through the motions because it looks good to those around them but in their heart, they are still dark. With this in mind, "let us throw off everything that hinders and the sin that so easily entangles and let us run with perseverance the race marked out for us." (Heb 12:1b NIV)

How, you may ask? How can we live such a life and not be self-centered? If we "fix our eyes on Jesus" (Heb 12:2a NIV), we are focusing on the best example of persevering there is, He prayed and talked to the Father for His guidance. We must remember that "God disciplines us for our good so that we may share in his holiness." (Heb 12:10b NIV) We are to live holy lives and live at peace with all, in love for one another. "Marriage should be honored by all, and the marriage bed kept pure," (Heb 13:4a NIV) is such good advice. Although there is no specific formula in the two chapters we are focused on today, we are reminded to "have a clear conscience and desire to live honorably in every way." (Heb 13:18b NIV)

Prayer: Father God, I long to live daily with a clear conscience that I might be pleasing to You. I am comforted that You will not forsake me, keep me always close to You so that I will not be taken in with teaching that is not from You. May I know your grace daily. In Jesus name, Amen.

Day 310

PERSEVERE
Read: James 1-3

When we have a right attitude in the midst of a testing time, we can better understand the advantages of the trial we are going through. We also understand that our assistance comes from the Lord, but He may send those in human flesh to help comfort us. Perseverance helps us to develop maturity. God desires us to be mature and stable, to believe and not let our emotions pull us first one way, then the other. Often, I have failed in this testing, but our Lord allows another test down the road.

In teaching us to persevere, God is also showing us what we must do as He guides us towards the final goal. We have already read in previous readings that we are to work hard, to provide for our family, to be kind to one another and care for them, to not be deceitful or perverted and so we have a better understanding that our behavior is what brings others to us or repels them away from us. We can say we love but unless our actions prove our love, we are not going to be believed. If our past behavior has been cruel, we will have to work even harder to prove we are a changed person. Do we truly care about the other person or are we still looking out for self?

"But the wisdom that comes from heaven is first of all pure, then peace-loving, considerate, submissive, full of mercy and good fruit, impartial and sincere." (James 3:17 NIV) This is the wisdom so many want but are not willing to work at, and thus, do not pass the test. Which are you?

Prayer: O Lord, may my mind be filled with purity that comes out in my behavior to others and especially when I think no one is looking. May I walk away from strife rather than saying something that is not pleasing to You. May I learn daily what You are teaching me, so I can be mature and complete in You. In Jesus name, Amen.

Day 311

SPIRITUAL MATURITY
Read: James 4-5

Spiritual maturity is our goal, one of the main themes to focus on in this life. We may have our moments of failure, but we dust ourselves off and get back to our calling. We are reminded to not squander what we have been given on our desires but to pray, asking God for direction. Then listen for His answer and do what He is calling us to do. As we obey Him, the evil one wants to discourage us and will use whatever he can to do so. "Come near to God and He will come near to you." (James 4:8a NIV) As we come before Him and confess our fears and weaknesses in humility, He lovingly carries us in His arms.

Here we are exhorted to watch what we say, not saying evil against a brother. We are encouraged to show patients toward others, standing firm just as Job persevered. Perseverance does bring us to maturity and teaches us to look beyond ourselves, praying for God's help. Confessing our sins keeps us humble but also brings healing to our bones. Please know this is a process along life's journey.

Finally, we are reminded to care for our fellow man enough to call them out when they sin. We are to walk alongside them, always covered with prayer, to bring them back to God. For the day will come when we sin, and that same person will gently restore us back to Christ. This is true love and true friendship!

Prayer: Heavenly Father, I have so much to learn and I fall short daily. Thank You for loving me where I am on this journey called life. Keep evil far from me as I persevere for I long for Your mercy and need Your compassion. In Jesus name, Amen.

Day 312

SUFFERING
Read: 1 Peter 1-5

"And the God of all grace, Who called you to His eternal glory in Christ, after you have suffered a little while, will Himself restore you and make you strong, firm and steadfast. (1 Pet 5:10 NIV) What? Once we have accepted Christ as our Lord and Savior, we will suffer? In 1 Peter 4:12, we are reminded, "Dear friends, do not be surprised at the painful trial you are suffering as though something strange were happening to you." (NIV) Indeed, as Christ followers, we will suffer for what we believe, one way or another.

We must know the Bible inside and out, we must behave differently than those in the world. Older Christ followers are to be shepherds, that is watch over and guide the younger ones. The younger ones are to submit to the older and learn with humility. We are to control ourselves and be alert for "your enemy the devil prowls around like a roaring lion looking for someone to devour." (1 Pet 5:8 NIV) Never in our own strength but in Christ are we able to resist this evil enemy.

This is what it means when we are told, "prepare your minds for action" (1 Pet 1:13a NIV). How else can we live holy lives? We must prepare our minds and our hearts by learning what being a Christ follower is all about. Not just receiving blessings but also willing to suffer for the cause of Christ. We must strive each day to live a holy life because we are a chosen people. Stay in the Word daily and sometimes throughout the day.

Prayer: Dear Lord, sometimes I feel like my life story is full of pain, I have been refined by the fires of this world. But I thank my God for each rejection, each blow to my body that He has allowed for it only draws me closer to Jesus, Who loves me deeply. Continue to prepare me to serve You daily and to recognize evil and be protected by the Word. In Jesus name, Amen.

Day 313

SPIRITUAL EFFECTIVENESS
Read: 2 Peter 1-3

Throughout the Bible we are given God's promises so that we can live spiritually effective lives and to stand firm against the evil pull of this world. Our growth in Christ depends upon our effort to follow His directions, once again we are encouraged to "make every effort to add to your faith goodness; and to goodness, knowledge; and to knowledge, self-control; and to self-control, perseverance; and to perseverance, godliness; and to godliness, bother kindness; and to brotherly kindness, love." (2 Pet 1: 5-7 NIV) We are encouraged to produce fruit, to change our behavior from our former way of life to show those around us that we are being led by the Holy Spirit.

We are also warned of the false teachers and leaders who deny the work of the Lord and because of their greed, be that for power, financial gain or self-gratification, will exploit the very people following them. They are bold and arrogant as they sin openly and encourage their followers to do the same.

I urge you not to follow such evil, keep your mind focused on God's Word. Memorize it. Meditate on the Bible. Read it daily and know that you are to stay true to wholesome thinking. "Make every effort to be found spotless, blameless and at peace with Him." (2 Pet 3:14b NIV) Watch out for those who seem to be educated and so knowledgeable but have no fear of what God is about to do, they are ill-informed and volatile people that distort the truth of God's Word. (see 2 Pet 3:16b)

> *Prayer: Lord Jesus, my desire is to be an effective vessel for Your Kingdom. Yes, I need self-control and godliness and love. May I yield to the Holy Spirit moment by moment to keep my mind focused on You. In Jesus name, Amen.*

Day 314

WALK AS JESUS WALKED
Read: 1 John 1-5

Are we hiding our sinful behavior in the darkness? Or are we walking in the light, in fellowship with Christ Jesus? The light reveals what God is calling for us to change. When we walk in the light, we will obey His command because this change is for our good and God's glory. When we surrender to God (see 1 John 3:9a) a change takes place in our hearts and as we grow in Christ, we develop a longing to be pleasing to Him. In the middle of this transformation, people we have known will see the change and will be drawn to us or will reject us.

If there is someone in your life whom you were cruel to or committed some other detestable act against that person, you cannot expect that they will trust you. When they see you or hear from you, the memories flood back, you have not given them reason to believe you are changed. Perhaps you need to check your reason for contacting them. Is it for their healing or to bring glory to yourself? Plus, perhaps they have forgiven you and moved on and have no desire for any further contact with you.

"We know that anyone born of God does not continue to sin; the one who was born of God keeps him safe, and the evil one cannot harm him. " (1 John 5:18 NIV) Today's reading has made it clear, we can go on as we did before, or we can ask forgiveness and make a life change. If we walk in the light, then we will want to please God by changing our observable behavior as well as our hearts.

Prayer: I acknowledge You Lord, as Savior and Master of my life. May Your light shine in my heart to reveal those areas that need Your changing power. May I draw close to You and love those You have brought into my path. In Jesus name, Amen.

Day 315

WALK IN OBEDIENCE
Read: 2 & 3 John and Jude

"I ask that we love one another. And this is love: that we walk in obedience to His commands." (2 John: 5b-6a NIV) Love. That word has been overused to the point that people love their children, their pet and the food they eat. It can be confusing for those listening. Indeed, when we love as Jesus loved, we are living that love in deep caring and protection for the other person. We put the other person's interest before our own. Jesus gave His life for us, the very people He loves. Now ask yourself if you are willing to give your life for those you claim to love?

In Jude we are warned about deceitful men who are godless. These men are depraved, they do all they can to destroy their own bodies and have no respect for anyone else as well as being full of slander and rejecting authority. These men are abusive and only desire to care about themselves. They will make it a point to divide mankind for their own pleasure. The ungodly acts they commit will be flaunted before the Godly as if there is nothing wrong with such behavior.

We, who are Christ followers, must stay in God's Word, where we can learn daily to be obedient, to show mercy to others and to give them the truth in love and kindness. We are to persevere when times are tough and to stand firm against the evil all around. We are called to love one another, and that love has nothing to do with what we can get but, quite the opposite, what we can give. To God's glory, let us live our lives as we serve Him through Jesus the Christ our Lord and Savior.

Prayer: Lord Jesus, I am learning the true meaning of love and work daily to live the type of life that You have called me to serve. Keep me from all that would pollute my body, for Your protection is my biggest need. May I show the same mercy as You have shown me! In Jesus name, Amen.

Day 316

TO HEAR
Read: Revelation 1-3

The book of Revelation shows us that there is triumph in the middle of tragedy. As John speaks to these seven churches, he is also speaking to us. We try to comprehend what he is saying and then to obey his words. Do not let anyone fool you, we are not just the church that John commends, we need to take the reproof to heart and fall on our knees in repentance. Each of us has areas where we need to improve, so, let us humble ourselves and see where we need to change.

Many of the letters written praise the people for persevering but in the United States that is not the case. We change churches as often as we change our cloths, looking for the church that makes us feel good but never challenging us to maturity. Many Christians are accepting the world's ways. If the government law says something is legal, then it is acceptable. We accept all forms of teaching because we have not read the Bible from cover to cover. As we read, we need to pray that God will open our heart and mind so that we will become more obedient. We need to pray that He will give us understanding to His Word!

Perhaps today's reading does not make you feel good, but it is a call for each of us to grow. It is time we look at our behavior and make sure we are pleasing to Jesus. Have we gotten so involved with the activities around us that we have put the Lord on a shelf? Are we afraid to make a deeper commitment? Have we become lukewarm in our walk with Jesus? It is a lot to think about but perhaps it is time to take that step.

Prayer: O Lord, how I long to be acceptable in Your sight yet I fall short. May I stay true to You and Your Word, even in the middle of persecution and suffering. May I always grasp Your Word and obey, to the best of my understanding. In Jesus name, Amen.

Day 317

GREAT GRIEF
Read: Revelation 4-7

"A rainbow, resembling an emerald, encircled the throne." (Revelation 4:3b NIV) Did you know that the rainbow is a complete circle? That is how it can encircle the throne. From beginning to end, the Bible is consistent. It may have many different writers but one Author. We are reminded of God's greatness, from the lightning bolts and thunder to the praising of Him who sits on the throne. He is worthy of our praise!

With deep grief John cried until the One Who is worthy stepped forward to open the scroll. None of us can ever match Jesus. He took our sins and washed them away. We will worship Him just as the elders are doing in today's reading. We should never stop praying for it is as fragrant incense to the Lord.

As the seals are opened, we can only comprehend a bit of what is about to happen. That is God's way of protecting us. But we must understand that God has given authority to some to carry out His plan. Our job is to pray and to remain in His arms. We are nearing the end of reading through the Bible for your first time, do not stop now. Finish with flying colors and then go back and start again. Each time through, He will encourage you and enlightened you in a different way. He will meet Your needs at that time with His Word of Love.

Prayer: Lord God, You are the One I seek daily and desire to please. I need You in my life, may I bring glory to Your name. May I hold on to Your faithful promises. In Jesus name, Amen.

Day 318

TRUMPETS SOUNDING
Read: Revelation 8-11

In today's reading, we see the seventh seal opened and the seven angels are given seven trumpets. We are not going to analyze these trumpets but rather look to ourselves and make sure we are ready for such a day as this. We read in Revelation 9:20-21 how the remaining people "did not repent of the work of their hands". We further read, "nor did they repent of their murders, their magic arts, their sexual immortality or their thefts." (NIV)

How could people be so evil and into their own pleasure that they would ignore or reject all the happenings going on around them? I mean, look one-third of the earth is burned up, one-third of the sea is blood, killing the creatures, then one-third of the waters are poisoned, and people die, and further destruction continues. The people are so hard-hearted that they will not give up their evil ways and turn to God. Even the two witnesses do not wake them up.

Each day we make choices on how to behave towards others and towards God. The time is now! Time to repent and turn to the living God! Time to turn from yourself and start letting God work in your life. Is your heart ready? Take that next step, Jesus is waiting with open arms.

Prayer: Heavenly Father, I turn my life and my heart over to You. I acknowledge my sinful ways and ask that You purify me with the blood of the Lamb, Who is the only One to take away the evil that is in me. Only You can make my heart new and renew my mind. You are my God, Whom I long to please. In Jesus name, Amen.

Day 319

PATIENT ENDURANCE
Read: Revelation 12-14

As our faithfulness grows, so does our patient endurance. The longer we walk with Christ, the more we will see how important endurance is. To endure those who cause pain and heartache, to learn how to react in the midst of an ungodly situation, and to learn the lessons that God means for only you. Yes indeed, we must learn patience along the way and to endure with joy, knowing that He will work each situation for our good.

We can see in today's reading that as time comes closer and closer to the end, we believers will have to stay close to God, to be in His Word as much as possible so that we can be strong for such a time as this. The only way we will overcome such evil as is about to come upon us is "by the blood of the Lamb and by the Word of their testimony; they did not love their lives so much as to shrink from death." (Rev 12:11 NIV) That's right, we should not fear of death. The evil one counts on us to be so fearful of death that we will turn away from our Lord and turn to him who wants to snatch us away from Jesus. But, may we, like Jesus, know Scripture so well as to use it against our enemy, the devil, and make him flee from us.

Be prepared. Know the Word of God and remember that you do not need to read the devils books. So many Christians today think they need to read about the enemy so as to know about him, but they have never read the Bible. When you read the Bible, you will recognize evil and not fall for evil deceptions. Stay strong, stay in the Word!

Prayer: Dear Lord, only You know what the future holds. May I endure what You have put in my path and mature in strength for each new day. My past is covered by the blood of Jesus so keep me pure and acceptable to You until I see you face to face. In Jesus name, Amen.

Day 320

THE LAMB WILL OVERCOME THEM
Read Revelation 15-18

Some might see the reading of Revelation as a bit frightening, but others will see that our God is victorious! The last plagues come when "God's wrath is completed. And I saw what looked like a sea of glass mixed with fire and, standing beside the sea, those who had been victorious over the beast and his image and over the number of his name. (Rev 15:1b-2a NIV)

We now see seven angels, each holding a bowl of destruction. For all those who took the mark of the beast and worshiped him, they suffered painful sores. Evil people caused God's holy ones to suffer, killing them and now tormentors are being judged with blood. Next, people "refused to repent and glorify Him" (Rev 16:9b) and experienced the sun's heat like never before. Once again, we see that men cursed God and refused to repent and are now thrown into darkness along with a terrible earthquake and huge hailstones. And yet, these people continued to curse God and not repent. What pride!

We see the evils of adultery and not repenting of their evil behavior. Sadly they seem be flaunting their evil and drawing others to follow them. People are led astray by their evil. As this evil continues to brag and pull people towards them, they have forgotten one thing as they "make war against the Lamb but the Lamb will overcome them because He is Lord of lords and King of kings—and with Him will be His called, chosen and faithful followers." (Rev 17:14 NIV) Each and every day, we must make sure our hearts are repentant and right with the Lord, for we must always be ready and certainly make the right choices. This is exciting, nothing to be afraid of!

Prayer: Lord Jesus, I come before You in humble repentance, asking that You not only forgive me but transform me daily to be more like You. I want to be one of Your chosen followers. In Jesus name, Amen.

Day 321

AMEN, COME, LORD JESUS
Read: Revelation 19-22

Twice in today's reading we read a list of those who never turned away from their evil practices. They are "the cowardly, the unbelieving, the vile, the murderers, the sexually immoral, those who practice magic arts, the idolaters and all the liars—" (Rev 21:8a NIV) And again, "outside are the dogs, those who practice magic arts, the sexually immoral, the murderers, the idolaters and everyone who loves and practices falsehood." (Rev 22:15 NIV)

Along with these two lists, we have read several other lists that should have our attention. But here at the end, right before our Lord comes back, we still find evil people who are not willing to turn from such detestable practices. Truly, such people are unrepentant. In Noah's day, God gave the people over 100 days to repent as Noah built an ark, the people would not listen to Noah but became more corrupt and grieved God. There will still be hard-hearted people at the end of time. We need to check ourselves against such lists and make sure that we take responsibility for our behavior and turn from our wickedness.

The blessings of reading the Bible will only be multiplied when you turn back to the beginning, yes, to Genesis and start all over again. You will be amazed what God will show you the next time around. "Behold, I am coming soon! Blessed is he who keeps the words of the prophecy in this Book." (Rev 22:7 NIV) May God watch over you and may you draw near to Him!

Prayer: Lord of Lord's, I thirst for You! You do care so deeply for me, wiping away my fears, drawing me ever closer to You and loving me more deeply than I could ever imagine. I look forward to Your coming, Lord Jesus! In Your Precious name, Amen.

ACKNOWLEDGMENTS

I am so grateful that Jesus, my Lord and Savior, would choose me to write *Faithful Promises of God*. I did not feel capable or worthy, but He used those around me to keep me writing.

Without that first challenge to read through-the-Bible, this book would not have come to fruition. Thank you, Pat Ankney, for that first challenge and your encouragement and mentoring through the years.

Lisa Pelto, you have made my life so much easier with your publishing expertise. I am ever grateful to each of you!

In our lives, we all need someone who listens to us and encourages us. My life is blessed with several such people, Terry, Sue, Deb, and Kay. I appreciate you all more than you will ever know.

Last, but certainly not least, I am blessed with the most amazing children: Teresa Ellert, Dawn Wiegand, and Sean Dunn. Their love and support was so needed as their talent helped make this book happen.

www.ingramcontent.com/pod-product-compliance
Lightning Source LLC
Chambersburg PA
CBHW032148080426
42735CB00008B/625